Economics and Politics
of Turkish Liberalization

Economics and Politics
of Turkish Liberalization

Edited by
Tevfik F. Nas and Mehmet Odekon

Bethlehem: Lehigh University Press
London and Toronto: Associated University Presses

Associated University Presses
440 Forsgate Drive
Cranbury, NJ 08512

Associated University Presses
25 Sicilian Avenue
London WC1A 2QH, England

Associated University Presses
P.O. Box 39, Clarkson Pstl. Stn.
Mississauga, Ontario,
L5J 3X9 Canada

The paper used in this publication meets the requirements
of the American National Standard for Permanence of Paper
for Printed Library Materials Z39.48-1984.

Library of Congress Cataloging-in-Publication Data

Economics and politics of Turkish liberalization/edited by Tevfik F. Nas and Mehmet Odekon.
    p.   cm.
    Includes bibliographical references and index.
    ISBN 0-934223-19-X (alk. paper)
    1. Turkey—Economic policy. 2. Turkey—Economic conditions—1960– 3. Turkey—Politics and government—1960– I. Nas, Tevfik F. II. Odekon, Mehmet.
HC492.E3   1992
338.9561—dc20
                                       91-60583
                                           CIP

Contents

Acknowledgments

We thank Gina Swift (Skidmore College) for her excellent typing, John Danison (Skidmore College) for his computer assistance, and Paula L. Nas and Ginny Egan Lagather for their support and editorial assistance.

The project was partially supported by a Skidmore College Faculty Grant and the Economics Department of the University of Michigan, Flint.

Economics and Politics
of Turkish Liberalization

1

The Impact of Turkey's Stabilization and Structural Adjustment Program: An Introduction

Tevfik F. Nas

The Turkish economy, after ten years of uninterrupted experimentation with economic liberalization, still lacks a sustainable balance among competing political and economic interests. Despite impressive accomplishments and considerable progress toward a free-market economy, trade and budget deficits remain, and more important, the problems of high inflation and political uncertainty continue to destabilize and delay the structural adjustment process.

Turkey's stabilization and structural adjustment program was introduced in 1980 to curb the growth of domestic demand and to simultaneously initiate supply-side adjustments.[1] Domestic demand was restrained by a combination of contractionary fiscal and monetary policies in order to generate excess capacity that was intended to meet the external demand; and supply-side measures were introduced to improve resource allocation both in the domestic and foreign sectors. As a result, trade volume quadrupled with an impressive export performance; the normalization of Turkey's creditworthiness eased some of the financial restraints; and the renovation of financial markets and liberalization of interest rates led to the establishment of a promising financial infrastructure.

Among other accomplishments, a newly established value-added tax raised hopes of furthering fiscal reforms; restructuring attempts culminated in improved public-sector efficiency; and privatization remained one of the government's priorities despite the adverse short-term outcomes usually expected of such sectoral changes.

On the negative side, inflation, caused by heavy debt servicing and excessive public-sector spending, continues to distort the commodity and financial markets; private sector investments are still

11

below expectations despite recent signs of substantial increases in industrial production; foreign investors have yet to find signals that indicate economic and political stability; and deteriorating income distribution has already begun to undermine the liberalization process, raising serious concerns even among the strongest advocates of current economic policies.

The causes of this mixed performance are numerous, but seem to center around the inadequacies of Turkey's institutional environment and the inconsistencies of the demand-management policies that accompanied the 1980 structural adjustment reforms. As hypothesized elsewhere, inconsistent monetary and fiscal expansion, the inability to generate sustained increases in savings and investment rates, and excessive reliance on exchange-rate adjustments may have led to counterproductive outcomes and delayed supply-side responses.[2]

Other equally important causes, which are hypothesized in this volume, stem from an institutional environment still reflecting the remaining influences of Turkey's long-standing pre-1980 protectionist and state-oriented economic structure. Despite the fundamental alterations and intensive restructuring, which have taken place in the economy since 1980, protectionist and statist reflections in economic policymaking still seem to condition and delay supply-side responses. In addition, redemocratization efforts have not yet produced the expected outcomes. After 1980, the center-Right coalition, which emerged under the leadership of Turgut Özal and his ruling Motherland party (MP), initiated fundamental structural changes to establish a competitive market economy and to complete Turkey's integration with Western democracies. However, despite impressive accomplishments in these areas, the coalition began to face considerable opposition toward the end of the 1980s and received mixed reviews due partly to the reemergence of inflation, and partly to growing public awareness and sensitivity over the issue of political legitimacy. The central theme of the institutional view of the delayed supply-side response is that Turkey's institutional incompatibility with free-market dynamics compounded the inconsistencies of the demand management policies, and that added to the severity of adverse macroeconomic outcomes and political uncertainty.

This chapter provides an overview of Turkey's experience with the 1980 stabilization and structural adjustment program. A summary of the main issues raised in this volume is preceded by a chronology of Turkey's major industrialization efforts, and followed by a brief commentary, providing a perspective for furthering Turkey's stabilization and liberalization process.

Pre-1980 Developments in the Turkish Economy

Turkey's first experiment with economic liberalization dates back to the early 1920s when a small-scale free trade−oriented economy emerged. Because it lacked a well-developed infrastructure, had limited resources, and had an agriculture-based economy, Turkey exported mainly primary products for which it held a comparative advantage and imported a wide range of consumption and capital goods under free trade arrangements. According to Kazgan (1985), the free-market outward-looking orientation of the economy in those years was somewhat comparable to the economic and policy environments envisaged in the 1980 program. In addition to the absence of trade barriers, both interest and exchange rates were determined through free-market forces, and the inflows of external capital and short-term credit provided the main sources of Turkey's domestic infrastructure and commercial capital investments.

During these early years of the republic, state intervention in the economy remained minimal. Such passive interventionism was not deliberate, however, but resulted from an inadequate tax base and a lack of financial intermediaries to carry out effective monetary and credit policies. State interventionism consisted only of laws and decrees to encourage private capital accumulation; to establish an effective banking system; and to direct foreign capital to essential infrastructure developments, particularly to railroad construction.

The role of the private sector in Turkey's industrialization was also minimal. Private initiative was felt mainly in the international trade and banking sector with negligible investments in selected food and textile categories. This was, perhaps, due to such legitimate reasons as the inadequacy of the existing capital base, the attractiveness of the trade sector due to the absence of protectionist measures, and the high risk involved in investing in import-competing industries due to foreign competition (Kazgan 1985; Sönmez 1982).

After a decade of economic liberalization, Turkey introduced protectionist policies in reaction to both the balance of payments crisis in 1926, and the domestic imbalances triggered by the Great Depression in 1929. These included higher tariffs, quotas, and strict foreign-exchange controls with few duty-free provisions for certain basic imported inputs. Consequently, protectionism improved the trade balance and led to some accumulation of private capital.

With the introduction of the first Five-Year Industrialization Plan in 1933, import substitution became the official priority, marking the beginning of an era of state-led industrialization, with a unique state-private sector partnership, which lasted more than four decades.[3] The state became the driving force of industrialization, establishing various essential enterprises that produced both consumption goods and essential inputs for the private sector, and provided prospects for the private sector to integrate vertically in both backward-and forward-linked industries.

After a short interruption due to the trade liberalization experience in 1950–52, Turkey began to diversify and deepen its import-substitution industries.[4] Under heavy protectionist measures, import substitution continued from nondurables to durables, and from intermediate inputs to capital goods. With the introduction of the first of the Five-Year Development plans in 1960s, government involvement in import substitution intensified, systematically reallocating society's resources to the manufacturing sector.

According to Keyder (1984), a unique state interventionism developed during the 1960s, reallocating resources by producing the intermediate inputs at subsidized values and by keeping the domestic prices of the imported goods below their world-price equivalence. These and other measures, like maintaining an overvalued domestic currency and redistributing income in accordance with state-oriented industrialization policies, kept the cost of production at low levels, thus helping the profit margin to rise in the industrial sector.

However, these measures did not prevent Turkey from becoming more dependent on imported inputs. During 1963–70, the economy managed a high rate of growth mainly fueled by domestic sources. This was followed by more rapid growth during 1970–77, primarily driven by workers' remittances and foreign savings. But an increasingly worsening balance of payments, accompanied by the external shocks of the mid-1970s, led to severe shortages of essential goods and resulted in the debt crisis of 1977.[5] In 1979, the annual percentage change in real GNP declined to −0.4 percent for the first time in more than two decades, and despite a stagnant economy and high unemployment, inflation rose by 110.2 percent in 1980, reaching its highest level ever.[6] The inability of demand-management policies to restrain domestic demand and the failure of 1978 and 1979 devaluations to improve current account balances, finally led to the introduction of the 1980 stabilization and structural adjustment program.

The Objectives and the Performance of the 1980 Program

The immediate goal of the 1980 program was to relieve the economy from a severe balance of payments crisis and rising inflationary pressures, and for that, the program proved to be fairly successful. Between 1980 and 1984, Gross National Product (GNP) growth averaged 3.6 percent annually, the current account deficit declined from 5 percent of GNP, to 2.8 percent of GNP, and despite increased protectionism among the Organization for Economic Cooperation and Development (OECD) nations, exports managed to rise from about $2.9 billion in 1980, to $7.4 billion in 1984, averaging a 28-percent annual increase. Twice during this period the current account deficit fell below its 1978 and 1979 levels, but this did not lead to serious policy reversals. With debt relief resulting from rescheduling agreements and from a slow but gradual increase in foreign direct investment, the program continued to achieve its stated objectives.

In the second half of the 1980s, the current account balance continued to improve, rising from a deficit of roughly −$0.5 billion in 1986, to a surplus of $1.5 billion in 1988, largely due to the increase in exports and restrictive import measures introduced in the first half of 1988. Exports rose from about $8 billion in 1985 to $12 billion in 1988, but began to show weaknesses toward the end of 1988. By 1989, real GNP growth also began to slow down. After reaching its highest level in 1986, GNP growth dropped to 3.4 percent in 1988, despite declining real wages and strong external demands.[7]

During the same period, inflation continued to rise. After dropping below its 1981 level in 1986, it climbed to 73.3 percent in August of 1989 due to high interest rates as well as a high budget deficit, and remains one of the most challenging problems of the 1990s.

Another remaining challenge is how to mobilize resources to encourage private investment in manufacturing, and thus sustain the export drive. Private investment, which was expected to accommodate the growth in exports, fell short of expectations.[8] Occasional upward trends in manufacturing investment were short-lived and largely induced by public expenditures. Even the recent change in government investment policy, which was intended to slow down public expenditures to allow increased private investment in manu-facturing, did not adequately strengthen the private sector so as to enable it to take the lead in promoting growth and in enhancing the export drive.[9]

The Limitations of the Program

Stabilization and structural adjustment programs are designed to generate long-term growth in real output and exports, and the following measures are prescribed to accomplish that goal:

1. restrain domestic demand by means of anti-inflationary monetary and fiscal policies;
2. restore competitiveness in external markets through exchange rate adjustments; and
3. stimulate aggregate supply through trade liberalization and improved market conditions.

The stabilization components in these programs usually empha-size demand-management measures, in the hope that they would induce supply-side responses within a reasonable time period. A combination of contractionary fiscal and monetary policies, for example, slows down the economy; this reduces real income and the price level, and, consequently, when expectations begin to change, the economy moves on with improved productivity and efficiency.

In this scenario, there is a possible risk of having a delayed supply-side response or policies with counterproductive outcomes. In either case, policy reversals are likely, and will remain so as long as society maintains an institutional environment incompatible with free-market forces. For example, it is unrealistic to expect a society to achieve induced supply-side adjustments, while at the same time functioning within an institutional structure that allows intervention and fails to comply with the rules and norms of a free-market system. Society will either have to introduce fundamental alterations in its economic and policy environments, or, instead, develop stabilization strategies in compliance with the dynamics of its economic policy-making process. To be more specific, em-phasizing improvements in the pricing mechanism alone, while keeping society's political and organizational structures ineffective and predominantly centralized, will not suffice. This will be es-pecially the case if the shortcomings of the political system generate uncertainties and cause frequent interruptions in the economic policy-making process.

Turkey still experiences difficulties in these regards, and thus needs to refocus its restructuring efforts. One area of focus is the issue of political legitimacy and its impact on macroeconomic outcomes. One of the frequent complaints raised by the private sector is the absence of a political tradition that would help expectation formation in the business world, bringing continuity to output and investment decisions. An electoral procedure ensuring democratic representation could probably minimize the risk of policy reversals; reduce political uncertainty, which during the last eight years led to six national elections and referenda; and most important, moderate the problem of inflation that reemerged during the second half of the 1980s.[10]

The following two chapters provide important linkages between Turkey's political realities and the macroeconomic outcomes. In chapter 2, Sayarı provides a chronology of political events in Turkey and reviews the dynamics of competing economic interests. Focusing on the 1980−88 period, Sayarı argues that the technocratic initiative to reform the economy benefited greatly from the absence of "public contestation and democratic liberties," but the redemocratization process that followed during the second half of the period led to considerable opposition. Threatened by the emergence of legitimate rivalry and by growing dissent with Turgut Özal's management style, MP's center-Right coalition implemented expansionary fiscal measures largely refocused on "patronage-oriented allocation," and that, according to Sayarı, partially caused the reemergence of inflation during the second half of the 1980s.

In chapter 3, Waterbury describes the "patronage politics" and the "interventionist" character of Turkey's public sector. Throughout the 1980s, MP's center-Right coalition initiated structural reforms to raise overall efficiency and introduced fiscal measures to maintain large public spending programs. The latter, Waterbury argues, is a unique form of state interventionism, which needs increased discretionary expenditures to sustain the coalition. According to Waterbury, both measures find wide support among external and domestic constituencies, and despite economic downturns that may be a disadvantage to these political allies, the delicate balance between the two sets of measures will very likely continue to have dim prospects for a viable rivalry in the foreseeable future.

Disappointing macroeconomic outcomes may also result from the inefficiencies involved in the society's organizational structure. The society's bureaucratic inefficiency may cause additional time and resource costs or seem to show resistance to the competitive forces of the free-market economy, and that may lead to delayed supply-side responses. Refocusing its restructuring efforts in this area, Turkey's center-Right coalition has been trying to remove impediments created by the Turkish bureaucracy and improve organizational efficiency. But as Öniş argues in chapter 4, these efforts have yet to change the "regulatory" character of the Turkish bureaucracy. Focusing on Turkey's foreign trade companies and the institutional environment within which they have been operating, Öniş claims that despite their important mission in promoting and furthering Turkey's export drive, they had little guidance from the state. It is this fact, the absence of a strategic plan that would guide "state-business interaction," combined with uncertainties and the distortionary practices characterizing the policy environment that may have been the primary reasons for their recent deterioration in performance. Öniş concludes by stressing the importance of considerable institutional and organizational changes to maintain the continuing momentum of the export drive.

THE INSUFFICIENCY, INCONSISTENCY, AND TIMING OF THE PROGRAM

In addition to the incompatibility of the institutional environment, adjustments in the interest rate and the exchange rate can cause a weak performance, delaying the supply-side responses.[11] The interest rate, combined with frequent adjustments in the exchange rate, is used to moderate the negative outcomes of trade liberalization policies. By depressing investment and consumption during the early stages of interest rate liberalization, private savings may be encouraged and the availability of loanable funds for capital formation increased.

However, frequent exchange rate adjustments, while helping the trade balance, could slow down the economy by lowering investment. Also, by affecting the supply side of the economy through imported goods, such adjustments could simultaneously generate high rates of inflation and unemployment.[12] In addition, interest rate decontrol could remove the credit squeeze and consequently lower the rate of inflation; but by raising the cost of working capital, it could also cause high rates of inflation and unemployment via the supply-side of the economy.[13]

In the case of Turkey, frequent exchange rate adjustments and gradual liberalization of financial markets were successful in strengthening the export orientation of the economy. But at the same time, they appear to be the primary reasons for increased inflation and nearly stagnant private investment in manufacturing.[14] In chapter 5, Aşıkoğlu finds the inconsistency between the exchange rate and demand management policies a drawback of the program. Despite the effectiveness of the exchange-rate strategy in preventing the overvaluation of the Turkish lira and in adapting to external conditions, the strategy failed to incorporate anti-inflationary measures. According to Aşıkoğlu, this is probably why frequent adjustments in the exchange rate, combined with interest rate decontrol led to high inflation.

As Conway argues in chapter 6, the structural adjustment reforms were constrained by insufficiently pursued stabilization policies. By emphasizing positive economic growth, Turkey incurred an unacceptable level of public sector dissaving, and that, in turn, undermined the long-term structural reforms.

In chapter 7, Uçtum blames the timing of the stabilization policies for the program's failure to achieve its long-term objectives. Because of the private sector's reluctance to participate in capital accumulation, the private to public sector ratio in resource allocation remained unchanged, with an investment level in the tradable sector inadequate to achieve the preferred outcomes. Uçtum argues that the contractionary policies implemented simultaneously with the liberalization measures were the likely cause of low investment in the tradable sector, and she concludes by suggesting that perhaps the outcome would have been more favorable had stabilization policies preceded liberalization measures.

In addition to these drawbacks, the program also may have been constrained by the failure of firms to respond to the proposed reforms. In support of this view, in chapter 8 Odekon reports the findings of a mail survey of Turkish industrial firms to determine both favorable and unfavorable aspects of the program, as perceived by firms classified by ownership, export-orientation, and size. According to the survey, the majority of firms shifted the burden of the value-added tax as well as the rising costs of working capital and imported inputs to the consumers, thus contributing to high and persistent inflation. Large firms that benefited from the structural reforms also contributed to the rise in unemployment as they began to adjust to international standards, which normally favor export-orientation and capital intensive technologies. Despite these adverse outcomes, the survey shows that most firms viewed the policy reforms as long-run phenomena and, overall, found the liberalization measures implemented thus far, to be favorable.

Another drawback of inconsistent stabilization policies is uncertainty and its impact on the country's relative attractiveness to foreign investors. Since 1980, gains in reinstating confidence and reestablishing Turkey's creditworthiness have been impressive. Despite conditions impeding an easy flow of international funds, Turkey managed to become a creditworthy participant, and now it has begun to enjoy the status of a voluntary borrower in international financial markets.

However, problems still exist. In addition to the inadequacy of social overhead capital, the risk of potential political instability raises concerns, making Turkey a less than ideal place for foreign investment.[15] Therefore, as Tırtıroğlu and Tırtıroğlu argue in chapter 9, Turkey needs to do more to attract foreign investment. Frequent exchange rate adjustments and interest rate liberalization were important steps in the right direction. These reforms and the direct participation of Turkish banks in the international banking community led to the development of a financial environment conducive to revealing the information needed to determine the return to political risk. What needs to be done now is to upgrade Turkey's economic and political environments by gradually implementing the proposed reforms.

A Perspective for Structural Reforms

From the preceding overview it is clear that a restructuring policy with priority given to Turkey's political and organizational effectiveness could substantially raise the overall efficiency of the economy. The implications of such restructuring can be analyzed in a general equilibrium framework, with a grand utility frontier and a social welfare function reflecting society's norms of efficiency and distributive justice.[16] At the frontier we envision a society where production is organized according to efficiency conditions commonly stated for social welfare maximization; property rights are sufficiently defined to assure the desired output mix; and the interrelationship among production, consumption, and distribution is legitimized within political and legal structures congruous to a welfare maximum setting. In this framework any strategy involving resource allocation is considered efficient and distributionally acceptable when it moves the economy toward the frontier, and at the same time, restores a new equilibrium with a private-public output mix determined in accordance with the social welfare function.[17]

Let us now consider a situation where society is inside the frontier and is encountering obstacles in adjusting its organizational, political, and legal structures to the preferred changes in the private to public output mix. The price mechanism works in accordance with the free-market system, but the organizational structure is nonoptimal. It biases resource allocation against the private sector and tends to fall behind in adapting to technological changes, assuming that such changes are driven more effectively by the private sector. Absence of market-oriented property rights legislation causes uncertainty, which distorts the exchange mechanism and generates externality problems leading to over- or underutilization of resources as well as vast inequities in income distribution. The absence of political institutions to monitor and improve the collective decision-making process, and more important, the lack of configurations to reveal individual political inclinations, are also obstacles leading to policy outcomes in conflict with the majority's expectations.

With these obstacles present, the outcomes of both liberalization and stabilization programs are likely to fall short of expectations unless they are accompanied by market-oriented structural reforms. Despite a reasonably effective competitive price mechanism, both stabilization and liberalization policies may yield short-lived outcomes with likely destabilizing effects. Even if society achieves temporary stability through the price mechanism, it will continue to incur losses in resource allocation and face critical macrochoices due to the fragility of policy outcomes.[18]

Under these circumstances, strengthening the competitive forces of the economy through an improved price mechanism alone may not be sufficient. In addition to assuring the workability of the exchange mechanism, the public choice configuration must improve in order to reveal realistically, individual political inclinations and to reflect society's preferences in allocating public services.[19] Organizational effectiveness must also be enhanced with free-market-oriented property rights legislation.[20] With this interpretation, law, economics, and democracy are inseparable, and efficiency and welfare maximization, as performance criteria, are more comprehensive than the more narrow norms of traditional welfare economics.

When Turkey's stabilization and structural adjustment reforms are viewed in this framework, many of the measures introduced during the 1980s appear to be consistent. Yet, they have been insufficient and lacked the necessary strength to move the economy toward the frontier. Further gains in social welfare could have been achieved by putting more emphasis on strengthening democratic practices. This could have substantially raised the overall efficiency and effectiveness of the economy and improved income distribution, which deteriorated during the last decade. Turkey could benefit greatly from increased citizen participation in the democratic process, allowing both institutions and individuals to reveal their actual inclinations regarding the use of public resources. In addition, a market-oriented property rights legislation could be an important source of improved economic efficiency. With such improvements in the economic and policy environment, stabilization and the structural adjustment reforms would be more effective, enabling the economy to achieve its most preferred macroeconomic objectives.

In this volume we examine some of the inconsistencies involved in the design and implementation of the stabilization and structural adjustments programs. Our curiosity takes us beyond the stylized comparisons of actual and a priori consequences. We trace the complexities and dynamics of Turkey's unique economic and policy environments, and by taking a political economy perspective, we hope to understand the expectations, the difficulties, and the politics of a society in transition. The findings in this volume are not conclusive, but we consider them to be valuable contributions to ongoing research aimed at developing a better understanding of Turkey's stabilization and liberalization process.

Notes

1. For more on Turkey's experience with liberalization see Arıcanlı and Rodrik (1990), Conway (1987), Şenses (1988), Kopits (1987), and Nas and Odekon (1988).
2. See in particular the chapters by Conway, Fry, Kumcu, and Şenses in Nas and Odekon (1988).
3. For the details of the industrialization plan see Sönmez (1982).
4. The liberalization experience of 1950−52 was the result of increased foreign exchange availability due to the Marshall Plan and easy credit markets. However, rising inflation, overvalued Turkish lira, and an increased trade deficit, led to renewed protectionist measures. For a full analysis of the period see Kazgan (1985), Krueger (1974), and Sönmez (1982).
5. For the causes and the consequences of the crisis see Pamuk (1982), Şenses (1983), Conway (1987), and Rodrik (1988).
6. The statistical information provided in this chapter is taken from the International Monetary Fund (IMF), *International Financial Statistics*, various issues, and the Central Bank, *Annual Report*, various issues, unless otherwise stated.
7. This decline was attributed to the contraction of output in the manufacturing and transportation industries as well as to the slowdown in total spending caused by contractionary fiscal policies in 1987 and a slowdown in investment.
8. Total investment, after declining below pre−1980 levels between 1980 and 1984, began to rise, reaching its highest level in 1988. The private sector followed a similar growth pattern, averaging roughly 9.6 percent of GNP during 1985−88,

but it remained below public investment levels. A more serious problem was the slow growth of private investment in manufacturing, averaging about 3 percent of GNP (see TÜSİAD 1989: 41−49).

9. In a recent survey conducted by TÜSİAD (the Turkish Industrialists' and Businessmen's Association), 26.7 percent of all businessmen surveyed, stated that economic and political instability was a significant factor adversely affecting capital investment in the private sector. Another situation adversely affecting capital formation is the withdrawal of public investment from the manufacturing industry. For more on this see Boratav and Turel (1988).

10. In the TÜSİAD survey, inflation, unemployment, and income inequality were also viewed as the most troubling issues adding to economic and political instability. Among those who responded to the survey, 25 percent viewed inflation as the most troubling problem in 1992. The response for unemployment and income distribution were 15 and 10 percent, respectively (TÜSİAD 1989: 119).

11. The downward rigidity of real wages, measured in terms of domestic prices, has been another supply-side explanation for the stagflationary trends in OECD countries (Helliwell 1988). In Turkey, however, such rigidity cannot be argued for the post−1980 period. Real wages deteriorated substantially after 1980 (OECD 1987).

12. The impact of exchange rate adjustments on the demand and supply sides are not necessarily concurrent. Supply-side effects are likely to precede demand-side effects the larger the share of imported inputs in the production cost; the lower the price responsiveness of demand for imported inputs; and the lower the responsiveness of aggregate prices, consumption, and investment to exchange rate adjustments (Conway 1988). For these and other contractionary demand and supply effects of exchange rate adjustments see Conway (1988), Cooper (1971), Krugman and Taylor (1978), and van Wijnbergen (1986).

13. This will especially be the case in financially repressed economies with weak equity and money markets. As argued by the new structuralists, the cost-push effect of interest rates (in particular, the cost of credit in the "curb market") reduces real output and raises prices via the supply side of the economy. See Bruno (1979), van Wijnbergen (1983 and 1986), Buffie (1984), and Lim (1987).

14. It is also claimed that Turkey's financial liberalization increased the degree of monetization in the financial system, raised the short-term indebtedness of both the corporate and public sector, and caused erosion in private wealth by accelerating real asset liquidation (Akyüz 1988).

15. See Erdilek (1988) and Rodrik (1988).

16. In this framework, the social welfare function is used in its general form. Its point of tangency with the welfare frontier determines the most desirable allocation among all possible efficient allocations. For more on the welfare frontier and the social welfare function see Ng (1979: 30−52) and Tresch (1981: 17−42).

17. Resource reallocation toward any point on the frontier is assumed efficient, including Kaldor's social improvement, which allows for gainers from the reallocation fully compensating the losers. For more on this see Ng (1979: 60).

18. In addition, forces to overcome structural barriers will be present to move society to another equilibrium, either through legitimate or illegitimate means, creating additional losses in social welfare (Nas et al., 1986: 112).

19. In this regard Elkin writes, "If the democratic state is to retain its legitimacy, it must develop additional institutional arrangements that will allow greater possibilities for individuals to define and pursue their own interest through various kinds of mutual adjustment processes" (1985: 15).

20. A legal structure compatible with the free-market system, redefining property rights and raising their congruence with the norms and dynamics of the market system, for example, could be an important source of improved efficiency.

References

Akyüz, Y. 1988. "Financial System and Policies in Turkey in the 1980s." Paper presented at the conference on Turkey's Economic Development in the 1980s: Changing Strategies and Prospects for the Next Decade, Harvard University.

Arıcanlı, T. and D. Rodrik, eds. 1990. *The Political Economy of Turkey: Debt, Adjustment and Sustainability*. London: Macmillan Publishing Co.

Boratav, K. and O. Türel. 1988. "Notes on the Current Development Problems and Growth Prospects of the Turkish Economy." *New Perspectives on Turkey* 2(1):37–50.

Bruno, M. 1979. "Stabilization and Stagflation in a Semi-industrialized Economy." In *International Economic Policy: Theory and Evidence*, edited by R. Dornbusch and J. Frenkel, 270–91. Baltimore, Md.: Johns Hopkins University Press.

Buffie, E. F. 1984. "Financial Repression, the New Structuralists, and Stabilization Policy in Semi-industrial Economies." *Journal of Development Economics* 14(3):305–22.

Central Bank of the Republic of Turkey. *Annual Report*. Various issues. Ankara: Central Bank.

Conway, P. 1988. "The Impact of Recent Trade Liberalization Policies in Turkey." In *Liberalization and the Turkish Economy*, edited by T. Nas and M. Odekon, 47–67. Westport, Conn.: Greenwood Press.

———. 1987. *Economic Shocks and Structural Adjustments: Turkey after 1973*. Amsterdam: North Holland.

Cooper, R. 1971. "Currency Devaluation in Developing Countries." *Princeton Essays in International Finance* 86:3–31.

Elkin, S. L. 1985. "Between Liberalism and Capitalism: An Introduction to the Democratic State." In *The Democratic State*, edited by R. Benjamin and S. L. Elkin, 1–17. Lawrence: University of Kansas Press.

Erdilek, A. 1988. "The Role of Foreign Investment in the Liberalization of the Turkish Economy." In *Liberalization and the Turkish Economy*, edited by T. Nas and M. Odekon, 141–59. Westport, Conn.: Greenwood Press.

Helliwell, J. 1988. "Comparative Macroeconomics of Stagflation." *Journal of Economic Literature* 26:1–28.

Kazgan, G. 1985. *Ekonomide Dışa Açık Büyüme* (Outward-looking Growth). İstanbul: Altın Kitaplar.

Keyder, Ç. 1984. "İthal İkameci Sanayileşme ve Çelişkileri" (Import Substituting Industrialization and its Inconsistencies). In *Krizin Gelişimi ve Türkiye'nin Alternatif Sorunu*, edited by K. Boratav, Ç. Keyder, and Ş. Pamuk, 13–35. İstanbul: Kaynak Yayınları.

Kopits, G. 1987. "Structural Reform, Stabilization and Growth in Turkey." International Monetary Fund Occasional Paper 52. Washington, D.C.: IMF.

Krueger, A. O. 1974. *Foreign Trade Regimes and Economic Development: Turkey.* New York: National Bureau of Economic Research.

Krugman, P. and L. Taylor. 1978. "Contractionary Effects of Devaluation." *Journal of International Economics* 8:445–56.

Lim, J. 1987. "The New Structuralist Critique of the Monetarist Theory of Inflation." *Journal of Development Economics* 25:45–61.

Nas, T. F. and M. Odekon, eds. 1988. *Liberalization and the Turkish Economy.* Westport, Conn.: Greenwood Press.

Nas, T. F., A. C. Price, and C. T. Weber. 1986. "A Policy-oriented Theory of Corruption." *The American Political Science Review* 80(1):107–19.

Ng, Yew-Kwang. 1979. *Welfare Economics.* London: Macmillan Press.

OECD. 1987. *Economic Surveys: Turkey.* Paris: OECD.

Pamuk, S. 1982. "İthal İkamesi, Döviz Darboğazları ve Türkiye" (Import Substitution, Foreign Exchange Bottlenecks, and Turkey). In *Krizin Gelişimi ve Türkiye'nin Alternatif Sorunu,* edited by K. Boratav, Ç. Keyder, and Ş. Pamuk, 36–68. Istanbul: Kaynak Yayınları.

Rodrik, D. 1988. "External Debt and Economic Performance in Turkey." In *Liberalization and the Turkish Economy,* edited by T. Nas and M. Odekon, 161–83. Westport, Conn.: Greenwood Press.

Şenses, F. 1988. "An Overview of Recent Turkish Experience with Economic Stabilization and Liberalization." In *Liberalization and the Turkish Economy,* edited by T. Nas and M. Odekon, 9–28. Westport, Conn.: Greenwood Press.

———. 1983. "An Assessment of Turkey's Liberalization Attempts since 1980 against the Background of Her Stabilization Program." *METU Studies in Development* 10(3):271–322.

Sönmez, M. 1982. *Türkiye Ekonomisinde Bunalım* (Crisis in Turkish Economy). Istanbul: Belge Yayınları.

Tresch, R. W. 1981. *Public Finance, A Normative Theory.* Plano, Tex.: Business Publications, Inc.

Turkish Industrialists' and Businessmen's Association, TÜSİAD. 1989. *1989 Yılına Girerken Türk Ekonomisi* (Turkish Economy at the Beginning of 1989). İstanbul.

Van Wijnbergen, S. 1986. "Exchange Rate Management and Stabilization in Developing Countries." *Journal of Development Economics* 23:227–47.

———. 1983. "Credit Policy, Inflation and Growth in a Financially Repressed Economy." *Journal of Development Economics* 13:45–65.

2

Politics and Economic Policy-Making in Turkey, 1980–1988

Sabri Sayarı

Introduction

Since its transition from an authoritarian one-party regime to competitive politics in the late 1940s, Turkey has experienced both democratic and military-authoritarian rules. Between 1950 and 1988, Turkey had elected civilian governments for nearly thirty-two years and experienced either direct or indirect military rule for about six years. While the tenure of elected governments in office have been periodically cut short by coups, military interventions in postwar Turkish politics (1960, 1971, and 1980) have all been followed by the journey back to democracy and revitalization of electoral politics. As a result, the dominant feature of the Turkish political system during the last four decades has been the absence of either a fully consolidated democracy or an institutionalized authoritarian regime. The pendulumlike swings between elected governments and military rule — followed by attempts to restructure political institutions and reformulate the rules of the democratic game under military aegis — underscore the failure of the contemporary Turkish political system to develop a durable solution to the critical problem of political legitimacy.[1]

The interruption of relatively extended periods of populist or semipopulist democratic governance (1950–60, 1961–71, and 1973–80) by military coups have typically occurred during a political crisis. The nature and intensity of these crises have varied considerably. For example, the military's decision to seize power in 1960 was prompted primarily by the growing polarization between the government and the opposition. This intense intraelite conflict, which was accompanied by the governing Democratic party's (DP) efforts to coerce the opposition led by the Republican People's party (RPP) into submission, undermined the legitimacy of democratic politics and paved the way for the modern Turkish Republic's first experience with a military coup in 1960.

The circumstances surrounding the breakdown of the Turkish democracy in 1971 were quite different. The late 1960s witnessed an upsurge of student political violence between the militants of the extreme left and right. While these bloody clashes on campuses created growing public concern, it was not until the emergence of the Marxist urban guerrilla groups in early 1971 that Turkey drifted into another major political crisis. By exposing the government's inability to control terrorist incidents, particularly those involving the kidnapping of several foreigners, and infiltrating the ranks of the military, the urban guerrillas managed to exacerbate the strains in civil-military relations and intensify the factional conflicts within the armed forces. Ultimately, the latter proved to be the decisive factor in the second breakdown of Turkish democracy in 1971 when senior military commanders toppled Prime Minister Süleyman Demirel's government in a pre-emptive move that was designed to forestall a possible coup by a group of radical officers.

In comparison with these earlier crises, the one that Turkey experienced in the late 1970s had a far stronger destabilizing effect on Turkish society and politics.[2] For much of the 1970s, and particularly toward the end of the decade, Turkey displayed the familiar signs of an embattled democracy on the brink of breakdown. They included increasing ideological polarization in the party system; rapid escalation of violence by organized terrorist groups; growing militancy of extremist parties and radical labor unions at both ends of the political spectrum; rising ministerial instability with short-lived coalition or minority governments; and frequent lapses into parliamentary deadlock and immobilism.[3] Among this multiplicity of problems, the most serious one was the dramatic increase in the level and scope of political violence that spread to most parts of the country and claimed more than 4,000 lives between 1976 and 1980. The problem of political instability was heightened by the simultaneous rise of a severe economic and financial crisis resulting from rampant inflation, declining terms of trade, economic stagnation, and Turkey's deepening debt to international governmental organizations and foreign banks. In addition to these domestic political and economic problems, developments in Turkey's external environment — the victory of Islamic fundamentalism in neighboring Iran and the Soviet invasion of Afghanistan — also contributed to the crisis atmosphere that seized Turkey in the late 1970s. By 1980, the possibility of another military takeover had become a matter of public discussion as many Turks, including some segments of the civilian political elites, began to express their open or tacit support for a military solution to the escalating crisis.

The extent of the Turkish military's efforts at political engineering following each intervention since 1960 has varied with the nature and intensity of the crisis preceding its seizure of power.[4] For example, in the case of the 1960 takeover, the officers saw the roots of the crisis primarily in the leadership strategies of the DP and in the legal/constitutional framework of electoral politics. Consequently, the military government of 1960–61 limited its political engineering to banning the DP, prosecuting its leadership, rewriting the constitution, and introducing a new electoral system. In 1971, the officers perceived the activities of the urban guerrillas and the militant Left as the principal threat to political stability and to the institutional unity of the armed forces. Hence, the intervention was followed by a massive crackdown on the Marxist terrorist groups, their real or imaginary supporters among the left-wing political forces, and a large-scale purge in the military.

Since the crisis that seized Turkish society and politics in the late 1970s was much more serious than its predecessors, the military's response in 1980 also proved to be far greater and repressive in its scope and objectives than in 1960 or 1971. Not only did the military stay in power longer than in earlier interventions, but it also engaged in an ambitious attempt to transform the major institutional pillars of Turkish politics. An important aspect of this political project concerned the military regime's efforts to restructure the traditional party system. This was to be accomplished by proscribing all existing political parties—including the RPP, the party that was formed by Ataturk in the early 1920s—banning former party elites from political activity for five to ten years, promoting the rise of a new centrist party with close ties to the military, and rewriting the constitutional and legal rules governing the Turkish political system.

In addition to politics, the 1980 coup also had a greater impact on economic policy-making in Turkey than it had been the case in earlier military interventions.[5] In January 1980, a few months before the military's seizure of power, Prime Minister Demirel's minority Justice party (JP) government launched a major economic stabilization program with the active support and the cooperation of the IMF. The stabilization initiative was designed to normalize an economy that had sprung out of control and had begun to show the signs of a general crisis—triple-digit annual inflation rate, exacerbation of the unemployment problem due to industrial slowdown, widespread shortages of even the most basic consumer goods, and a rising trade imbalance that created additional constraints on the country's dwindling foreign exchange reserves.

Although the generals who planned and executed the coup terminated Prime Minister Demirel's tenure in office, they entrusted economic policymaking to his chief economic advisor and the principal architect of the stabilization program, Turgut Özal. This proved to be a momentous decision since Özal not only shaped economic policies throughout the next decade, but he also emerged as a powerful political figure who played a central role in Turkish politics during the 1980s.[6] First, as the "economic czar" of the military regime, and later as prime minister and leader of the newly founded Motherland party (MP), Özal became the leading proponent of economic liberalization and market-oriented policies. For a country that had a long tradition of state-controlled and inward-oriented economic strategies, Özal's neoliberal strategy of economic growth, with its emphasis on an outward-looking economy, represented a significant new phase in its postwar development.

Özal's efforts to reshape the economy during 1980−88 took place in the context of three different phases of political change from authoritarian rule to democratic politics. From 1980 to 1983, economic policies were formulated under an authoritarian military government. After 1983, Turkey gradually moved from military rule to limited political liberalization (1983−87), and then to greater political opening and redemocratization. The transition from authoritarian rule in the 1980s was initially controlled from "above" and engineered by the military leadership; the restructuring of civil society was not mediated through political pacts between the key actors such as the leaders of the principal political parties and the top military command; and the transition has not yet culminated in a fully consolidated democratic regime despite significant progress toward legitimizing democratic institutions since 1987.[7]

The Political Context of Economic Stabilization under Military Rule, 1980−1983

The generals who came to power following the coup in September 1980 faced two pressing problems. One concerned restoring political order and suppressing the terrorist organizations of the extreme Left, far Right, and Kurdish separatism. Following a large-scale antiterrorist campaign, which involved mass arrests and extensive

use of Martial Law powers, the military brought terrorism under
control within a fairly short time. The other pressing problem on
the military government's agenda was the state of the Turkish
economy. Prior to the coup, the military had given its tacit support
to the Demirel government's stabilization program. After the
coup, it continued its support and, by appointing Özal as deputy
prime minister for economic affairs, fully endorsed his plan for
economic recovery. This plan rejected the economic growth strategy
pursued by the populist governments of the 1960s and the 1970s,
which was based on import-substituting industrialization, extreme
protection with high tariff walls, dramatic wage increases, and low
public sector prices. According to Özal, this strategy had brought
the Turkish economy to the brink of breakdown for two main
reasons: it tended to promote domestic industries that were not
internationally competitive, and it gave rise to a large and inef-
ficient public sector that perennially proved to be one of the main
causes of Turkey's inflation problem.

Özal's immediate objectives in 1980 were to check the three-digit
annual inflation rate, to end the shortages of basic consumer goods,
and to improve the foreign exchange deficit. His longer-term goals
were to replace import-substitution with export-promotion; to trim
down the subsidies to state economic enterprises and eventually
privatize them; to increase foreign investment in Turkey; and to
initiate various market-oriented measures that would enable the
Turks to "get the prices right" in their domestic and international
economic activities. Within a year after the 1980 takeover, considerable progress was made in economic recovery. The annual
inflation rate dropped from about 140 to 35 percent, shortages
of consumer goods and petroleum came to an end, and Turkey's
balance of payment accounts began to improve. In addition to
various austerity measures — a 48-percent devaluation of the Turkish
lira against the dollar, large price increases for a variety of products produced by the public sector, reduction of governmental
subsidies and expenditures, and wage restraints for public sector
employees and workers — economic recovery was positively influenced by the financial backing that the military government
received from international financial agencies and from Turkey's
Western allies.[8]

An equally important factor in the successful implementation
of the stabilization and austerity program was the political context
of economic policy-making in the early 1980s. The stabilization
effort took place within a political system in which there was little
room for opposition to, or dissent from, the policies adopted by

the government. Under normal democratic conditions, groups whose interests were adversely affected by the neoliberal stabilization policies, such as organized labor, would have expressed their opposition through political channels. But Turkey's military regime ruled out this possibility by imposing strict control over potential sources of opposition, namely, the political parties, trade unions, universities, and the press.

Since the military leadership, along with a sizable segment of the Turkish population, blamed the political parties and their leaders for the deterioration of the political and economic conditions in the late 1970s, parties appeared to be high on the military's list of the political organizations that needed to be "disciplined" and "reformed." The officers held Bülent Ecevit and Süleyman Demirel —leaders of Turkey's two major parties of the center-Left (RPP) and the center-Right (JP), respectively—along with the leaders of the two extremist minor parties, personally responsible for Turkey's drift into terrorism and civil strife. The ruling junta headed by Gen. Kenan Evren dissolved all political parties and banned 240 politicians from politics for five to ten years. Thus, for the first time since the founding of the Republic in the early 1920s, the Turkish political landscape was totally devoid of any legal party activity between late 1981 and early 1983.

While the military leadership blamed parties and their leaders for failing to unite when the democratic regime was under attack from the extremist forces, it held the radical trade unions responsible for exacerbating the political and economic problems during 1976—80 through politically motivated strikes and militant protest activities. In the aftermath of the coup, the large Marxist trade union confederation DİSK (Devrimci İşçi Sendikaları Konfederasyonu— Revolutionary Trade Union Confederation) and the much smaller extreme right-wing MİSK (Milliyetçi İşçi Sendikaları Konfederasyonu—Nationalist Trade Union Confederation) were both banned and their leaders were imprisoned. The generals permitted the centrist trade union confederation Türk-İş (Türkiye İşçi Sendikaları Konfederasyonu—Turkish Trade Union Confederation) to function. But the authorities banned all strikes and introduced new regulations for wage increases to replace collective bargaining procedures.

The universities and the press were similarly brought under strict governmental control and supervision. A newly established Higher Education Council was empowered to control all aspects of university education and administration, while the students and the faculty were banned from participating in political organizations. At the same time, a large number of professors were purged from the universities due to their alleged or real involvement in "subversive" activities prior to the coup. Although the military regime did not formulate a special policy for the press, Martial Law commanders in İstanbul and Ankara closed down several newspapers and periodicals and imposed temporary bans on the publication of a number of prominent dailies. To avoid these sanctions, newspaper editors chose to exercise self-censorship and avoided printing news or editorial comments that were critical of the government's policies.

By removing the channels of representation, by sharply reducing the political space for public discussion of governmental policies, and by curtailing civil liberties, the generals created a political environment suitable for a new style of policy making—one that weighed heavily toward centralization and technocratic initiatives. The most telling sign of the centralization of political authority was the consolidation of power in the National Security Council (NSC). Composed of Chief of Staff General Evren and four top military commanders, the NSC had, for all practical purposes, both executive and legislative powers. The newly drafted 1982 constitution, which was approved by a large majority in a nationwide referendum that took place under nondemocratic circumstances, also reinforced the trend toward centralized policy-making style. For example, the new constitution expanded the power of the presidency, promoted it to the position of a strong executive, and legalized the centralization of university administration under the Higher Education Council.

Technocratic policy making on economic and social issues also became the hallmark of the military regime. The Turkish military had traditionally viewed economic policies as a technocratic matter, which would best be left above "narrow" political concerns. For example, the 1971 coup was followed by the formation of a military-backed civilian government in which technocrats and academic economists occupied central positions in economic policy-making. This tendency was reinforced in 1980 when the generals entrusted the management of the Turkish economy to Turgut Özal, a seasoned technocrat who had previously been the director of the State Planning Organization (SPO). Özal not only centralized policy making and emerged as the undisputed "economic czar," but he also gave other technocrats—many of them his colleagues from the SPO, other young economists working at the IMF, the World Bank, and various American universities—strategically important roles in the economic policy process. The net results of this new economic management style in Turkey were similar to those that had taken place in Latin America a decade earlier when technocrats became "intellectual brokers between their governments and international capital, and symbols of the government's determination to rationalize its rule primarily in terms of economic objectives."[9]

The absence of public contestation and democratic liberties under military rule made the task of implementing the neoliberal stabilization policy considerably easier than it would have been otherwise. However, this task was also made easier by the fact that the near-collapse of the Turkish economy in the late 1970s had created a suitable milieu for the implementation of a radically new strategy of economic development. The poor performances of the populist coalition governments of Ecevit and Demirel between 1974 and 1980 discredited the statist variations of the import-substitution policies. Many, especially among the influential business and military elites, were convinced of the need for a new approach to resolving the Turkish economy's recurrent problems. The prevailing trend toward market-oriented policies and liberalization in the world economy also strengthened the arguments for economic and financial reforms within the parameters suggested by the IMF and by the World Bank.

The technocratic initiative for the stabilization of the economy initially benefited from the popular support that the military regime enjoyed as a result of its ability to end the deadly spiral of political terrorism and violence. This, coupled with the government's success in terminating the shortages of consumer goods, won the backing of the urban middle classes. In addition, the groups that stood to benefit most from the new economic policies and enjoyed direct access to Özal and his team of technocrats, were especially supportive of the military regime's stabilization drive. In particular, the new powerful financial interests related to the promotion of nontraditional exports, companies and individuals linked to multinational enterprises, and some segments of the banking sector with an international economic orientation, figured prominently in the support coalition behind the stabilization measures.

Political Liberalization and the Ascendancy of a New Center-Right Coalition, 1983–1987

Between 1983 and 1987, Turkish politics moved from military authoritarian rule toward gradual political opening accompanied by the strengthening of civil society.[10] This intermediary phase between authoritarianism and redemocratization was characterized by political liberalization—a period when the military permitted the revitalization of electoral politics within narrowly drawn limits and removed some of the restrictions on civil liberties. Although the initial phase of the political liberalization process took place under the generals' supervision, it nevertheless proved to be an important step toward the civilianization of Turkish political life.

Following the 1980 coup, the ruling NSC had declared its commitment to return Turkey to democracy. But the generals did not specify a timetable and repeatedly stressed the need to move with caution to avoid repeating the "past mistakes" of the earlier military interventions and withdrawals. These declarations reflected the military's desire for a fundamental restructuring of the Turkish political system instead of partial measures aimed at removing a particular party from politics or rewriting a new constitution. During its first two years in power, the military government approved a large number of new laws that were mostly designed to prevent the recurrence of the problems that the generals perceived to be the main causes of political and social instability in the past. At the same time, the ruling NSC also took steps that would enable the military to retain its political influence after an eventual transition to electoral politics. The two most important of these measures concerned the presidency of the Republic and the structure of the party system: the office of the presidency would be occupied by the leader of the 1980 coup, and party politics would be purged of the precoup political organizations and dominated by a newly established military-backed centrist party.

A provisional article in the new constitution submitted to a nationwide referendum in November 1982 provided for the automatic election of General Evren to a seven-year presidency. Consequently, Evren resigned his military post as head of the NSC and took up the office of the presidency. The four other military commanders of the NSC also resigned from the military and joined a newly formed Presidential Council, which was to advise the president and the cabinet on important policy questions. Following Evren's election as the new president, the military regime also initiated its centrist-dominant party project along with the gradual opening up of the political space.

By early 1983, there were growing indications that the generals had decided, after considerable internal factional debates between the soft-line officers and the hard-liners, to initiate a gradual, controlled, and limited political liberalization.[11] The decision itself, as well as its timing, reflected the influence of a multiplicity of factors: the military clearly expected that it could control the transition and its outcome, it was concerned about the effects of prolonged stay in power on the unity of the military establishment, and it came under growing pressure from Turkey's West European allies and international organizations to make liberalizing concessions. The generals' decision was also influenced by the successful recovery of the Turkish economy after the coup. In this respect, the Turkish transition from authoritarian rule differed from the recent Latin American experience. In the latter, the worsening of economic conditions and the growing debt problem helped pave the way for the transfer of power from the military to the civilian governments during the 1970s. In Turkey, the economic recovery of the early 1980s facilitated the beginning of political liberalization. The softliner generals saw it to their interests to support liberalization while the military still enjoyed fairly extensive popular support due to its success in combatting terrorism and stabilizing the economy.

In accordance with its plans, the ruling military government orchestrated the initial phase of liberalization in 1983.[12] From April, when the NSC permitted the formation of new political parties, until the national elections in November, it vetoed scores of individuals from becoming founding members of the new parties, and/or standing as their candidate in the elections. The regime also banned two newly formed parties widely recognized to be the heirs of Turkey's two major parties prior to 1980, and it used the powers of Martial Law to ban or restrict the activities of various political organizations. Although the military stopped short of creating an official party, it clearly supported the formation of a new centrist party by a retired general. The leadership ranks of the Nationalist Democracy party (NDP) included scores of individuals who were closely identified with the military regime of 1980–83. The government also permitted two other parties to compete in the 1983 elections—the Populist party (PP), which claimed to represent the social democratic voters, and the MP, formed by Turgut Özal. While the officers expected the PP to play the role of the "loyal opposition" in a parliament dominated by the NDP, they did not seem to assign any particular role for the MP in their scenarios for the near future.

Due to the restrictions within which it took place, the 1983 elections were, at best, semicompetitive.[13] But the results of the elections deviated sharply from the expectations of the generals, revealed the shaky assumptions on which their political project for a new party system rested, and ultimately lessened the military's ability to control the transition process. Özal's MP scored a major upset victory over the NDP and the PP. The MP captured nearly a majority of the votes (45 percent) and an absolute majority of the parliamentary seats. The PP came in second with about one-third of the electoral votes. The biggest loser of the 1983 elections was the military's favorite, the NDP, which did very poorly and won less than a quarter of the total votes. The MP's unexpected electoral success was largely, though not exclusively, due to its image as the only party that did not appear to be too closely identified with, or indirectly controlled by, the military.[14]

Following its rejection by the Turkish voters, the NDP's assumed central role in the transition process dissipated almost overnight. Instead, the 1983–87 period witnessed the ascendancy of Özal and his MP. As the coercive and manipulative capabilities of the authoritarian regime gradually gave way to a phased return to civilian government, Özal emerged as one of the central political figures in the transition from authoritarian rule. Several factors contributed to the MP's dominant position in Turkish politics. First, thanks to the new electoral system, which was designed to produce a large parliamentary majority for the strongest party, Prime Minister Özal and his MP enjoyed a comfortable majority in the National Assembly. By scoring another big victory in the local elections of 1984, the MP also established itself as the major political force in many municipal and local administrations, including the electorally important large cities such as İstanbul, Ankara, and İzmir. Second, the two other parties in the Parliament failed to function as effective opposition parties. Both the PP and the NDP were in a state of disarray and experienced frequent defections from their ranks. Third, despite the move toward liberalization of the political system, Turkish politics still operated within narrowly defined limits for most of the 1983–87 period. Former party elites were still barred from political activity and the restrictions on trade unions and the universities remained intact.

Özal's predominance in Turkish politics during 1983–87 had a significant impact on economic policy making. Most importantly, there was a basic continuity with the economic stabilization and liberalization policies that were initiated in the early 1980s. The maintenance of political stability under a government that had strong parliamentary support enabled Prime Minister Özal to pursue policies that were consistent with his general economic strategies. In particular, the strategy of economic growth through export-promotion continued to receive much governmental emphasis and support. The notable expansion of Turkey's exports to the West European and the Middle Eastern markets contributed significantly to another major objective of the government, namely, the maintenance of high growth rates. In other areas, Özal's vision of economic liberalization and market-oriented policies had less striking but nevertheless important results: the cutback of subsidies and the lifting of price ceilings forced the State Economic Enterprises to be more competitive; the level of foreign investment in Turkey continued to increase; the transformation of the country's economic infrastructure—especially communications and transportation facilities—proceeded at a rapid pace, and preparations got underway for various privatization schemes.

But the MP's political dominance also created problems in the management of the economy. Özal's penchant for technocratic, centralized, and personalized policy-making style had become apparent while he served under the military regime from 1980 to 1982. After he became prime minister in 1983, this free handed style of policy making became even more pronounced. As he consolidated his political power, Özal increasingly bypassed the cabinet, the Parliament, and the MP and consulted mostly with his team of young technocrats, his brothers and close relatives, and a few trusted aides. The prime minister's highly personalized style of governing not only led to growing resentment and criticism from the bureaucracy, political parties, and the press, but it also deprived the government from incorporating constructive criticisms from a wider circle of policy makers into the decision-making process. In particular, middle-and upper-echelon bureaucrats who were left out of policy making, became increasingly embittered over the weakening of their political role and influence. The bureaucratic response to the growing power of the technocrats—especially the young economists brought in by Özal from abroad—took the form of delaying tactics, excessive emphasis on legal measures, and insistence on established bureaucratic procedures. These, in turn, created a host of problems for the government in implementing its policies.

Redemocratization and Challenges to the Governing Center-Right Coalition

The year 1987 marked the beginning of the third phase in Turkey's transition from authoritarian rule to democratic politics. Political developments in the four years following the semicompetitive 1983 elections dramatically highlighted the pitfalls in the military regime's political project concerning the transition process. This was particularly true with respect to the generals' efforts to do away with the traditional parties and to revamp the party system. Beginning with the local elections of 1984, the precoup political parties reemerged on the Turkish political landscape. Operating under new names, they nevertheless retained much of their organizational links with the past. The prominent leaders of the 1970s such as RPP's Ecevit and JP's Demirel were still legally barred from former political activity. However, as Turkey journeyed back toward democracy, they began to defy these legal restrictions by unofficially resuming their leadership roles.[15]

The distortions that were created in Turkey's electoral politics were partly removed by a constitutional referendum and by a national election, held in September and November of 1987, respectively.[16] The referendum was about a constitutional amendment that would abolish the political ban on Demirel, Ecevit, and other party elites. The decision to lift the ban won by a very small majority — 50.3 percent versus 49.7 percent — with only the governing MP campaigning against the constitutional amendment. The close outcome of the referendum led Prime Minister Özal to call an early election in November 1987. Unlike in 1983, the 1987 election was contested by all parties and with the participation of the politicians who had been barred from politics until then. Hence, the election represented an important threshold in Turkey's transition to democracy.

Prime Minister Özal's MP did reasonably well in the election and finished first despite a strong challenge for the center-Right votes by Demirel's True Path party (TPP). The MP received 36.3 percent of the total votes — down from 45 percent in 1983 — and captured 292 parliamentary seats out of 450. The MP clearly benefited from a change in the electoral system in 1987, which increased the already substantial rewards received by the strongest party in the allocation of the parliamentary seats. While the center-Left Social Democratic Populist party (SDPP) led by Erdal İnönü emerged from the election as the main opposition force with 24.7 percent of the votes, Demirel's TPP came in third after receiving 19.1 percent. Ecevit, who chose to establish a new Democratic Left party (DLP) instead of joining the SDPP, finished a distant fourth with 8.5 percent of the votes and failed to get elected to the parliament.

Although the 1987 election enabled Prime Minister Özal to remain in power with a comfortable parliamentary majority, the MP's dominant position in Turkish politics began to weaken after 1987. The main reason for this was the growing public disenchantment with the government's management of the economy, particularly regarding the problem of inflation. The second half of the 1980s witnessed the rise of a runaway inflationary trend that reached an annual rate variously estimated to be around 80 percent in 1988. Although the Turkish economy continued to grow at a fairly impressive rate, and the country's export performance maintained its momentum, the steep inflation rate coupled with rising unemployment figures led many voters to desert the MP. Fixed income groups—government employees, retired people, and organized labor—were among the hardest hit by the spiraling inflation rate. Furthermore, the government's neoliberal economic measures resulted in worsening the gap between the rich and the poor, while the latter experienced a decline in their real wages and standard of living.

Political factors played an important role in the reemergence of the inflation problem in the second half of the decade. The redemocratization process inevitably introduced new political variables into economic policy making. These stemmed from the resumption of competitive elections and the replacement of the artificial party system that was created by the military with a more representative one. To ensure his and the MP's political survival in the face of growing competitive pressures from rival parties—particularly from Demirel's TPP—Prime Minister Özal chose to significantly expand public expenditures before the referendum and the national election in 1987.

Given the importance of political patronage in retaining supporters and winning new ones, governing parties in Turkey had often sought to manipulate public policy to influence electoral outcomes.[17] In the case of the MP, the need to allocate resources for patronage-oriented government expenditures became all the more pronounced due to the electoral calendar of 1987—88. In addition to a national election and a constitutional referendum in 1987, there was also another referendum in September 1988 over a minor issue concerning the issue of early local elections.[18] Since the opposition parties turned both of these referendums into a public poll over the government's popularity, they too assumed the characteristics of national elections with full-scale campaigning by political parties.

The impact of increased public expenditures before the electoral contests of 1987—88 was reflected in steep rises for most products and services, which defied the government's rhetoric regarding the imminency of a decline in annual inflation figures. The problem of inflation, coupled with the reemergence of alternatives to the MP on the center-Right and the center-Left, figured prominently in the declining personal political popularity of Turgut Özal as well as his MP. In the months following the 1988 referendum, opinion polls showed a steady erosion of voter support for Özal's leadership and for the MP's governmental performance. The government's strategy of accepting the inflation and promoting expansion—through increases in exports and imports with changing exchange rates— appeared to be a growing political liability for the MP.

The problems encountered by the MP in retaining its popular support were compounded by the cracks in the coalition on which it was built. When Özal formed his party in 1983, it represented a new coalition of center-Right political forces. The MP's organizational ranks included individuals who had previously worked for the center-Right Justice party (JP), as well as the two extremist right-wing minor parties, the Islamic fundamentalist National Salvation party (NSP) and the neo-Fascist National Action party (NAP). Özal himself had been a political protégé of the JP's leader Demirel and he had also maintained close ties with the NSP in the late 1970s.[19] But the MP's leadership ranks also included many newcomers to politics. Most of them were engineers and technocrats with conservative political and religious orientations.

Özal's coalition-building efforts initially achieved considerable success and contributed significantly to the MP's electoral victories. The new center-Right coalition maintained its unity until the late 1980s despite the frequent rise of factional conflicts between the so-called liberals and the political religious right-wingers—dubbed the "holy alliance" by the Turkish press—among the party's deputies in the Parliament. Most of the liberals were either newcomers to politics or had previously supported the JP. The right-wing faction was mostly made up of the former supporters of the NSP and the NAP.

The MP's broader support coalition comprised voters who had, in the past, traditionally supported center-Right parties such as the JP, as well as those who had drifted to the Islamic fundamentalist and the militant rightist parties during the polarized politics of the 1970s. In an effort to broaden its electoral appeal, the MP employed a typical "catchall" strategy and managed to build an interclass nucleus of social support including urban middle classes, business interests—especially the burgeoning export sector and large domestic industries that linked up with foreign capital through joint ventures—and some segments of the peasantry and the urban poor.

By 1988, there were growing indications of major cracks in the social and political coalition that was put together by Özal in the first part of the decade. The tensions and conflicts between the rival factions in the MP's leadership ranks began to surface with much greater force than before and seriously threatened party unity. The balancing act that Özal performed between the liberals and the right-wingers among the MP's parliamentary deputies became more precarious as a result of growing signs that Demirel's TPP might well replace the MP as the main political force of the center-Right in the Turkish party system.

The electoral basis of the center-Right coalition also showed signs of major defections from the MP as the party slipped in the polls and in public opinion surveys. While some voters shifted their loyalties to the TPP and to the minor parties of the political Right, many were still in search of possible new alternatives to the MP. Although this search was likely to continue in the immediate near future, all signs pointed to the fact that 1988 marked the beginning of the end of the dominance that the MP had enjoyed in Turkey's politics for the better part of the 1980s.

Notes

1. For an analysis and an explanation of the development of Turkish democracy, see Sunar and Sayarı (1986: 165−86). For general overviews of recent Turkish politics, see Rustow (1987) and Harris (1985).

2. On the political context of the crisis and democratic breakdown in 1980, see Dodd (1983) and Karpat (1981: 1−43). For a useful journalistic account of the military's perception of the crisis, see Birand (1984).

3. See Sayarı (1981: 1).

4. On the politics of military interventions in Turkey, see Turan (1988). For an interesting Turkish perspective, see also Özdemir (1989).

5. For some perspectives on economic policies in the 1980s, see Nas and Odekon (1988), Ebiri (1980: 209−54), and Şenses (1981: 409−53).

6. For a brief political biography of Özal, see Sayarı (1990: 395−401).

7. Viewed from a comparative perspective, the transition process in Turkey has more in common, for example, with the recent Brazilian experience than it does with the democratization of Spain following Franco's rule. For comparative case studies, see O'Donnell, Schmitter, and Whitehead (1986).

8. See Rodrik (1986).

9. See Kaufman (1979: 189).

10. For a description of the initial phase of this period, see Ahmad (1985: 211−26) and Ergüder (1988: 115−45).

11. See Doğan (1985).

12. See Sunar and Sayarı (1986: 184−86).

13. For a useful analysis and interpretation of the election results, see Ergüder and Hofferbert (1987: 23−30).

14. Although Özal was the chief architect of the military regime's economic policies, his resignation from the government in 1982 following a major financial scandal and his decision to form a political party in 1983 had created some strains in his relations with the generals. In addition, the MP's image was bolstered by President Evren's sharp denunciation of Özal in a nationwide television address shortly before the polling took place.

15. For developments in party politics, see Turan (1988: 63−80).

16. For an analysis of the results of the referendum and the national elections, see Ergüder (1988: 115−45).

17. See Sayarı (1977: 103–13). For comparative case studies and a major theoretical statement on this issue see Ames (1987).

18. The referendum in 1988 turned out to be an electoral disaster for Özal. His position on the proposed constitutional change for the scheduling of local elections was soundly defeated by a 65-percent margin.

19. Özal was a parliamentary candidate from the National Salvation party in the 1977 national elections but failed to get elected from his electoral district in İzmir. His brother Korkut was a leading member of the NSP and served as a minister in the coalition governments of the mid-1970s.

References

Ahmad, F. 1985. "The Transition to Democracy in Turkey." *Third World Quarterly* 211–26.

Ames, B. 1987. *Political Survival: Politicians and Public Policy in Latin America*. Berkeley: University of California Press.

Birand, M. A. 1984. *12 Eylül: Saat 04.00* (September 12: 4:00 a.m.) İstanbul: Karacan Yayınları.

Dodd, C. H. 1983. *The Crisis of Turkish Democracy*. Walkington, England: Eothen Press.

Doğan, Y. 1985. *Dar Sokakta Siyaset (1980–1983)* (Politics in the Alley). İstanbul: Tekin Yayınevi.

Ebiri, K. 1980. "Turkish Apertura." *METU Studies in Development* 7(3–4): 209–54.

Ergüder, Ü. (1988). "Post-1980 Politics and Parties in Turkey." In *Perspectives on Democracy in Turkey*, edited by E. Özbudun, 115–45. Ankara: Turkish Political Science Association.

Ergüder, Ü and R. I. Hofferbert. 1987. "Restoration of Democracy in Turkey? Political Reforms and Elections of 1983." In *Elections in the Middle East: Implications of Recent Trends*, edited by Linda Layne, 23–30. Boulder, Colo.: Westview Press.

Harris, G. S. 1985. *Turkey: Coping With Crisis*. Boulder, Colo.: Westview Press.

Heper, M. and A. Evin, eds. 1988. *State, Democracy, and the Military: Turkey in the 1980s*. New York: Walter de Gruyter.

Karpat, Kemal. 1981. "Turkish Democracy at Impasse: Ideology, Party Politics, and the Third Military Intervention." *International Journal of Turkish Studies* (Spring-Summer), 1–43.

Kaufman, R. 1979. "Industrial Change and Authoritarian Rule in Latin America: A Concrete Review of the Bureaucratic Authoritarian Model." In *The New Authoritarianism in Latin America*, edited by D. Collier, 189. Princeton, N.J.: Princeton University Press.

Nas, T. and M. Odekon, eds. 1988. *Liberalization and the Turkish Economy*. Westport, Conn.: Greenwood Press.

O'Donnell, G., P. Schmitter, and L. Whitehead, eds. 1986. *Transitions from Authoritarian Rule: Prospects for Democracy*. Baltimore, Md.: Johns Hopkins University Press.

Özdemir, H. 1989. *Rejim ve Asker.* (Regime and Military). İstanbul: AFA Yayınları.

Rodrik, D. 1986. "Macroeconomic Policy and Debt in Turkey during the 1970s: A Tale of Two Policy Phases." Harvard University, Kennedy School of Government. Mimeo.

Rustow, D. A. 1987. *Turkey: America's Forgotten Ally.* New York: Council on Foreign Relations.

Sayarı, S. 1990. "Turgut Özal," In *Political Leaders of the Contemporary Middle East and North Africa,* edited by B. Reich, 395–401. Westport, Conn.: Greenwood Press.

———. 1981. "The Crisis of the Turkish Party System, 1973–1980." Paper presented at the Conference on History and Society in Turkey. Berlin.

———. 1977. "Political Patronage in Turkey." In *Patrons and Clients in Mediterranean Societies,* edited by E. Gellner and J. Waterbury, 103–13. London: Duckworth's.

Şenses, F. 1981. "Short-Term Stabilization Policies in a Developing Economy: The Turkish Experience in 1980 in Long-Term Perspective." *METU Studies in Development* 8(1–2).

Sunar, I. and S. Sayarı. 1986. "Democracy in Turkey." In *Transitions from Authoritarian Rule: Prospects For Democracy,* edited by G. O'Donnell, P. Schmitter, and L. Whitehead, 165–86. Baltimore, Md.: Johns Hopkins University Press.

Turan, I. 1988. "Political Parties and the Party System in Post-1983 Turkey." In *State, Democracy and the Military,* edited by M. Heper and A. Evin, 63–80.

3

Export-Led Growth and the Center-Right Coalition in Turkey

John Waterbury

Introduction

Since the early 1980s Turkey has resolutely and fairly successfully pursued an economic strategy of export-led growth. In that respect it has joined the ranks of a number of East Asian economies, and, like them, provides lessons in the political economy of transition for the many developing countries contemplating similar strategies. The argument here will focus on three basic variables that circumscribe the transition. First is the export-led strategy itself; second, the use of public expenditures to promote exports largely through the private sector; and, third, the use of public expenditures to maintain a minimal winning electoral coalition.

There are a number of assumptions associated with these variables. With respect to public expenditures, they can be seen as two kinds: enhancing productivity and exports in a straightforward way, and maintaining the coalition and compensating losers in the new strategy through discretionary funds. These two kinds of public expenditure yield two kinds of discourse: one in which the efficiency of the market is lauded, and one in which traditional patronage politics, centered in the government and the governing party, predominates. International creditors and business elites are attuned to the first discourse, while potential and actual voters listen to the second.

A second assumption is that Turkey has established itself as an electoral system in which the center-Right predominates. Among the heterogeneous elements that make up the center-Right, a party or parties can fashion a fairly narrow winning coalition under current electoral law. One segment of that coalition is the large business sector that is undertaking the export drive and making heavy claims

44

on the public budget. But that sector can neither openly align itself with a specific party nor can it deliver votes commensurate with its financial claims. Therefore, the governing coalition must use large amounts of discretionary funding to keep other allies, richer in votes, in the coalition, as well as to neutralize broad segments of the population that experience a relative loss of income as the new strategy unfolds.

Third, the large business sector will tolerate the use of these discretionary funds that do not have a direct payoff in increased production or efficiency, because they do provide that level of political stability necessary to sustain their activities.[1] This point needs some elaboration.

All of Turkish enterprise is highly leveraged and must walk a tightrope — of working at near full capacity and meeting payments on increasingly costly debts. No matter how dynamic the economy is, it has the appearance of a house of cards. Widespread default on debt held by the banking system could end the miracle. The loss of a few foreign markets could lead to such a default. If external creditors find their confidence in the export drive flagging, the flow of external credits that have sustained Turkey's high rate of imports, themselves crucial to sustaining the export drive, could come to an end. For the economy as a whole, repeated devaluations of the Turkish Lira (TL) and continued foreign borrowing have produced an external debt that is over 55 percent of GNP with servicing obligations in the coming years that will average $7 billion per annum, or approximately 60 percent of visible export earnings. The economic stakes are very high, and the political arrangements that keep Turkey on its tightrope are of paramount importance.

Turkey's public sector, in its broadest sense, encompasses all the instruments of state intervention in the economy and the use of public resources by state agencies, writ large. In a more narrow sense it refers to the financial and nonfinancial State Economic Enterprises (referred to henceforth as SEEs). It is argued here that the public sector in its broad sense, and perhaps in its narrow sense, is necessary to the maintenance of the center-Right coalition. Its ability to control or neutralize strategic blocks of organized labor and white-collar employees, to supply key private enterprises, and to service geographically dispersed constituencies is essential to maintaining the minimal winning coalition — something in the range of 35–40 percent of all validly cast votes. In addition, it is not important to this argument that MP (Motherland party) per se holds this coalition together; any other coalition of center-Right elements would presumably face the same challenge.

In sum, the logic of Turkey's current economic and political system can be analyzed in very different, and frequently contradictory terms. Specifically, the Özal government favors turning the economy over to the private sector *and* reinforcing the state. It has promoted deregulation and liberalization in the name of efficiency *and* increased the scope of discretionary allocations in the economy. It has promoted survival of the fittest in the export sector *and* built entitlements elsewhere.

The Center-Right Coalition

Turkey is not alone in witnessing the emergence of an electorate with a center of gravity in the center-Right. Even accepting the volatility of that vote, its existence requires some explanation. What we may be seeing are the results of decades of the failure of interventionist states to incorporate the bulk of active adults into the formal economy and polity. The result has been the expansion of the informal, nonregulated, and unmeasured economy; the atrophy of formal corporatist political organizations; and the formation of parties that reflect new economic interests. Informal does not necessarily mean poor, and there is material wealth and political resentment in abundance to sustain the new coalitions. In short, in contrast to what one would have observed in the 1950s and 1960s, there is now present in Turkey and elsewhere, a large middle class, covering a range of incomes, many of whose members are self-employed or otherwise engaged in private markets at least part of the time. They may deal with the state and extract resources from the state, but they are not of the state (see Ergüder and Hofferbert 1987).

The shift to an openly center-Right coalition in Turkish politics is certainly discernible in 1950 and throughout the ensuing decade of Demokrat party domination. However, there was no clear center-Left alternative, but rather one between statism of greater or lesser degrees. It is significant that despite the proclaimed intention of the Demokrat party to divest from and to privatize public enterprises, the SEE sector actually expanded during the 1950s. Turkey witnessed the proliferation of so-called election factories, especially in sugar and cement, through which the Demokrat party could shore up its coalition (Ahmad 1977: 128; Roos and Roos 1971: 43).

After the 1960 military coup, the center-Right reestablished its electoral predominance under the Justice party (JP), which alone won 53 percent of the vote in the parliamentary elections of 1965.

It was apparent that even recent migrants to the cities were attracted to the JP (Özbudun 1980: 76 and 1987: 343). Indeed, the transformation of the RPP to an openly Left-Center position was probably driven by the 1965 success of the JP (Sunar and Sayarı 1986: 176). After 1969, the center-Left began to gain strength, and the existence of a kind of natural constituency for it, with the potential to dominate electoral politics, seemed a likely outcome. Since the first Demokrat victory in 1950, Turkey had changed immensely. The urban population had grown from 4,000,000 to around 12,000,000. Membership in labor unions had grown from a few tens of thousands in the early 1950s to about 1.2 million in 1969 (part of the growth is of course attributable to the legalization of a broad range of union activities in the 1961 constitution). If one combined these new and growing constituents with an already entrenched technocracy and white-collar strata in public employ (including parts of the military), then a projection of a stable center-Left dominant coalition does not seem at all farfetched.

Once Ecevit had gained full control of the RPP, that coalition made itself felt, winning 33 percent of the vote in 1973 and 41 percent in 1977. The center-Right had splintered among the Justice, National Salvation, National Action, and Democratic parties, which together took 56 percent of the vote in 1973, and 54 percent in 1977. The RPP had to govern in coalition with center-Right partners. This notwithstanding, the center-Left appeared to be gaining at the expense of the center-Right. That was an illusion. In the partial elections of 1979 for one-third of the Senate and five empty seats in the Grand National Assembly, the Justice, National Salvation, and National Action parties won 63 percent of the vote. The JP alone won 48 percent.[2]

The three years of military rule after 1980 saw the same pattern reestablished, although the names of the players had changed (see table 3.1). The two major center-Right formations — MP throughout the period, and the TPP beginning in 1984 — locked up 65, 54, and 55 percent of the vote. MP's share has settled at around a third of the total. To describe this narrow coalition as stable and dominant requires an act of faith. The odds for its continuation may be poor. Inflation and worsening income distribution eroded the legitimacy of MP, which paid the price in the municipal elections of March 1989. Nonetheless, the center-Right still won 61 percent of the vote. However, if current growth rates of GDP are maintained, then it is likely that they were MP's constituent parts (the notorious *kutsal ittifak*) to come unglued, other center-Right parties, principally TPP, would pick up the pieces. There would be no

Table 3.1 Distribution of Votes in Turkish Elections: 1983–1989

	Party	General Elections 1983	Municipal Elections 1984	By-Elections 1986	General Elections 1987	Municipal Elections March 1989
Center Right	MP[a]	45.2	41.5	32.0	36.2	22.0
	TPP[b]	–	–	–	–	25.0
	WP[c]	–	13.0	23.4	19.2	25.0
	NWP[d]	–	–	–	7.2	10.0
	Subtotal	45.2	57.5	55.4	62.6	61.0
Center Left	SDPP[e]	–	24.0	22.8	24.7	28.0
	DLP[f]	–	–	8.6	8.5	9.0
	Subtotal	54.0	24.0	31.4	33.2	37.0
Ephemeral	NDP[g]	23.5	7.1	–	–	–
	PP[h]	30.5	8.7	–	–	–

Source: Sunar (1987); *The Middle East*, January 1988: 15; *Cumhuriyet*, March 28, 1989.
Columns do not add to 100% as not all parties are listed.

Notes: [a] Motherland party (Özal); [b] True Path party (Demirel); [c] Welfare party (Erbakan); [d] Nationalist Labor party (Türkes); [e] Social Democratic Populist party (İnönü); [f] Democratic Socialist party (Ecevit); [g] National Democracy party; [h] Populist party.

major swing to the center-Left. Moreover, the left itself is divided between Erdal İnönü's SDPP and Bülent Ecevit's DLP. Thus, with the center-Left and the center-Right divided, Özal may be able to survive with a third of the vote; the minimal winning coalition.

The center-Right will, under any conceivable alignment, present two economic faces. It will pursue liberalization, privatization, and private sector expansion in key export sectors, while borrowing heavily (perhaps printing money as well as issuing Treasury Bonds) in order to maintain large public spending programs. The center-Right coalition's alternatives can be rendered as follows:

Enhance Economic Efficiency and State Fiscal Strength	*Coalition Maintenance through State Patronage*
Liberalization	Neutralize Organized Labor
Deregulation	Control Discretionary Credit
Public Sector Reform	Service Scattered, Private
Privatization	Sector Constituents
Reduced Public Spending	Subsidize Private Sector
	Export Drive

The left-hand measures are the features of the face Özal wishes to show the donor community, the European Community (EC), and international business. The right-hand measures are the features of the face that Özal turns toward his domestic political allies, and it is the policy area in which he took direct control prior to his election to the presidency in November 1989. Theoretically, with time the policies on the left hand could create new organized interests in the private sector that could sustain the center-Right coalition. Then Özal or any successor could reduce the flow of resources through the policies on the right hand. But that moment is, if it is ever reached, fairly far in the future.[3] All of the external and domestic constraints that Turkey faces would argue for a continuation of both sets of policies. Perhaps only Turkey's full integration into the EC would solidify a new, entrenched, export-oriented private sector, controlling sufficient resources and people to build a new coalition. Even then, as the Japanese experience tells us, there will be great pressure on any center-Right coalition to make large side payments to guarantee political peace. Moreover, important segments of the existing center-Right coalition look with misgiving on entry into the EC and, indeed, on the export orientation itself. Like the Japanese small business sector, they may make substantial claims on public resources and find in the SEE sector a natural ally in favor of tariff protection, production subsidies, and public pump priming.

Etatism under Özal

The public sector in its broadest sense has not diminished its
weight in the Turkish economy; rather, it has regrouped. In many
ways more discretionary power and resources have been concentrated in the state, and, more specifically, in the prime minister's
office than is generally recognized. The volume of public outlays
remains very large in relation to all economic measures. For instance, the public share in total fixed capital investments stood at
50 percent at the beginning of Turkey's adjustment crisis in 1979.
Total fixed capital investments in that year represented 22 percent
of GNP. By 1981 the public share had risen to 62 percent while
total investment to GNP declined to 19 percent. In 1988, total
fixed capital investment reached 25 percent of GNP, while the
public share in total investment stood at 47.5 percent (see table
3.2). The public sector borrowing or financing requirement has
moved erratically since 1980 but within a fairly narrow range
and with little overall decline. In 1980 it stood at 6.4 percent of
GNP, rose to 7.7 in 1984, and declined to 5.5 percent in 1988 (see
table 3.3).

Table 3.2   Relative Share of the Public and Private
Sectors in Total Fixed Capital Investments
(TL Billion)

Years	Total Fixed Investment	Public Fixed Investment TL	%	Private Fixed Investment TL	%
1973	53.4	25.1	47.0	29.3	54.9
1974	73.0	35.0	47.9	38.0	52.1
1975	106.7	53.8	50.4	52.9	49.6
1976	146.0	75.2	51.5	70.8	48.5
1977	195.0	108.0	55.4	87.0	44.6
1978	280.0	135.0	48.2	145.0	51.8
1979	479.0	238.0	49.7	241.0	50.3
1980	864.0	482.0	55.8	382.0	44.2
1981	1,254.0	780.0	62.2	474.0	37.8
1982	1,664.0	1,023.0	61.5	641.0	38.5
1983	2,192.0	1,226.1	56.2	955.9	43.8
1984	3,285.7	1,775.5	54.0	1,510.2	46.0
1985	5,554.7	3,228.4	58.1	2,325.7	41.9
1986	9,120.7	5,299.4	58.1	3,821.2	41.9
1987	13,886.2	7,550.1	54.4	6,336.1	45.6
1988	25,524.0	11,641.0	47.5	12,883.0	52.5

Source: TÜSİAD 1988: 9, and TÜSİAD 1989: 11.

Table 3.3 Consolidated Budget, 1973–1986
(TL Billion, current)

	Budget Deficit (A)	Financial Requirements of SEEs (B)	Budget Transfers to SEEs (C)	Public Sector Borrowing Requirement (A + B − C)	Public Sector Borrowing Requirement/GNP
1973	5.1	14.2	6.1	13.2	4.3
1974	7.4	22.3	7.2	22.5	5.3
1975	8.5	30.6	10.3	28.8	5.4
1976	13.6	47.8	16.2	45.2	6.7
1977	53.1	58.3	27.8	83.0	9.6
1978	37.1	86.3	39.5	83.9	6.5
1979	87.1	186.1	83.4	189.8	8.6
1980	171.6	264.1	152.9	282.8	6.4
1981	112.8	434.7	229.5	318.0	4.9
1982	197.2	464.7	191.4	470.5	5.4
1983	344.2	594.7	278.1	660.8	5.7
1984	902.2	753.3	238.8	1,416.7	7.7
1985	635.0	968.6	171.0	1,432.6	5.2
1986	1,073.0	1,008.0	140.0	1,941.0	4.9
1987	2,598.0	1,821.0	446.0	3,973.0	6.8
1988	3,440.0	1,580.0	1,019.0	4,001.0	5.5

Source: SPO, Ministry of Finance, as presented in Öniş and Özmucur (1988), and the Central Bank of the Republic of Turkey (1988). Figures for 1988 are estimates based on SPO data presented in Turkey: 1989 Almanac, Turkish Daily News, Ankara.

Note: Public Sector Borrowing Requirement: Budget Deficit + Financial Requirements of SEEs − Budget Transfers.

Not only has the flow of public investment remained very high, but a growing proportion of it has been disbursed through off-budget, discretionary funds. Estimates of the total number of funds range from 96 to 134, and total assets in 1987–88 at $3.5 to $5.7 billion (see Celâsun and Rodrik 1987; and Oyan 1987, 1988). In 1988, the Mass Housing and Public Participation Fund (MHPPF) was valued at about $2.1 billion at the prevailing exchange rate. The funds are financed through various earmarked revenues. They are disbursed, nominally, with specific targets in mind, such as public housing, but because their budgets are not subject to prior approval by the Grand National Assembly and few of them are scrutinized by the High Auditing Council, disbursements can be guided by political as well as economic motives.

The MHPPF is the single most important fund and demonstrates the uses to which such funds can be put. Its revenues come from shares in the whiskey tax, the exit fee charged all Turks traveling abroad, sales of revenue-sharing certificates,[4] and foreign loans guaranteed by the Central Bank. The proceeds of all sales of equity in privatization moves will revert to the fund. Under Law 3291 of May 1986, all publicly owned shares in SEEs designated for privatization are transferred to the fund.

The MHPPF, along with other funds, has directed a large flow of public resources into housing, power generation, roads, and other forms of infrastructure (see figs. 3.1a and 3.1b). The flows are largely under the control of the prime minister and the State Ministry for the Economy. Their combined resources can be called upon to target flows strategically, especially before elections and in order to serve important coalition interests. The flows may act as matching funds for large municipal undertakings or to complement regional development programs such as the gigantic Southeast Anatolia Project (GAP).[5] This pattern, it should be noted, was well established by Demirel and the JP coalition in the middle 1970s.

The funds and the state investment budget have combined to bring about a major shift in sectoral investment patterns. Public investment has swung markedly into infrastructure, communications, and energy, while it has dropped in manufacturing and mining. But private investment in manufacturing has begun to fall off as well, while it has grown rapidly in housing, due in part to subsidized credits from special public funds (see figs. 3.1a and 3.1b).

This brings us to the question of the state enterprise sector. It is made up of some 39 firms, run on a commercial basis but not registered under the commercial code, and another 47 establishments

Figure 3.1a. Sectoral public investment (as share of GNP)

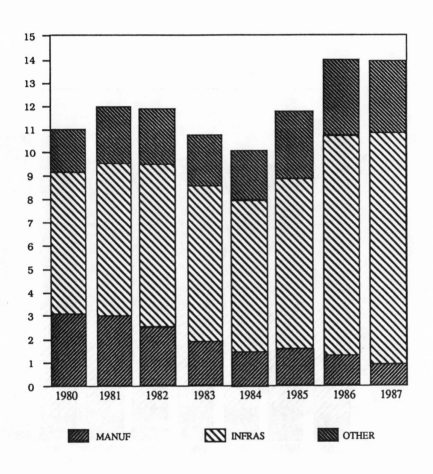

Figure 3.1b. Sectoral private investment (as share of GNP).

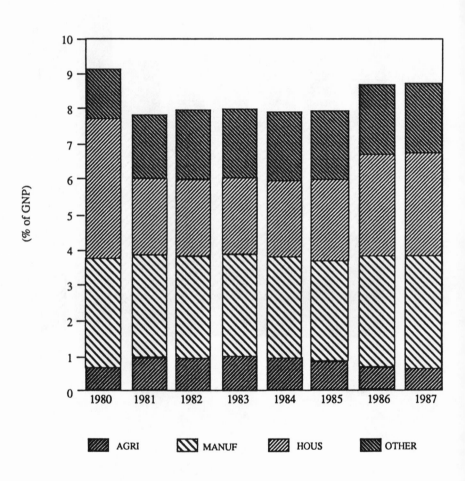

Source: Rita Anand, et al. (4/88).

that are either monopolies or companies registered under the commercial code in which the state owns part of the equity. Özal, as late as the summer of 1987 (August 23rd press conference), set privatization as the most important economic task facing his government. On balance, however, since the adoption of the structural adjustment programs in 1980, three failing private sector enterprises (a bank, a textile plant, and a steel plant) have been taken over by the state, while four significant privatizations had been completed by the end of 1989.[6]

The overall configuration of the SEEs has changed. On the one hand, the weight of the SEEs among the top 500 public and private corporations has increased since the early 1980s (see fig. 3.2 and TÜSİAD 1988; and Kamu-Özel Sektör Dengesi). Their share of total production has declined slightly but is still around 45 percent, but their value-added increased from 11 percent of GNP in 1980, to 17 percent in 1985. Over the same period, their share of total *industrial* value-added rose from 24 to 27 percent (see Celâsun and Rodrik 1987). Similarly, their share of sales revenue and net profits has increased substantially, due, no doubt, to the series of price increases after 1980. As is shown in table 3.4, the share of SEEs in total investment has risen from 33 percent in 1981, to 40 percent in 1985, while their share of *public* investment has increased from 53 to 68 percent over the same period. By 1988 the SPO and Treasury Undersecretariat had concluded that the SEEs had been pressured to undertake too many projects and new investments and a major cutback was being contemplated. But until such cutbacks are implemented, it is safe to say that the SEE sector in most ways remains the center of gravity of the organized, nonagricultural sector of the economy.

On the other hand, levels of employment in the SEEs have been frozen or have actually declined. It is generally conceded that the Özal administration has ended the practice of using the SEEs as employers of last resort or as sources of employment patronage in electoral politics. There was an apparent surge in SEE employment between 1983 and 1984, but that was the result of the conversion to the legal status of operating SEE of TEKEL (the State Alcohol Monopoly), TİGEM (the General Directorate for Agricultural Operations), DHMI (the State Airports Authority) and USAŞ (an airline catering company). Some 80,000 employees were thus added to the SEE work force. If one were to net out these new additions, it would be the case that SEE employment had actually declined from its previous peak of 650,000 in 1978. Civil service employment has grown slowly, so that the government-SEE sectors as a whole

Figure 3.2 The share of public establishments in the top 500 corporations.

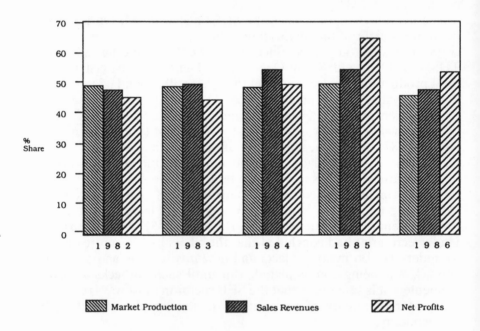

Source: TÜSIAD,   1980 Sonrası Ekonomide Kamu-Özel Sektor Dengesi,
          Istanbul, 1988: 14

Table 3.4   Comparison of SEE Investment Expenditures with General
and Public Investment Expenditures
(TL Billion)

Year	General Investment	Public Investment	SEE Investment	SEE Share in Gen. Inv. %	Public Inv. %
1974	73	35	17	23.29	48.57
1975	107	54	26	24.30	48.15
1976	146	75	35	23.97	46.67
1977	200	108	46	23.00	42.59
1978	267	135	60	22.47	44.44
1979	415	238	128	30.84	53.78
1980	723	423	281	38.87	66.43
1981	1,241	767	406	32.72	52.93
1982	1,647	1,005	533	32.36	53.03
1983	2,153	1,300	733	35.90	59.46
1984	2,859	1,724	1,171	40.96	67.92
1985	4,254	2,493	1,704	40.06	68.35
1986	9,626	5,258	2,405	25.00	46.00
1987	14,823	7,558	3,168	21.00	42.00
1988	24,971	12,053	4,838	19.00	40.00

Source: T. C. Başbakanlık, Hazine ve Dış Ticaret Müsteşarlığı (1986) for
figures through 1985. Central Bank, *1988 Annual Report*, Ankara
for 1986–88. The Central Bank uses SPO figures, which do not
always exactly match those of the Treasury and External Trade
Ministry. The discrepancies are minimal.

(not including the armed forces) employed over 2.3 million people
in 1987 (see table 3.5). This represents 14 percent of the entire
civilian work force and 33 percent of the nonagricultural work force.
To reiterate an earlier point, no politician would unhesitatingly
weaken that strategic grip on the organized work force.

The general issue of reforming SEE activities will be taken up
next. At this point, however, it is important to mention the weight
of SEE deficits in the overall deficits of the Turkish government
and in the economy as a whole. That weight has diminished substantially mainly because the major reform undertaken by the Özal
government has been to allow SEEs to raise their prices regularly
and to operate at profit. This has allowed the state to reduce its
financing of SEE operations through budgetary transfers and loans
from the State Investment Bank (indeed, the latter has been trans-

Table 3.5　Employment by SEEs, 1970–1987
(Thousands)

Year	Administrative Personnel	Labor	Total	Civil Service
1970	165.738	196.562	362.300	—
1971	170.601	204.020	374.621	—
1972	179.921	212.462	392.383	—
1973	192.360	233.502	425.862	—
1974	179.291	324.543	503.834	—
1975	195.979	348.399	544.378	—
1976	216.624	368.964	585.588	—
1977	225.441	410.758	636.199	—
1978	233.998	416.309	650.307	—
1979	159.945	390.371	550.316	—
1980	159.476	381.317	540.793	1,381.431
1981	160.389	369.698	530.087	1,411.053
1982	159.030	370.423	529.453	1,407.905
1983	177.030	403.195	580.225	1,431.479
1984	190.781	467.315	658.096	1,518.737
1985	202.854	479.842	682.696	1,560.934
1986	224.704	497.308	722.012	1,601.142
1987	205.810	477.190	683.000	1,647.135
1988				1,658.125

Source: 1970–78 SPO Annual Programs. SEE employment 1979–1987
SPO *The Fifth Five Year Development Plan: 1988 Program*
Ankara, 1988:89; civil service figures from T.C. Maliye ve
Gümrük Bakanlığı, *1988 Mali Yili Bütçe Gerekçesi*, Ankara,
1988:87. Note that the civil service figures include permanent
and temporary "workers," averaging about 15 percent of the
total figure in the last column in each year.

formed into a new Ex-Im Bank), and to allow the SEEs to borrow
directly from the commercial banking sector and from abroad (the
latter with Treasury guarantees). The financial requirements of the
SEEs peaked in 1979, at the height of Turkey's crisis, at 8.5 percent
of GNP, but declined to 5.5 percent of GNP in 1988 (percentages
derived from table 3.3). This substantial turnaround cannot be
attributed to increases in efficiency and productivity but rather to
the monopolistic and oligopolistic status of many SEEs that have
allowed them to pass on large price increases to final consumers.
Many SEEs are heavily subsidized by the state. In 1986 total
subsidies reached TL 358 billion. By far the largest recipient was

TZDK, the state fertilizer manufacturing and supply firm, with TL 161 billion in subsidies, followed by the railroads with 38 billion, TMO, the Soils Products Office, with TL 81 billion, and TEK, the electricity organization with TL 26 billion.

The 1960s was a time in which no one questioned the existence of the SEEs. As Keyder (1987) and others have pointed out, after the military coup and the Constitution of 1961, all parties accepted an economically interventionist state, and no one advocated, as in the early 1950s, the gradual sale of the SEEs to private capital. Law 440 of 1964, which governed all state enterprises other than monopolies and firms in which the state was not the sole owner, was a state capitalist manifesto. Law 3460 of 1938, which it replaced, embodied Atatürk's vision of a transfer of state assets to the private sector at the same time that it stressed the social equity obligations that state enterprise must meet. Neither theme resurfaced after 1961, while the stress was put upon increased efficiency (Walstedt 1980: 38–39). Before the issuance of Law 440, the draft five-year plan of 1962 had explicitly called for the reorganization of the SEEs along capitalist lines. Feroz Ahmad claims that this terminology was dropped at the insistence of private sector interests with access to the High Planning Commission. They, it seems, had no desire for the SEEs to become more efficient (Ahmad 1977: 275).

The different pieces of the center-Right joined in the expansion of the SEEs. Alparslan Türkeş, one of the so-called radical officers in the 1961 coup, was hostile to large corporate interests in the private sector and championed the small business and the state sector. For its part, the National Salvation party, in control of the Ministry of Industry from 1973 to 1978, advocated heavy industrialization under state auspices and aimed at putting a factory in every district (see Toprak 1984: 126, and Hale 1981: 125). The center-Right coalition of the Justice and National Salvation parties between 1975 and 1978 led to a rapid expansion of the state enterprise sector. With the expansion came a marked deterioration in performance: gross losses of the SEEs grew from TL 4.4 billion in 1975 to TL 71.5 billion in 1979; budgetary transfers alone to the SEEs grew from TL 10.5 billion in 1975 to TL 83.4 billion in 1979 and TL 153 billion in 1980 (World Bank 1982: 426–27). This transpired against a backdrop of rising imported oil prices, growing union demands and militancy, the maintenance of consumer and producer subsidies, and rapidly growing external debt (see the discussion of the convertible lira accounts in Celâsun and Rodrik 1987). The center-Left Ecevit government was granted only a brief moment to try to deal with an intolerable situation.

The Ecevit government resigned after the defeat of the RPP in the 1979 by-elections, but it had begun to take the first painful steps of structural adjustment, including a devaluation of the TL. The new Demirel government, which lasted only half a year before being deposed by the military in September 1980, continued the adjustment process, and Turgut Özal was one of its chief architects. The philosophy that prevails today regarding reform of the SEEs became apparent at that time. Put crudely, it is guided by the assumption that *structural* reforms of the SEEs are not worth the effort and that real efficiency in production can be achieved only through privatization.

The single most important policy innovation has been to free SEE prices. This had already been begun in the late 1970s, but in 1980 the lid was entirely removed. In that year fertilizer prices rose by 824 percent, paper by 231 percent, cement by 177 percent, electricity by 153 percent, and pig iron by 121 percent. More modest price increases continued in subsequent years at rates that generally exceeded that of domestic inflation. Within a year after 1980 the SEEs had become "profit-making," and their net sales rose from −1 percent of GDP to 4.7 percent by the end of 1981. The proportion of Central Bank credits directed to the SEEs declined from 50 percent in 1980, to 13 percent in 1985 (see Celâsun and Rodrik, 1987, especially table 4.4). In early 1984 the Treasury converted nearly TL 1.5 trillion in SEE debt to equity (or about $4 billion), thereby greatly reducing the interest burden born by the enterprises.

In addition, SEEs benefited from preferential exchange rates and from subsidized interest rates on domestic borrowing. The latter may have yielded in monetary terms a cumulative subsidy of TL 2.7 trillion over the period 1980−84, or about twice the cumulative net income of the SEEs for the same period (estimates from an unpublished World Bank report). Similar and more recent conclusions are reached by Mertoğlu (1987: 46−7) who argues that

> SEE balances by year-end 1986 and forecasts for 1987 do not show any significant changes over 1983 or even the pre-1980 period. In real terms, SEE investments have declined during these last two years. Exchange rate differences and interest payments which are included in the investments not only show the investment amount higher than it really is, but also turn losses into profit.

Because many of the SEEs enjoy monopoly or quasi-monopoly status, they have been able to pass on their large price increases to final consumers. Some of those are private sector firms producing for export. They in turn raise their prices while the private sector

Table 3.6   Export Credits, 1977–1986 (TL Million, %)

	Export Credits	Share of Export Credits Central Bank Credits	Share of Export Credits Commercial Bank Credits	Exports Credits Total Exports
1977	15.157	4.4	2.8	48.4
1978	26.848	6.4	3.8	48.4
1979	40.614	6.4	3.7	53.6
1980	91.290	7.3	5.5	41.2
1981	206.911	12.2	7.1	39.0
1982	479.767	11.1	21.0	51.2
1983	728.741	14.7	22.6	56.1
1984	594.517	6.8	17.8	22.8
1985	724.942	0.5	12.9	17.5
1986	1,576.894	0.1	18.8	3.1

Source: Central Bank; as presented in Öniş and Özmucur (1988).

trading companies that handle the bulk of the exports, are partially compensated for the price increases through credit subsidies, tax rebates, and export subsidies (see, e.g., table 3.6, and Baysan and Blitzer, 1988, esp. table 2). Many of these export subsidies will have to be phased out in order to comply with GATT regulations, at which point the policy of allowing SEEs to constantly raise prices may come in direct conflict with Turkey's export drive. Indeed, in 1989 the rate of increase in exports slowed markedly.

Another set of reforms has been legal. Once again, after the 1980 military intervention, specialized committees were formed to look into the reorganization of the SEEs. After the Banker Kastelli scandal and the brief eclipse of Özal, the 1982 Ulusu government put Mustafa Aysan, the minister of transport, in charge of a team of experts to draw up new legislation, accounting procedures, training programs, and computerization. Aysan came up with a set of proposals and a draft bill (see Karataş 1986), but the Ulusu administration adopted a modified version, which became Law 2929 of October 1983. The old division of SEEs on the one hand and, on the other, enterprises that were monopolies or providers of public services were kept. The SEE sector was divided into 31 Sector Holding Companies. The Boards of Directors of the Sectoral Holdings were to have broad powers within their sectors and to insulate them from political interference. No general manager would have had less than ten years' management experience in the public sector. The general manager was to be jointly appointed by the related ministry and the Ministry of Finance. They would report to the High Economic Coordination Council, chaired by the prime minister, and that would be charged with developing long-term strategy for the SEEs.

Once Özal returned to power as Turkey's elected prime minister in 1983, he scrapped Law 2929, and, in October 1984, put into effect Decree-Law 233. This incorporated many of the clauses of Law 2929, including the division of the public sector into commercially run SEEs and public service monopolies. Importantly, however, it did away with the sectoral holding companies, nominally to avoid bureaucratic sprawl. A practical effect was to give the Prime Ministry direct access to all SEEs, and there was, in fact, a wholesale change in top management. The law stipulated that new SEEs could be founded only by action of the Council of Ministers, while they could be dissolved by action of the High Economic Coordination Board (presided over by the prime minister; see Karataş, 1986: 158).

There are two other initiatives that reflect the spirit in which the Özal government has approached public sector reform: the spread of contract personnel and the use of the MHPPF as the primary agency for implementing privatization. Contract personnel is hired into management or into the work force on the basis of an individual contract as opposed to civil service and collective agreement hiring laws. The contractee may be dismissed with relatively few administrative impediments and he does not have the right to be a member of a union. One high official in the Treasury Undersecretariat told the author that the intention was to convert the *entire* SEE management and work force to contract status within two years. The deal that appears to be offered would include higher wages in exchange for less job security. Any individual might understand the broad implications for reduced employment but still hope to be the lucky one who survives the cuts. The conversion of managers to contract status has proceeded fairly rapidly: in 1984 there were 674 such administrators (*memurlar*); in 1985, 3,491; and in 1986, 26,578 or about 10 percent of the administrative corps (Yüksek Denetleme Kurulu 1988: 33). More recent figures are not available.

Seen in a positive light, the contract system has enabled the SEEs to offer salaries to qualified managers as much as three times the levels attainable under the collective and civil service systems. But the contract system is a clear threat to organized labor, and the SDPP (but apparently not Türk-İş) has challenged the constitutionality of the system. In early October 1988, the Constitutional

Court handed down a ruling that in fact declared the system unconstitutional, with consequences that it is too early to assess (*Cumhuriyet*, October 7, 1988).

According to Law 3291 of 1986 on Privatization, all outstanding shares of companies designated for privatization are transferred in their entirety to the MHPPF. Already several SEEs and an even greater number of firms in which the government has an equity position have had their shares handed over to the Public Participation Fund (PPF): Citosan, Petkim, Turban, and Sümerbank are among the most important. The goal is, of course, that the MHPPF will prepare these firms for privatization by restructuring management and debt, perhaps shedding loss-making units and activities and identifying potential buyers. This process, even if the political context permits, is lengthy, and in the meantime the MHPPF becomes a large public sector holding company under the supervision of the minister of state for the economy. To the extent that privatization proceeds, the MHPPF will retain the so-called golden share in all privatized companies that will give it effective veto power over the management and board of directors (the MHPPF retains the golden share with respect to Teletaş). In some ways then, the agency in charge of privatization can be seen as yet another large public holding company, and one might expect its management to think twice before relinquishing control of its assets. It is also a holding company over which the prime minister and the minister of state for the economy can exercise direct control.

The Center-Right Coalition and Income Distribution

In the expansionary 1970s, center-Right and center-Left coalitions spread public resources around in prodigal fashion. Between 1974 and 1978 real public sector wages increased by 58 percent, total employment increased by 28 percent, and value-added fell by 20 percent. Whereas wages stood at about 27 percent of value-added at the beginning of the period, they had risen to 38 percent by its end. In explaining these figures, Boratav captures part of my argument on the nature of center-Right side payments (Boratav 1986: 136; see also Celâsun 1986).

> (T)hanks to the existence of a parliamentary regime, the popular classes are able to influence political decision-making in areas related to their short-term economic interests, but the same classes are not organized at a level at which they can play roles as alternatives to or junior partners in the political power structure.

Figure 3.3   Real income, real expenditures, real wages, and agricultural terms of trade.

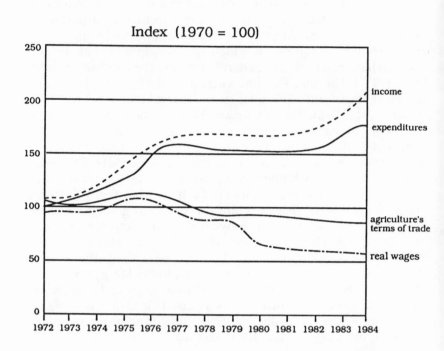

Index (1970 = 100)

Source: Celasun and Rodrik (1987).

For the most part, all sectors of society held their own economically during the 1970s or improved to varying degrees. Until about 1977 the domestic terms of trade for agriculture remained favorable, industrial wages rose in real terms, and private investment was growing.

Since the first steps toward structural adjustment in 1979, both the agricultural terms of trade and real wages fell sharply (see fig. 3.3). "Open unemployment," that is, people not working but actively seeking work, by 1987 stood at 1.2 million, or over 7 percent of the entire work force. The number of unemployed and underemployed not seeking work stood at double that figure.

Both categories are growing at rates in excess of that of the work force itself (see TÜSİAD 1988: 38–40). Certain kinds of social welfare expenditures, crucial in other times and other settings to the maintenance of social pacts, have been cut. As proportions of GDP, expenditures on public health and education declined from 3.3 and 1.1 percent in 1980, to 2.4 and .6 percent in 1985 (Celâsun 1988). In sum, the trend lines represented in figure 3.3 should delineate a scenario of political disaster. How have center-Right coalitions been able to survive while simultaneously reducing the relative incomes of cultivators and of wage and salary earners?

First, it may be that the Turkish people have been willing to put up with austerity and inflation in order to support a return to civilian politics after 1983. They voted for the 1983 constitution to end military rule, and they voted against the military's party and preferred candidate in the 1983 elections. Second, austerity has not fallen uniformly on all sectors of the population, but rather has been targeted, perhaps, deliberately, by policymakers. Third, there have been the compensatory flows consisting of outlays on housing and public works, revenue sharing certificates, and rebates on the value-added tax (VAT). Finally, there has been real growth in the economy, although much of it appears to accrue to the "coupon clippers" who earn over two-thirds of the national income (see table 3.7 and Boratav 1988).

Let us look more closely at the decline in real wages. As a proportion of national income they had declined from 33 percent in 1979, to 18 percent in 1985–86. Similarly, according to Celâsun and Rodrik, gross government salaries and wages dropped from 9 percent of GNP in 1980, to 6 percent in 1985. Official figures show that the share of wages and salaries in the value of SEE production declined from 47 percent in 1979 (in its own right an amazing figure), to 19 percent in 1986 (Yüksek Denetleme Kurulu 1988: 33). However, it appears that in the public sector as a whole it is the civil service that has suffered the greatest absolute and relative declines in salaries (some 50 percent since 1979: see Boratav 1988: 26), and, according to the postcoup labor legislation, they do not have the right to unionize. By contrast, the real decline in the wage of SEE employees has been much less dramatic. In relative terms, the Özal government has been somewhat more solicitous toward organized labor and, in particular, toward the major peak organization, Türk-İş.

The fundamental calculus of Özal may be that he needs a third of the Turkish electorate to keep his center-Right coalition in power. Moreover, barring a collapse of the export drive and a wave of

Table 3.7 Functional Distribution of Income in Turkey, 1967−1988 (%)

Year	Agricultural Incomes	Wages and Salaries[a]	Incomes from Interest, Rent, and Profit[b]
1963	41.19	21.50	37.31
1964	38.67	23.72	37.60
1965	35.83	27.01	37.17
1966	36.19	27.13	38.68
1967	34.53	28.51	36.95
1968	32.44	29.31	38.25
1969	31.58	31.38	37.05
1970	31.08	31.15	37.77
1971	31.31	31.33	37.37
1972	30.32	31.57	38.11
1973	29.13	31.56	39.31
1974	30.20	29.77	40.03
1975	30.76	31.51	37.73
1976	31.28	33.11	35.60
1977	29.12	36.81	34.07
1978	26.66	35.19	38.15
1979	24.33	32.79	42.88
1980	23.87	26.66	49.47
1981	23.06	24.57	52.36
1982	21.82	24.62	53.55
1983	20.52	24.78	54.69
1984	20.44	21.57	57.99
1985	19.08	18.84	62.08
1986	18.09	17.70	64.21
1987	17.10	17.00	65.00
1988	14.00	15.80	70.20

Source: See Öniş and Özmucur (1988), for 1963−86. For 1987−88, see Rodrik (November 1989).
[a] Nonagricultural wages and salaries.
[b] Interest, rent, and profit incomes from nonagricultural activities.

bankruptcies, even if Özal or his successor were to fall, some new center-Right coalition would pick up the pieces. What patterns of public spending and investment will best serve the minimal winning coalition? We should expect a continuation of the following: continued medium to high inflation (fueled in part by continuous devaluation of the TL) with stagnant and in some instances declining real incomes for large portions of the population. These would have to be offset by selective resource flows. The off-budget funds (unless the IMF is able to force them on-budget) can alleviate some of the equity strain through public works and housing. The GAP project will address the gross regional disparities that effectively separate southeast Turkey from the rest of the nation.[7] VAT rebates and revenue-sharing certificates may supplement the incomes of some portion of the lower middle class. If privatization gathers momentum, we may see a few worker stock option programs. (Gürol 1989).

The real question in selective rewards lies in the farming sector and in the small-and medium-enterprise sector. Both have been hit hard in recent years, the first through soaring production costs and deteriorating terms of trade, and the latter through soaring interest rates and decreasing protection against foreign imports. While large firms and trading companies have been able to counterbalance rising production costs with investment incentives, tax rebates, and export subsidies, the private sector depending solely upon the domestic market, has not enjoyed such privileges. It is hard to imagine a center-Right coalition that could ignore these constituents for long, and the increase in agricultural prices preceding the 1987 elections shows that the government is aware of this.

Where might the public sector fit into all this? Ownership in some entities surely will be relinquished, and some chronic losers will be liquidated. But the economic gains of privatization are not sufficient to offset the potential political costs at a time when the MP coalition cannot afford to alienate any potential allies. It is quite conceivable that a large SEE sector will be tolerated by the center-Right (just as it was actually promoted in the late 1970s). It could serve to neutralize a significant segment of the organized work force. It could be used periodically to create jobs at crucial moments in the electoral cycle, and it can continue to provide goods and services to the private sector on favorable terms, even if SEE accounts are not always in the black. There will not be much effort made to promote real efficiency through internal restructuring of the SEEs. The center-Right will have little interest in building a managerial technocracy that takes the task of public enterprise seriously and that might constitute a strong internal lobby that could claim larger flows of public resources and perhaps sabotage center-Right programs (Walstedt 1980: 187, saw just such a group as having emerged sometime in the 1960s). In some ways then, the SEE sector would continue as milch cow and whipping boy.

It should not be concluded from this that this strategy is in fact politically viable. Özal's economic and political strategies are both tightrope walks, and the need to shore up one (e.g., the large wage concessions to labor and the civil service and higher agricultural prices to farmers made in the summer of 1989) could undo the other by changing basic costs upon which the export drive has been founded. Domestic banks may be holding as much as TL 6 trillion (or over $4 billion at the 1988 exchange rate) in nonperforming loans, and a wave of bankruptcies is not improbable. Foreign creditors may become alarmed at Turkey's debt-to-GNP ratio and its annual servicing burden and decide to loan no further. In other words, the equilibrium that has ben established between the export sector and the nontraded sector and between the needs of producers and political allies is dynamic and fragile. But its continuation will have to involve some of the mechanisms just outlined, and it is highly probable that the center-Right will continue to control the levers.

Acknowledgments

This chapter was originally prepared for the panel, "Dynamics of a Mixed Economy: The Turkish Case," organized by Marcie Patton for the annual meeting of the Middle East Studies Association, Los Angeles, November 2–6, 1988. I am grateful to Yeşim Arat, Şevket Pamuk, Ahmet Kuyas, and Kent Calder for subsequent comments.

Notes

1. My argument here has been substantially inspired by Kent Calder's 1988 analysis of the forty-year dominance of Japan's center-Right coalition embodied in the Liberal Democratic party.
2. Sunar and Sayarı (1986: 177) characterize both the NSP and the NAP as being on the extreme right. In terms of socioeconomic programs, however, they were as statist as any other political formation.
3. This conundrum is well-known in more abstract terms. Theoretically, the gains from increased trade should outweigh the aggregate losses of specific interests harmed by trade. Some of the gains can be redistributed to compensate the losers; the real question is how much is redistributed and who is compensated (see Rogowski 1989: 170–71).
4. Revenue-sharing certificates in power plants and the bridges over the Bosphorous are the principal manifestation of what might be called popular capitalism in Turkey. Earnings on the certificates are implicitly guaranteed by the state to yield a real positive rate of return. In the face of high inflation, they have been a popular instrument for the small investor.
5. The big spending programs of several municipalities included running up substantial foreign debts: İstanbul, $900 million; Ankara, $200 million; Cukurova

Region, $120 million; and İzmir, $200 million. Uncontrolled foreign borrowing by the public sector accounted for $23 billion of Turkey's total foreign debt of $38 billion (*Dateline*, June 18, 1988).

6. The first sale in February 1988 involved the state's 22 percent in Teletaş, a manufacturer of switchboard equipment, which in fact was already a private company. In the first half of 1989, 90 percent of the state's equity in the large cement firm, Çitosan, was sold to Société Ciment Français, and 70 percent of USAŞ, an airline catering service, was sold to Scandinavian Airlines (SA). Four small feed production units were also privatized.

7. The State Statistical Institute recently reported geographical shares in national income. It was found, for instance, that average per capita income in Istanbul was the equivalent of $1,180 per annum, while that of Hakkari in southeast Anatolia was $105 (*Dateline*, May 21, 1988).

References

Ahmad, F. 1977. *The Turkish Experiment in Democracy, 1950–1975*. London: Hurst & Co.

Anand, R., A. Chibba, and S. van Wijnbergen. 1988. "External Balance and Sustainable Growth in Turkey: Can They Be Reconciled?" Paper presented at the conference on Turkey's Economic Development in the 1980s, Harvard University, April.

Akyüz, Y. 1988. "Financial System and Policies in Turkey in the 1980s." Paper presented at the conference on Turkey's Economic Development in the 1980s, Harvard University, April.

Arat, Y. 1987. "Social Change and the 1983 Political Elite in Turkey." Unpublished mimeo.

Balassa, B. 1983. "Outward Orientation and Exchange Rate Policy in Developing Countries: The Turkish Experience." *Middle East Journal* 37(3).

Baysan, T. and C. Blitzer. 1988. "Turkey's Trade Liberalization in the 1980s and Prospects for Sustainability." Paper presented at the conference on Turkey's Economic Development in the 1980s, Harvard University, April.

Bianchi, R. 1984. *Interest Groups and Political Development in Turkey*. Princeton, N.J.: Princeton University Press.

Boratav, K. 1988. "Inter-Class and Intra-Class Relations of Distribution under 'Structural Adjustment': Turkey during the 1980s." Paper presented at the conference on the Political Economy of Turkey in the 1980s, Harvard University, April.

———. 1986. "Import Substitution and Income Distribution under a Populist Regime: The Case of Turkey." *Development Policy Review* 4:117–39.

Calder, K. 1988. *Crisis and Compensation: Public Policy and Political Stability in Japan, 1949–1986*. Princeton, N.J.: Princeton University Press.

Çavdar, T. 1988. "Erken Seçim'in Düşündürdükleri" (Thoughts on Early Elections). *Mülkiyeliler Birliği Dergisi* 23(91):3–7.

Celâsun, M. 1988. "Turkey: Fiscal Aspects of Adjustment in the 1980s." Conference on Turkey's Development in the 1980s, Harvard University, April.

———. 1986. "Income Distribution and Domestic Terms of Trade in Turkey."

METU Studies in Development. Special issue on the Turkish economy, 1977–84. 13(122):193–216.

Celâsun, M. and D. Rodrik. 1987. *Debt, Adjustment and Growth: Turkey*. National Bureau of Economic Research Project on Developing Country Debt. Preliminary draft.

Central Bank of the Republic of Turkey. *Annual Report*. Various issues.

Coşan, F. M. and H. Ersel. 1987. "Turkish Financial System: Its Evolution and Performance, 1980–1986." *Inflation and Capital Markets*. Ankara: Capital Market Board Publications.

Cumhuriyet, March 28, 1989.

Dateline, June 18, 1988

———, May 21, 1988

Economic and Social Studies Conference Board. 1969. *State Economic Enterprises*. Istanbul: Economic and Social Studies Conference Board.

Ergüder, U. and R. I. Hofferbert. 1987. "Restoration of Democracy in Turkey? Political Reforms and the Elections of 1983." In *Elections in the Middle East: Implications of Recent Trends*, edited by Linda Layne, 19–46. Boulder, Colo.: Westview Press.

Ekzen, A. 1981. "Kamu İktisadi Kuruluşlarının Yeniden Düzenlenmesi Yaklaşımları ve Dördüncü Beş Yıllık Plan'ın Politikaları" (Approaches to the Reorganization of the State Economic Enterprises and the Policies of the Fourth Plan). *METU Studies in Development*. Special issue. 227–60.

Ersel, H. and G. Sak. 1987. "Ownership Structure of Public Corporations in Turkey." *Yapı Kredi Economic Review* 1(2).

Ertan, I. 1969. "The Problem of the Reorganization of State Economic Enterprises." *State Economic Enterprises* 133–69. Istanbul: Economic and Social Studies Conference Board.

Gürol, M. A. 1989. "Privatization and Labor Relations in Turkish State Economic Enterprises." The Wharton School, Philadelphia, Unpublished monograph.

Hale, W. 1981. *The Political and Economic Development of Turkey*. New York: St. Martin's Press.

Heper, M. 1985. *The State Tradition in Turkey*. Walkington, England: Eothen Press.

Karataş, C. 1989. "Privatization in the U.K. and Turkey." University of Bradford, Bradford. Unpublished paper.

———. 1986. "Public Economic Enterprises in Turkey: Reform Proposals, Pricing and Investment Policies." *METU Studies in Development* 13:135–69.

Kepenek, Y. 1983. *Turkiye Ekonomisi* (Turkish Economy). Ankara: Orta Doğu Teknik Üniversitesi.

Keyder, C. 1987. *State and Class in Turkey: A Study in Capitalist Development*. London: Verso.

Kopits, G. 1987. *Structural Reform, Stabilization and Growth in Turkey*. IMF Occasional Paper 52. Washington, D.C.: IMF.

Mertoğlu, H. 1987. "Increasing Indebtedness and Decreasing Investment in SEE Balances Expected." *Yapı Kredi Economic Review* 1(2): 43–47.

The Middle East, January 1988.

Öniş, Z. 1988. *The Role of the Financial System in the Creation and Resolution of Macroeconomic Crises in Turkey*. Istanbul: Boğaziçi University.

Öniş, Z. and S. Özmucur. 1988. *Supply Side Origins of Macroeconomic Crises in Turkey*. İstanbul: Bogaziçi University.

Özbudun, E. 1987. "Turkey." In *Competitive Elections in Developing Countries*, edited by M. Weiner and E. Özbudun, 328−65. Durham, N.C.: Duke University Press.

————. 1980. "Income Distribution as an Issue in Turkish Politics." In *The Political Economy of Income Distribution in Turkey*, edited by E. Özbudun and A. Ulusan. New York: Holmes & Meier.

Oyan, O. 1988. "Fonlar, İstikrar Programı ve Özelleştirme" (Funds, Stabilization Program, and Privatization). *Mülkiyeliler Birliği Dergisi*, January 20−26.

————. 1987. "An Overall Evaluation of the Causes of Use of Special Funds in Turkey and Their Place in the Economy." *Yapı Kredi Economic Review* 1(4):83−116.

Rodrik, D. 1990. "Premature Liberalization, Incomplete Stabilization: The Özal Decade in Turkey." Unpublished paper.

————. 1988. "Some Policy Dilemmas in Turkish Macroeconomic Management." Prepared for the conference on Turkey's Economic Development in the 1980s, Harvard University, April.

Rogowski, R. 1989. *Commerce and Coalitions: How Trade Effects Domestic Political Alignments*. Princeton, N.J.: Princeton University Press.

Roos, L. and N. Roos. 1971. *Managers of Modernization: Organizations and Elites in Turkey (1950−1969)*. Cambridge: Harvard University Press.

Sağlam, D. 1981. "Türkiye' de KIT Reform Çalışmalarının Değerlendirilmesi" (Evaluation of State Economic Enterprises Reform Studies in Turkey). 2. *Türkiye İktisat Kongresi Kalkınma Politikasi Komisyonu Tebliğleri*, October 2−7. İzmir, Turkey.

Saybaşılı, K. 1976. "Türkiye'de Özel Teşebbüs ve Ekonomi Politikası." (Private Enterprise and Economic Policy in Turkey). *METU Studies in Development* 4:83−97.

State Planning Organization (SPO). 1988. *The Fifth Five Year Development Plan: 1988 Program*. Ankara: SPO

Sunar, I. 1987. "Redemocratization and Organized Interests in Turkey." Unpublished mimeo.

Sunar, I and S. Sayarı. 1986. "Democracy in Turkey: Problems and Prospects." In *Transitions from Authoritarian Rule*, edited by G. O'Donnell, P. Schmitter, and L. Whitehead, 165−86. Baltimore, M.: Johns Hopkins University Press.

T. C. Başbakanlık Hazine ve Dış Ticaret Müsteşarlığı 1986−88. *Kamu İktisadi Teşebbüsleri 1980−1986 Yıllığı*. (State Economic Enterprises: 1980−1986 Yearbook). Ankara.

T. C. Maliye ve Gümrük Bakanlığı. 1988. *1988 Mali Yılı Bütçe Gerekçesi* (Justification for the 1988 Fiscal Year Budget). Ankara.

Toprak, B. 1984. "Politicization of Islam in a Secular State: The National Salvation Party in Turkey." In *From Nationalism to Revolutionary Islam*, edited by S. Arjomand, 119−33. Albany, N.Y.: SUNY Press.

Turkey: 1989 Almanac. Turkish Daily News, Ankara.

TÜSİAD. 1989. *Turkish Economy '89*, İstanbul, Turkey: TÜSİAD.

————. 1988. *1980 Sonrası Ekonomide Kamu-Özel Sektör Dengesi*. (Public-Private Sector Balance in Turkish Economy after 1980). İstanbul: TÜSİAD.

————. 1988. *Turkish Economy '88*. İstanbul: TÜSİAD.

Walstedt, B. 1980. *State Manufacturing Enterprise in a Mixed Economy: The Turkish Case*. Baltimore, M.: Johns Hopkins University Press.

World Bank. 1988. *Turkey: External Debt, Fiscal Policy and Sustainable Growth* 1, The Main Report, 7, Methodological and Statistical Annex. Washington, D.C.: World Bank.

————. 1986. *Turkey: Adjusting Public Investment* 2, Main Report and Statistical Annex. Washington, D.C.: World Bank.

————. 1982. *Turkey: Industrialization and Trade Strategy*. Washington, D.C.: World Bank.

Yüksek Denetleme Kurulu. 1988. *Kamu İktisadi Teşebbüsleri Genel Raporu (Report on State Economic Enterprises), 1985 and 1986*. Ankara.

————. 1987. *Kamu İktisadi Teşebbüsleri Genel Raporu (Report on State Economic Enterprises), 1985 and 1986*. Ankara.

4

Organization of Export-Oriented Industrialization: The Turkish Foreign Trade Companies in a Comparative Perspective

Ziya Öniş

Introduction

The fundamental transformation in the Turkish economy during the 1980s occurred in the sphere of exports. The following facts are worth considering. The share of exports in GNP rose from 3.9 percent, on average, during 1975−79, to 12.2 percent during 1980−88, and to 16.4 percent by 1988. Rapid export growth, in combination with large inflows of external finance, contributed to a significant expansion in import volume. Consequently, the share of foreign trade in GNP expanded from 14.7 percent during the 1975−79 phase, to an average of 30.8 percent during the course of the 1980s. A parallel phenomenon involved the dramatic shift in the composition of exports in favor of manufactured commodities. The share of manufactured exports increased from an initial base of 36.0 percent in 1980, to 75.3 percent in 1985, and reached a peak of 76.7 percent in 1988. Turkey's export boom contributed to the economic recovery of the 1980s with GNP growth averaging 4.5 percent during 1981−84, and 6.8 percent during 1985−87, respectively, as compared with an average growth rate of 0.5 percent during the crisis period of 1978−80.[1]

The Turkish experience does not represent a paradox for neoclassical economic theory. Turkey experienced an economic crisis during the late 1970s due to an inappropriate combination of industrialization and trade policies. Policy makers persevered with import substitution industrialization (ISI) during the 1970s, in the context of the third and fourth Five-Year Development plans, following the completion of the "easy phase" by the late 1960s. The very instruments required to sustain the momentum of the ISI strategy, namely, high levels of effective protection and overvalued exchange rates, aggravated the import dependence of the economy and resulted in a stagnation of exports. The consequent balance of payments disequilibrium, in turn, placed definite limits on the feasible rates of economic growth. External factors such as the oil shock, explain the timing and magnitude of the crisis. Yet, the origins of the crisis that emerged in the late 1970s can ultimately be traced back to domestic factors in the form of inappropriate economic policies.[2]

The structural adjustment program introduced in January 1980, in collaboration with the IMF and the World Bank and supported by the leading OECD nations, represented a fundamental break with the import substitution policies of the previous two decades. In fact, Turkey emerged as a "model" of orthodox economic policies during the early 1980s. Important steps were taken in the direction of liberalizing the trade regime and the capital account. Furthermore, a decisive shift occurred with respect to exchange rate policy. Following the discrete, large-scale devaluations of 1980, a flexible exchange rate regime was introduced in 1981. Exchange rate adjustments engineered throughout the 1980–88 period have more than compensated for the differential between domestic inflation rates and the inflation rates of major trading partners. Exchange rate policies were established as the principal instruments for the promotion of exports. Hence, a favorable policy environment was created, which laid the foundations of rapid export growth and the subsequent economic recovery.

The neoclassical perspective provides a coherent account and captures important aspects of the Turkish experience. The focus on the exchange rate is also particularly appropriate. The ability of the authorities to generate *real* devaluations of the exchange rate throughout the 1980–88 period was clearly a key factor underlying rapid export expansion, an observation that is unambiguously supported by several econometric investigations.[3] The *consistency* with which the authorities have been able to achieve real devaluations over a considerable time span clearly distinguishes the Turkish case from the experiences of a number of other countries that have also embarked upon an export-led industrialization strategy.

Nonetheless, the neoclassical account is seriously incomplete in terms of comprehending the *pattern* of export-led growth, both in the Turkish case as well as in the context of other semi-industrialized economies. Our central claim is that an analysis of the *institutional framework* and the manner in which export growth has been organized is essential for understanding both the *dynamics* as well as the *long-term viability* of an export-led growth strategy.

We ought to recognize from the outset that the Turkish government has sought to establish right from the very beginning, a highly concentrated export sector as a basis for reaping economies of scale and for penetrating international markets. The state has provided explicit incentives for the formation and the subsequent development of foreign trade companies, the inspiration for which was derived directly from the Japanese and South Korean experiences with general trading companies. Since then, a select group of Turkish foreign trade companies have steadily expanded their share in total exports, currently accounting for about half of all Turkish exports. Now, an "institutional model" based on a limited number of large-scale foreign trade companies is not consistent with a "liberal vision" founded upon the ideal of free markets, focusing on import liberalization and exchange rate policies as the central ingredients of export success. This apparent duality between a concentrated export sector, on the one hand, and the adoption of market-oriented policies, on the other, may explain the lack of interest so far concerning the characteristics and performance of the Turkish foreign trade companies.

The major objective of the present paper is to try to remedy this deficiency by investigating the contribution of the Turkish foreign trade companies in a comparative framework. Our basis for comparison is the stylized facts associated with the Japanese and South Korean models which, hitherto, represent the outstanding success stories of sustained export expansion. Our preference for a comparative framework is motivated by the fact that Turkish authorities have deliberately tried to adopt certain basic features of the Japanese and Korean models. In that sense, our comparative framework provides a basis for studying the more general problem, namely, to what extent can organizations developed in a certain socioeconomic environment be tansplanted and replicated in quite dissimilar institutional or political contexts.

The Institutional Basis of Export Performance: Characteristics of Turkish Foreign Trade Companies

The legal framework underlying the formation of foreign trade companies was established during the first year of the structural adjustment program in 1980. The various requirements for setting up a foreign trade company were specified by a Government Decree issued on July 18, 1980. The conditions for qualifying as a foreign trade company (FTC) were outlined as follows:

1. Minimum export earnings of $15 million during the year preceding the application, with the additional condition that at least 50 percent of all exports would consist of mineral and manufactured products.
2. An initial capital of at least TL 50 million (equivalent of $640,000) paid up over a twelve-month period.
3. Export growth at a rate of 10 percent per annum.

The next decisive step in legislation with respect to FTCs occurred at the beginning of 1984. The decree issued in January 1984 revised the conditions required for qualifying as a foreign trade company. The minimum export requirement was raised to $30 million and the requirement for paid-up capital was extended to TL 500 million. Furthermore, the share of the mineral and manufactured exports was raised from 50 to 75 percent. Finally, the scope of FTCs was broadened in 1984 and the name was changed from "export corporations" to "foreign trade corporations," reflecting the desire of the policymakers to extend the range of the companies' activities to include import as well as export trade.

Companies that managed to comply with these requirements and gained the status of a FTC became eligible for the following set of privileges:

(a) The ability to use credits from the Central Bank rediscount facilities with one-year maturity and favorable interest rates amounting to 50−60 percent of commercial rates, covering as much as 90 percent of all export commitments.

(b) Allocation of foreign exchange from the "Export Promotion Fund" for importing raw materials required in the manufacture of products to be subsequently exported.

(c) Permission to import investment goods and spare parts of up to 60 percent of projected exports. These privileges were extended in 1984 by a new set of additional export incentives.

(d) Export tax rebates corresponding to 6 percent of export value, in addition to tax rebates for which all exporters qualified on an item-by-item basis.

(e) The right to maintain foreign currency holdings on a global basis, to be used in importing raw materials for the manufacture of exportable commodities embodied in the FTC's program.

(f) Incentive certificates automatically awarded up to 50 percent of their export budget to be utilized in importing raw materials and packaging materials. FTCs were allowed to import these commodities without seeking prior government approval.

(g) The ability to contract (with government approval) medium term foreign credits of up to two years.

(h) Monopoly rights (jointly with state economic enterprises) for importing commodities from countries associated with COMECON.[4]

Hence, it is quite obvious that an explanation based exclusively on exchange rate policies complemented by import liberalization provides a highly partial and misleading picture of Turkish export performance. Exchange rate policies were undoubtedly very important in terms of removing the bias against exports that had previously existed under the import-substitution regime. Yet, exporters in the 1980s, especially those who qualified for FTC status, benefited from a multitude of incentives of which tax rebates, duty-free imports of raw materials, and the ability to borrow from external financial markets were probably the most significant.

Foreign trade companies steadily expanded their share of Turkish exports during the course of the 1980s. The share of FTCs in total exports rose from 5.8 percent in 1980, to a peak of 49.4 percent in 1986. In spite of the marginal decline in their relative shares, twenty-four FTCs accounted for 46.3 percent of all total Turkish exports in 1988 (see table 4.1).

The major breakthrough in Turkish export performance occurred in 1981. It is interesting to observe that FTC exports expanded at a phenomenal rate during that particular year. In fact, FTC exports grew at a significantly higher rate as compared with total national exports over the 1980–88 period as a whole. Yet, rather surprisingly, we do not observe a close correspondence between the growth of FTC exports, on the one hand, and total Turkish exports, on the other. The absence of a parallel pattern is illustrated by the fact that FTCs recorded rapid increases of exports during 1983 and 1986 at a time when the overall export performance displayed a tendency toward stagnation (see table 4.2).

Finally, we ought to emphasize the high degree of concentration of FTC exports. In spite of the fact that there existed a total of twenty-four FTCs in 1988, four companies contributed 29.3 percent and eight companies accounted for 49.0 percent of total FTC exports (see table 4.3).

Legally, FTCs are prohibited from participating in manufacturing

Table 4.1   Share of FTCs in Total Turkish Exports,
1980−1988 ($ U.S. Million, %)

Years	FTC Exports	Total Exports	FTC Share
1980	171.0	2,910.1	5.8
1981	642.1	4,702.9	13.6
1982	970.4	5,746.0	18.4
1983	1,643.4	5,727.8	28.6
1984	3,261.8	7,133.6	45.7
1985	3,376.2	7,958.1	42.4
1986	3,689.1	7,456.7	49.4
1987	4,496.9	10,190.0	44.1
1988	5,403.2	11,662.1	46.3

Source: Turkish Foreign Trade Association.

Table 4.2   Comparative Performance of
FTC Exports and Total Turkish Exports,
1980−1988 (Annual rate of change, %)

Years	Total Exports	FTC Exports
1980	28.7	———
1981	61.6	275.5
1982	22.2	51.1
1983	−0.3	69.4
1984	24.5	98.5
1985	11.6	3.5
1986	−6.3	9.3
1987	36.7	21.9
1988	14.4	20.2

Source: Turkish Foreign Trade Association.

or investment activities. Nonetheless, organic links exist between FTCs, on the one hand, and major domestic industrial, trading, or construction conglomerates, on the other. Almost all of the major FTCs were originally established as the marketing outlets of domestic corporations (see Appendix, table 4.A1). Two of the largest foreign trade companies, RAM and EXSA, were founded with the explicit objective of marketing exclusively the multitude of products manufactured by the two leading industrial conglomerates, KOC and SABANCI, respectively. In fact, only one

Table 4.3   Degree of Concentration in FTC Exports, 1980–1988
(Relative Shares, %)

Years	Top Four FTCs	CR[a]	Top Eight FTCs	CR[b]	Number of FTCs
1980	72.5	50.0	100.0	100.0	8
1981	40.5	20.0	62.6	40.0	20
1982	51.2	23.5	74.2	47.1	17
1983	45.2	20.0	69.9	40.0	20
1984	28.8	16.0	47.9	32.0	25
1985	25.7	15.4	44.8	30.8	26
1986	25.5	14.8	43.6	29.6	27
1987	26.3	16.7	46.0	33.3	24
1988	29.3	16.7	49.0	33.3	24

Source: Turkish Foreign Trade Association.
[a] Four firm concentration ratio.
[b] Eight firm concentration ratio.

company, PENTA, may be classified as a "pure" foreign trade company, in the sense that it is totally independent, with no affiliation to any major domestic enterprise.

The organic link that exists between FTCs and domestic conglomerates, is particularly significant for Turkey's political economy during the 1980s. It suggests that, in general, there was no conflict of interest between large firms oriented toward internal and external markets, respectively, in striking contrast to the rather profound conflicts of interest that appear to characterize the Latin American experience. In retrospect, major domestic conglomerates that had performed an instrumental role in the import-substitution process during the 1960s and the 1970s, adjusted to the novel circumstances of the 1980s by taking advantage of the new export opportunities, while at the same time continuing to maintain their stronghold over the domestic market.

Many of the largest FTCs were established as the foreign trade outlets of major corporations during the 1970s, long before they actually obtained the status and privileges associated with a foreign trade company during the 1980s. Yet, we should not deduce from this observation that FTCs are engaged exclusively in marketing the products of their parent companies. In fact, the majority of FTCs, especially medium- and small-scale FTCs, are engaged in "passive export trade," acting as intermediaries for small-scale exporters and manufacturers. A study recently commissioned by the Undersecretariat of Treasury and Foreign Trade, discovered that up to 50 percent of all total export earnings of FTCs are derived from "passive exports," although considerable variation exists between different FTCs in this respect.[5]

Towards a Comparative Analysis of Japanese Sogo Shosha, and the Turkish Foreign Trade Companies

Sogo Shosha have been a major driving force in the Japanese export offensive during the postwar period. Sogo Shosha is a general trading company, engaged in both export and import trade, involving a wide range of products. The key comparative advantage of Sogo Shosha lies in the spheres of marketing and finance. Sogo Shosha typically command extensive marketing expertise, maintained through a dense network of offices throughout the world and controls enormous financial resources via the close links that they have established with commercial banks.[6]

There are currently nine Sogo Shosha in Japan and these constitute only a small subset of the number of general trading companies that exist in the country. A typical Sogo Shosha differs from an ordinary general trading company in several crucial respects. First, the size of Sogo Shosha is considerably greater, measured both in terms of the volume of sales and the range of products handled. Second, Sogo Shosha is a truly independent company, whereas an ordinary trading company is typically an affiliate of a domestic manufacturing conglomerate. Yet, a key point ought to be emphasized from the outset. In spite of the fact that Sogo Shosha are autonomous institutions, they have, nevertheless, established close, organic links with both manufacturing corporations and commercial banks.

Furthermore, Sogo Shosha undertake various activities including warehousing, transportation, resource development, and manufacturing to complement its trading activities. It is interesting to observe that 90 percent of the working and investment capital originates from bank loans and only 10 percent of investment capital is derived from equity. Still, Sogo Shosha have established themselves as a major form of financial intermediation. The explanation offered to resolve this apparent paradox is that commercial banks needed an escape route for evading the constraints imposed by the Ministry of Trade and Industry (MITI) on extending loans to small companies and enterprises. In the Japanese context, small firms have made a disproportionate contribution to exports. Sogo Shosha have performed a key role in this respect by helping to overcome the financial constraints confronted by small-scale enterprises. In fact, Sogo Shosha have extended credit to both companies whose products they wished to handle, as well as providing working capital to small-scale manufacturers. Currently, all Sogo Shosha, as parent companies, own numerous manufacturing subsidiaries as affiliated companies. There are growing indications that Sogo Shosha may evolve progressively toward a conglomerate type of organization, with general trading constituting only one dimension of the corporation's activities.

Having provided a broad overview of Sogo Shosha, we are in a position to focus explicitly on issues of comparative interest, concerning organizational characteristics, interactions with other institutions, and the environment external to the firm. We may argue that in certain important respects, the Turkish FTCs have performed a major developmental role, parallel to the role undertaken by Sogo Shosha in the Japanese economy. They have managed to exploit economies of scale in marketing and have been instrumental in penetrating foreign markets in the early stages of Turkey's export drive. Furthermore, the FTCs acted as key intermediaries to a large number of small-scale exporters or manufacturers who lacked the necessary expertise for establishing a stronghold in external markets on an individual basis.

Our interviews revealed that FTCs have been a source of financial assistance to small-scale exporters. They have also provided information relating to technology and product development. Small-scale companies also benefited indirectly from the fierce competition that has taken place between the FTCs themselves.[7] The available evidence suggests that FTCs have opted for the objective of long-term expansion at the expense of short-term profitability. Vigorous competition for market shares, combined with fragile financial structures, resulted in the majority of cases in extremely low or even negative profit margins.[8] Consequently, a disproportionate share of the additional 6 percent tax rebate to which FTCs were entitled to was, in fact, directed to small-scale producers or exporters. Informal or unofficial figures, based on our interview data, reveal that typically around 1.5 percent of the additional tax rebate is claimed by the FTCs, while 4.5 percent is directed to small-scale manufacturers or exporters. If these figures are generally valid, then there does not seem to be a fundamental conflict of interest between FTCs and small-scale exporters excluded from the FTC status.

On closer examination, however, a number of differences between

Sogo Shosha and the Turkish FTCs arise. One of the fundamental strengths of the Japanese economy derives from a "Zaibatsu" type of organization, which involves a close, triangular pattern of interaction between a bank, a trading company, and an industrial corporation, respectively. The tight network linking the various key organizations in the economy has equipped Sogo Shosha with a solid financial base on which to coordinate and expand their marketing activities. In contrast, the Zaibatsu type of organizational network has, on the whole, been absent in the Turkish case. Only in a very limited number of cases, of which RAM and EXSA are the principal examples, do we observe a duplication of the Japanese pattern involving close collaboration between a bank, an industrial conglomerate, and a trading company under the banner of a single holding company.

The vast majority of Turkish FTCs are, in essence, subsidiaries of domestic corporations. The tight, organic links with commercial banks and financial institutions, which characterize the Japanese pattern, is largely absent in the Turkish context. Consequently, Turkish FTCs display highly fragile financial structures which, in turn, place considerable restrictions on the scope of their activities.

More significantly, the parent company itself is constrained by a weak financial structure. The available evidence indicates that Turkish manufacturing corporations exhibit extremely high debt-equity ratios and excessive levels of dependence on bank finance for short-term working capital purposes. The high debt-equity ratios, themselves, are the by-products of two mutually reinforcing forces. First, in spite of a recent upsurge since 1986, the development of capital markets has hitherto been rather limited. Second, major Turkish companies, which are essentially family concerns, have been reluctant to lose control over their businesses, which an extension of ownership via the issue of shares in the Stock Exchange might entail.[9]

Hence, we hypothesize that one of the central motives for establishing a foreign trade company was to relieve the financial constraint, not only on the FTC itself, but also on the parent company. Tax rebates, the ability to borrow from international markets and maintaining funds in foreign currency were all conceived of as mechanisms for relieving the company's short-term financial problems. Our interviews with FTC managers pointed unambiguously toward a common pattern. They all regarded export tax rebates as an important instrument for satisfying their short-term working capital requirements, especially in the presence of high domestic loan rates of interest. Export incentives, therefore, emerged as a substitute mechanism for overcoming the underlying weakness of the financial system. What is crucially significant at this point is that the FTCs were sidetracked from their main function, with potentially negative repercussions on their subsequent economic performance.

The Macro Institutional Environment for Export Success: The Nature of Government-Business Interactions in South Korea and Japan

The Japanese experience testifies the crucial significance of a favorable political environment for long-term industrial growth. Japan may be described as an example of a guided market economy, in which the state has performed a central role in the process of economic transformation. One of the paradoxes of the Japanese pattern is that the public sector is comparatively the smallest among the leading industrialized nations. Similarly, the scale of the bureaucratic apparatus is also quite restricted, with the well-known MITI being one of the smallest ministries in the Japanese government.[10] Yet, the Japanese case clearly demonstrates that a state can perform a developmental function quite independently of the size of the public sector and the scale of the bureaucratic apparatus. What really matters is the *mode of intervention* as opposed to the scale of public sector involvement in the economy.

The fascinating aspect of the Japanese experience is the remarkable symbiosis or convergence of interest between the government and private business. Japan is first and foremost a market economy in the sense that initiative rests mainly with private companies, profit remains the company's principal objective, and companies that fail to generate profits are squeezed out of business. Yet, the state, in spite of its restricted size, performs a key role in guiding the market as opposed to direct regulation or production. State ownership matters very little in Japan since Japanese bureaucrats can rule more effectively by guiding private firms and by capturing the efficiency of private markets for public ends. Japanese policymakers are fiscally conservative; they favor balanced budgets and maintain a strong anti-inflationary bias.[11] Furthermore, the commitment to spend on welfare and other direct forms of social support are extremely limited. Hence, many features of the Japanese environment conform rather closely to the "ideal type" depicted by advocates of free markets.

Nonetheless, the state provides a *strategic direction* to the Japanese economy, which is largely absent in other advanced market economies. The crucial aspect of state intervention is the industrial policy, administered by the MITI. Industrial policies involve the formulation of long-term policies for investment and for the identification of key sectors or industries that possess dynamic comparative advantages. The market is guided by a conception of long-term rationality of investment formulated by government officials. Hence, industrial policy is a form of indicative planning, whereby policymakers attempt to anticipate systematically, future market prospects, and initiate a dialogue with private business on how to generate an appropriate response to these developments at the level of specific sectors or industries. Industrial policy is formed through a process of "reciprocal consent" with private business. In fact, the Japanese state negotiates and formulates a dialogue as opposed to assuming a direct leadership role.

A political environment is established in which corporations can take long-term risks (e.g., lifetime employment) because they know that the government stands behind them providing long-term credits, export market information, and favorable tax treatment for promising industries. The essence of the growth-promoting environment is the *predictability* of both leadership and commercial policy.[12] The role of the MITI, via the medium of industrial policy, is to provide a "strategic vision" of the future, whereby private actors can anticipate and adjust smoothly to external market conditions. The MITI maintains close contacts with industry groups such as steel, automobiles, and chemicals; major business management associations; as well as organizations representing medium- and small-scale business. The aim of the policy has been to create a flexible industrial structure such that the economy can respond quickly to changes in world market conditions and thereby reduce its vulnerability to interruptions in the supplies of imported inputs.

At a deeper level, the notion that the state and individuals necessarily form an adversarial relationship is in conflict with the traditional concept of the "nation family." The state and the market are interwoven parts jointly constituting the nation's economy. Japan adopted capitalism from the West in the nineteenth century, but it was capitalism without the Western ideology of individualism and economic freedom. Hence, the strength of the Japanese economy stems from the fact that it is a form of "organized capitalism," with the developmental dynamic originating from a kind national crusade led by an alliance of state and economic managers.

From a comparative perspective, Japan is characterized by highly centralized and tightly organized "policy networks." Japan has a long tradition of competent bureaucracy. Many of the nation's best-educated minds enter the civil service. When bureaucrats retire at the age of fifty-five, they either join political parties or become managers of private firms. Hence, a close interaction is established between the bureaucracy and private business, on the one hand, and the bureaucracy and Parliament, on the other. The bureaucratic elite is highly centralized and exhibits a high degree of unity, a process that is closely associated with its relatively small size. Investigators point toward the presence of intra-bureaucratic or intraministerial conflicts; but, on the whole, these tend to be negligible.

A unified and tightly organized bureaucracy confronts a similarly tightly structured and concentrated private business. One of the striking organizational attributes of the Japanese economy concerns the significant links that exist between giant industrial corporations (Keiretsu), trading companies (Sogo Shosha), and commercial banks. In spite of the autonomous status of these three groups of entities, a close collaboration and division of labor has been established between them. Furthermore, an organic relationship appears to exist between big business and small-scale enterprises in the Japanese context. We have already pointed out the important intermediating role performed by Sogo Shosha in conjunction with small-scale producers who account for a significant share of all total Japanese exports.

The pattern that we have, hitherto, described is not unique to Japan and can be identified in other East Asian contexts, notably in the cases of South Korea and Taiwan. In fact, a remarkable duplication of the Japanese pattern can be observed in the South Korean context.[13] This correspondence of experience is not a paradox, considering the fact that the roots of South Korean development can be traced back to the time when the country was colonized by Japan. South Korea, like other East Asian economies, embodies a common heritage with Japan that include (a) Confucian principles; (b) an historical legacy of strong and economically active states; (c) traditions of social and political hierarchy; and, (d) strong nationalist sentiments influenced by cultural homogeneity and reinforced by external threats.

An explicit industrial policy engineered by a strong and monolithic bureaucracy, under the direction of the Ministry of Economic Planning (the counterpart of the MITI), has been a cornerstone of South Korean development. In South Korea, industrialization has been the main objective, as opposed to the neoclassical principle of maximizing profitability on the basis of *current* comparative advantage. South Korean governments have not limited themselves to macroeconomic policy and the provision of infrastructure. Nor, have they intervened at the industry level, when the industry is already in trouble, as in the case of the West. Instead, they have intervened on an active, nonetheless highly selective basis at the industry level. Some industries have been highly subsidized and directed by the government, while others have experienced policy intervention only intermittently. Others that have not been regarded as priority sectors have been left to take care of themselves within an explicit framework of regulation. The state has maintained significant instruments of control at its disposal such that, whatever happens in the rest of the economy, enough investment is forthcoming in strategic projects.

South Korea, like Japan, is yet another case of a guided market economy. Yet, one could argue that the Korean state has been more interventionist, reflecting the lower degree of the development of the economy. The directional thrust provided by the Korean state has assumed a more active and vigorous form. For example, the Korean state has been able to impose strict discipline on the private sector. Korean corporations have been heavily dependent on borrowed funds and bank finance for their long-term expansion. Hence, the state was able to impose discipline via a strict control over the banking sector and other financial institutions. The state either directly owned or indirectly regulated the banking sector of the economy. The rigid control exercised over financial resources restricted the avenues for the major conglomerates (Chaebol) to engage in rent-seeking activities and guided them in the direction of productive and accumulation-oriented activities. Similarly, strong controls have been instituted on the transfer of foreign exchange abroad, as a consequence of which the potential problems associated with "capital flight" have been eliminated. The Korean state has also been influential in terms of restricting the number of firms in an industry, as a basis for realizing economies of scale. Yet, monopoly power has, in turn, been regulated by extensive price controls, a practice that has persisted up to the present day.

In spite of the fact that the Korean state appears to be more interventionist than its Japanese counterpart, the policy networks in both countries are very similar. The South Korean case is also characterized by a process of policy formation based on "reciprocal consent," involving a highly cohesive and centralized bureaucracy, on the one hand, and a similarly tightly structured and concentrated private sector involving industrial conglomerates, trading companies, and financial institutions, on the other.

Sustainability of Turkish Export Performance: The Turkish Foreign Trade Companies in the Presence of Institutional Constraints

The Turkish foreign trade companies were designed explicitly to replicate the Japanese and Korean models. Yet, the Turkish FTCs originated and matured in a very different institutional and political environment, with direct repercussions on their subsequent economic performance. Striking contrasts are evident with respect to the nature of the businesses as well as the pattern of government business interactions.

In a number of important respects, the Turkish state represents the antithesis of the stereotype East Asian state. It is generally recognized that Turkey has a strong "state tradition" that she has inherited from the Ottoman era. Subsequently, the first major industrialization drive occurred in Turkey during the etatist period of the 1930s. The bureaucratic elite assumed the task of transforming the economic structure in the absence of an indigenous business elite; state economic enterprises were established during the 1930s and represented a major effort to initiate industrial production in a number of key sectors.

Private business in Turkey has developed under the explicit influence of the subsidies and incentives provided by the state and progressively assumed a significant role in the industrialization process, during the peak years of import-substitution in the 1960s and the 1970s. Nonetheless, the state has continued to perform a central role in the industrialization drive both through its direct participation in capital formation and also indirectly via extensive interference in the operation of the market mechanism. The public sector typically accounted for more than a half of fixed capital formation and the state economic enterprises have been a major contributor to industrial production. Indirect intervention in the operation of the market mechanism involved heavy tariff protection, quantitative controls on trade, a fixed exchange rate in the presence of accelerating inflation, price ceilings on the products of the state economic enterprises, as well as price support schemes for agricultural products. The SPO was established as the major layer of bureaucracy dealing with economic affairs in the 1960s and 1970s. In addition to the task of formulating and implementing medium-term economic plans, the SPO possessed extensive discretionary powers to intervene at the microlevel via its influence on tariffs, quotas, subsidies, and investment allowances.

The nature of the state's participation in the economy resulted in an ambiguous pattern of government-business interaction. Private business developed in Turkey under strong state protection and has been heavily dependent on state subsidies for its long-term viability. Yet, an extensive set of regulations combined with a large public sector and the absence of fiscal discipline resulted in a dislocation of private business and negative repercussions on overall economic performance. This apparent duality in government-business relations generated an unstable environment with two important corollaries for business behavior. First, the presence of an extensive regulatory framework and direct controls on the operation of markets encouraged pervasive "rent-seeking." Second, private business was encouraged to adopt a progressively myopic approach and to concentrate on investment with an explicit short-term bias, in the absence of an adequate longer-term perspective concerning the future course of the country's economic development.

Following the crisis of the import-substitution regime in the late 1970s, a major transformation was initiated in 1980. The structural adjustment program that was introduced in that year was designed to dismantle all the elements associated with the inward-oriented industrialization strategy. The new strategy aimed to liberalize the economy and to promote market forces in economic decisions, via a reduction in both the scale of the public sector and the degree of state intervention in the operation of the market mechanism. The nature of the policies adopted and the subsequent economic performance have been extensively analyzed in the literature.[14] What is significant for our purposes is that certain key elements of the pre-1980 system survived and, hence, conditioned the pattern of liberalization that emerged during the course of the 1980s. We would like to substantiate this hypothesis with specific reference to the pattern of export-oriented growth and the contribution of the foreign trade companies.

In a comparative context, a central feature of the Turkish case involved a decline in the economic strength of the bureaucracy, at a time when a significant process of restructuring in the economic system was in progress. Although Turkey had a strong bureaucratic tradition, the relative decline of the bureaucracy was already under way during the 1960s and the 1970s and the process continued in an accelerated form during the 1980s. In contrast to the East Asian cases that we have examined, joining the bureaucracy became an increasingly unattractive option for the new wave of graduates in the 1980s.

A parallel phenomenon involved the emergence of a highly fragmented bureaucratic structure in conjunction with trade policy and the implementation of export incentives. The MITI has been invested with the sole responsibility of formulating and implementing trade policy in the Japanese context. The Turkish case, in contrast, has been characterized by the participation of several government agencies, following the relative decline in the power of the SPO during the 1980s. Hence, in marked contrast to their Japanese and South Korean counterparts, Turkish FTCs have to deal with the SPO in matters relating to incentives, subsidies, and tax rebates and with the undersecretariat of treasury and foreign trade for issues concerning export and import permits and the overall trade regime. Furthermore, the Central Bank is authorized in matters relating to currency transfers, disbursements of export tax rebates, and export credits, while the Ministry of Finance is invested with responsibilities concerning exchange and customs matters. This highly fragmented structure undoubtedly restricts the speed of operations and limits the effectiveness of FTCs.

In fact, it is paradoxical that the fragmented nature of the bureaucracy is rather unique to the implementation of trade policy and is not duplicated in other spheres of economic activity. For example, we observe highly unified bureaucratic structures in the 1980s, with respect to the implementation of the privatization program and policy toward foreign direct investment. The newly created "Board of the Mass Housing and Public Participation Fund" was invested with the sole responsibility for administering the privatization program. Similarly, the Foreign Investment Department of the SPO was assigned the task of dealing with issues relating to foreign direct investment. Hence, the "bureaucratic fragmentation" thesis does not apply with equal force across other issue areas.

Another striking contrast between the Turkish case and her East Asian counterparts concerns the absence of a clearly defined national export strategy, which itself is part of a broader strategy for industrial transformation. There appears to be a profound absence of strategic direction in the Turkish case concerning export priorities and targets, in terms of markets, sectors, or products to be developed; encouraged and supported FTC managers have increasingly voiced their complaints regarding the absence of a well-defined, long-term strategy compounded by the fragmentation in their relations with government agencies.

Hitherto, we have emphasized two important features of the Turkish state, namely, the fragmented bureaucratic structure and the absence of a longer-term "strategic vision" of the economy. Our account would be incomplete, however, if we fail to consider two additional dimensions of state intervention. The first element concerns the nature of export incentives. While the policy-making elite displayed a high degree of consistency with respect to exchange rate policy, the same degree of consistency was absent in conjunction with other policy instruments. Export tax rebates (as a ratio of total exports) displayed considerable fluctuations during the 1980−88 period. The following pattern is worth considering. Export tax rebates were established as a major instrument for export promotion during the 1980−84 period. The second phase involved a significant reduction in export tax rebates during 1985 and 1986, reflecting the desire of policymakers to concentrate on the exchange rate as the sole instrument for export promotion. Yet, the experience of negative export growth in 1986 resulted in a reinstitution of tax rebates, on a large scale, during the course of 1987. Export tax rebates were progressively reduced during the course of 1988 and were finally abandoned by the beginning of 1989 (see table 4.4). They were replaced by a new incentive involving the provision of low interest credits and subsidies on key inputs such as energy.

An exclusive focus on the exchange rate policy tends to disguise the lack of continuity of export incentives provided in Turkey during the course of the 1980s. Moreover, the lack of continuity was accentuated by the incoherent nature of government's macroeconomic policies. The post-1984 period, in particular, has been characterized by macroeconomic policies of an expansionary nature in attempt to accelerate the pace of economic growth. Economic growth, itself, was conceived as an instrument of "coalition-building" in

Table 4.4　Evolution of Export Tax Rebates,
1980−1988 (TL Billion, %)

Years	Total Tax Rebates	Tax Rebate Ratio[a]	Tax Rebates/ Total Exports
1980	4.9	8.9	2.2
1981	24.7	14.2	4.7
1982	86.7	21.0	9.3
1983	149.0	22.3	14.2
1984	329.1	20.8	13.2
1985	287.4	12.7	6.9
1986	258.4	10.3	3.5
1987	605.5	N.A.	6.8
1988	603.9	N.A.	3.6

Source: SPO.
[a] Tax rebate ratio is defined as total tax rebates divided by "eligible exports."

the presence of electoral constraints following the reestablishment
of parliamentary democracy in November 1983. Attempts to increase the pace of GNP growth resulted in fiscal disequilibrium,
accelerating inflation, and rapid buildup of domestic and external
debt. Hence, the macroeconomic environment that emerged, made
a strong contrast with the predictable and stable macroeconomic
environment that lay the foundations of long-term export success
in the East Asian context.[15]

The fragmented structure of private business constitutes yet
another striking characteristic of the Turkish environment. With
few notable exceptions, the Zaibatsu type of economic organization based on close links between banks, industrial corporations,
and trading companies are absent in the Turkish case. In general,
Turkish FTCs could not obtain a solid backing from commercial
banks and from other financial institutions, as a consequence of
which they were left with a highly vulnerable situation. A similar
pattern was also evident in the case of the vast majority of manufacturing firms, which were also negatively affected by high loan
rates of interest.

The fragmented nature of the business sector also implied that
the "FTC model," based on a highly select group of large trading
companies, could not elicit wholesale support from other segments
of the business community. The legitimacy of FTCs have been questioned by both small exporters as well as business corporations
with a predominantly internal market orientation. In spite of the
advantages provided by FTCs to small-scale exporters, the latter
have progressively conceived themselves as competitors for the
available pool of incentives, which, according to them, has been
directed on a disproportionate scale to large FTCs. Hence, the
absence of a clear-cut consensus on the desirability of FTCs as a
basis for long-term export expansion yet again differentiates the
Turkish case from the East Asian pattern.

The environment that we have described encouraged myopic
behavior on the part of FTCs, as well as "export-oriented rent-
seeking." The phenomenon known as "overinvoicing," or in more
popular language, as "fictitious exports," emerged as an acute
problem in the 1980s and raised serious questions against both the
short-term success and the long-term viability of the export-led
growth strategy. The dimensions of the problem are illustrated in a
recent study that compares export figures to OECD countries
derived from Turkish sources with OECD imports to Turkey based
on OECD data. The findings of the study concerning the degree of
overinvoicing are presented in table 4.5.

Table 4.5   Turkish Exports to OECD
Countries and Dimensions of "Overinvoicing," 1980–1988 U.S. Million, %

Years	Turkish Data	OECD Data	Degree of Overinvoicing
1980	1,634	1,789	−8.0
1981	2,282	2,239	1.9
1982	2,576	2,328	10.7
1983	2,771	2,461	12.6
1984	3,172	2,903	27.9
1985	4,084	3,773	8.3
1986	4,311	4,578	−5.8
1987[a]	2,349	1,535	53.0

Source: Rodrik (1988), based on the OECD
        Monthly Bulletin of Foreign Trade
        Statistics and Devlet İstatistik Ensti-
        tüsü Aylık Dış Ticaret İstatistikleri
        Bulteni (Çeşitli Sayılar).
[a] January-May period.

A remarkable degree of overinvoicing appears to characterize
1987, a year distinguished by the reinstitution of export tax rebates,
following the negative growth in exports recorded in 1986. The
precise contribution of FTCs to overinvoiced exports is not clear.
Yet, there exists sufficient indirect evidence that through their
superior organizational skills FTCs have made a disproportionate
contribution to the problem of overinvoicing or fictitious exports.
It is also interesting to note that the Turkish state, in spite of its
strong regulatory and interventionist character, has made little
attempt to discipline the companies concerned, although export
tax rebates were finally eliminated by the end of 1988.

Conclusions and Future Prospects

According to neoclassical economic theory, exchange rate policy
and a liberal foreign trade regime constitute the central ingredients
of successful export performance. The outstanding success stories
in this respect, namely Japan and subsequently South Korea and
Taiwan, are identified as cases that confirm decisively the validity
of the neoclassical "logic." We do not dispute the claim that

exchange rate policy is a necessary condition for export success. Nor do we suggest that exports can flourish in an environment characterized by high rates of effective protection. We do argue, however, that an excessive emphasis on exchange rate policy and the nature of the trade regime, distracts attention from the more fundamental institutional factors at work, which provide the true dynamic of rapid and sustained export growth. Hence, our central claim is that to be able to explain rapid and sustained export growth, we need to focus explicitly on how the export offensive has been organized in the first place. The logical corollary of this perspective is that we need to concentrate our analysis on the manner in which the "state" and "private business" are organized as well as the specific patterns of state-business interactions.

Japan and subsequently South Korea could sustain a major export offensive because of the conducive political and institutional environment. We have drawn attention to three major institutional forces that account for the success of Sogo Shosha in the Japanese context. First, the state performed a crucial developmental role via its selective industrial policy, which provided a predictable environment and a strategic view of long-term growth prospects. The developmental role of the Japanese state was accentuated by the fact that it intervened to supplement the market and did not engage in direct production or regulatory activities. Second, the private sector was tightly organized along a Zaibatsu type framework, involving close collaboration and division of labor between banks, trading companies, and industrial conglomerates. Hence, Sogo Shosha were endowed with a solid financial backing to perform their essential and primary task, namely, marketing and financial intermediation. Third, the policy formation process involved a tight policy network based on the close collaboration of state and business elites, in a process of mutual negotiation and consent. South Korea could successfully adopt the Japanese Sogo Shosha model, because basically, similar institutional and environmental conditions were also available in the South Korean context.

In contrast, the Turkish foreign trade companies could not replicate the Japanese success because they were originally transplanted and forced to operate in a very different and comparatively unfavorable political and institutional environment. The Turkish case differed from the Japanese and South Korean experiences in three fundamental respects. First, the "regulatory" character of the Turkish state outweighed its "developmental" contribution. Trade policy was formulated and implemented by a highly fragmented bureaucratic structure that nevertheless intervened regularly at the microlevel by frequent changes in decrees involving subsidies, tax rebates, and other export incentives. Yet, the bureaucratic elite provided little strategic direction to private business. The absence of a long-term strategy combined with expansionary monetary and fiscal policies increasingly generated an unstable and unpredictable macroeconomic environment, which progressively undermined the conditions necessary for sustained export success. Second, the business sector also displayed a highly fragmented structure. Turkish FTCs lacked a solid financial base due to the absence of close and organic links with commercial banks. In fact, the principal objective of many FTCs became that of obtaining short-term finance, as a means of supporting their parent companies, which themselves displayed highly fragile financial structures. Due to intense competition and a weak financial base, most FTCs were forced to operate with extremely low or even negative rates of profit. Third, the policy formation process was characterized by loose policy networks, as a consequence of the fragmented structures of both the state bureaucracy and private business. In comparative terms, the relationship between private business and the bureaucracy has been unstable and involved mutual distrust, again restricting the possibilities for formulating and implementing a coherent long-term strategy.

In spite of the structural constraints within which they operate, the Turkish FTCs have undoubtedly made a major qualitative impact on Turkish export performance. New markets, networks, and contacts have been established without which a major surge in exports would not have been feasible. In retrospect, the fundamental problem of Turkey during the early 1980s was a marketing problem, namely, how to direct existing capacity from the depressed domestic market into external markets. The Turkish FTCs have performed a crucial role in resolving the marketing problem by establishing extensive networks with external markets. They also contributed to a generalized learning process from which small companies also benefited in terms of the transfer of up-to-date technologies as well as the design and development of new products.

The problem, in the second half of the 1980s, was transformed, however, as rates of capacity utilization in most manufacturing sectors reached their maximum feasible levels. It is evident, therefore, that export growth cannot be sustained in the absence of additional investment in key sectors of the economy. Hence, there is increasing recognition that production and marketing need to be integrated into a coherent industrial strategy. In the absence of such a strategy plus the institutional environment to implement such a strategy, the comparative advantage of the FTCs will increasingly be irrelevant for the novel conditions confronting the Turkish economy by the end of the 1980s.

There is growing evidence that many FTCs have become instruments of "export-oriented rent-seeking," a process that has been encouraged by the broad macroeconomic environment as well as the counterproductive measure of tax rebates. Export tax rebates have, hitherto, been provided in a generalized fashion, and not in the context of a clearly defined long-term strategy. A casual examination of the available data suggests a strong association between the size of the tax rebate ratio and the dimensions of the overinvoicing problem. Following the abolition of tax rebates by the end of 1988, the future of many FTCs seem uncertain. The preliminary evidence points toward a significant deterioration in their performance, as of 1989. The most recent policy response has been to replace tax rebates by a new incentive regime, in the form of subsidized energy inputs and low cost credit, with a clear shift of focus from marketing to production for export markets. Consequently, the gap between incentives granted to FTCs and small-scale exporters have been reduced considerably in the early months of 1989, which also accentuates the uncertainty surrounding the future of FTCs in Turkey.

At present, Turkey's export strategy is at an impasse. Considerable institutional and organizational changes are required for overcoming the current impasse and for maintaining the momentum of the export drive over the next decade.

Acknowledgments

This paper is part of a broader project entitled "The State, Policy Networks and the New Economic Strategy in Turkey," supported by the Middle East Research Committee of the Ford Foundation. This paper was completed while I was a Visiting Fulbright Fellow at the Center of International Studies, Princeton University. I would like to acknowledge the assistance of Murat Tuna, the General Secretary of the Turkish Foreign Trade Association, in arranging the informal interviews with the executives of selected foreign trade companies that provided background information for this study. I would also like to thank Hakan Batur for his able research assistance.

96   EXPORT-ORIENTED INDUSTRIALIZATION

Notes

1. We made extensive use of certain concepts without fully defining them. The concept of "policy networks" is based directly on Katzenstein's comparative analysis of the foreign economic policies of advanced industrial states (Katzenstein 1977). For a comprehensive discussion of "rentseeking," see Buchanan, Tollison, and Tullock (1980). Finally, the distinction between a "developmental" state and a "regulatory" or "predatory" state is developed by Evans (1987) who outlines the central ingredients of the "new comparative political economy," which provides the broad theoretical framework underlying the present study.

2. Krueger (1974) and Derviş and Robinson (1979) contain the best neoclassical accounts of the problems associated with the import-substitution strategy in Turkey and the underlying causes of the crisis that emerged by the end of the 1980s.

3. See Togan, Olgun, and Akder (1988), Riedel (1988), and Öniş and Özmucur (1988a) in this context.

4. In spite of the considerable advantages provided, especially in conjunction with bilateral trade involving Eastern Bloc countries, import trade has not emerged as a major activity of Turkish FTCs. FTCs, in fact account for less than 10 percent of total Turkish imports. The relative insignificance of import trade is another factor that distinguishes Turkish FTCs from Sogo Shosha and Korean general trading companies.

5. Extensive information concerning the operation and performance of Turkish FTCs are provided by Kozlu (1988); Özel (1988); and Togan, Olgun, and Akder (1988). The findings of the study undertaken by the Undersecretary of Treasury and Foreign Trade concerning the significance of "passive exports" in the overall contribution of FTCs is reported in an article published in the national newspaper, *Dünya* (1989).

6. Our discussion of Sogo Shosha draws extensively from Yoshihara (1982), Yoshino and Lifson (1986), Kojima and Ozawa (1984), and Hofheinz and Calder (1982). Yoshihara consists of a valuable study on the interaction of Sogo Shosha with their broader external environment, while Yoshino and Lifson concentrate more specifically on the internal organizational attributes of Sogo Shosha.

7. See Özel (1988) in relation to the nature of benefits provided by FTCs to small-scale exporters.

8. An interesting puzzle that future research ought to address concerns the possible reasons underlying the companies' decision to maintain their FTC status in spite of the fact that they operated with extremely low or negative rates of profit. One hypothesis is that the companies' basic strategy was long-term profit maximization, which entailed an expansion in market shares in the long-run, by driving competitors out of business in the short-run. Another possible hypothesis is based on the practice of "transfer pricing" between the "subsidiary," namely the FTC and the "parent company," the industrial corporation. The hypothesis suggests that the overriding objective was to maximize the profits of the parent company. Hence, the FTC sacrificed its own profitability objective in order to contribute to the maximization of overall profits by the parent company. While the latter hypothesis is especially suggestive, at the same time it is very difficult to test.

9. For evidence concerning the fragile financial structures of Turkish firms and their dependence on short-term bank finance, see Yaser (1988). The behavioral characteristics of private business in Turkey, including the reluctance of Turkish entrepreneurs to surrender control over their business via the issue of share

certificates, are investigated by Buğra (1988). For an overview concerning the characteristics and the limitations of the Turkish financial system, see Öniş and Özmucur (1988b).

10. Our discussion of the Japanese experience is based upon Hofheinz and Calder (1982), Johnson (1982), Özaki (1984), and Samuels (1987). The discussion of the MITI and the nature of industrial policy draws extensively from Johnson and Özaki.

11. See Özakı (1984) and Hofheinz and Calder (1982) in this context.

12. See Özakı (1984) and Samuels (1987) in this context.

13. Our discussion of the South Korean case has been heavily influenced by White (1988). See, in particular, the article by Wade and White on the characteristics of "developmental states" of East Asia, as well as the specific articles by Wade (1988) on Taiwan and Luedde-Neurath (1988) on South Korea; in the same volume Deyo (1987) has also been valuable in this context. The strong impact of Japan on Korean development is highlighted by Cumings (1984). For an influential neoclassical account of the East Asian experience, see Little (1982).

14. Celâsun and Rodrik (1988); Nas and Odekon (1988); and Togan, Olgun, and Akder (1988) represent the major contributions in this context.

15. For attempts to explain the adoption of incoherent macroeconomic policies during the 1983–87 period on the basis of "political rationality" or "coalition-building," see Öniş and Riedel (1989) and Waterbury (1988).

Appendix

Table 4.A1 Turkish Foreign Trade Companies: Sources of Affiliation and Contribution to Export Performance

Name of FTC [a]	Year of Establish-ment	Export Cont. (Million Dollars) [b]	Source of Affiliation	Nature of Parent Company [c]
ENKA	1972	2,162.4	ENKA	CC
RAM	1970	1,692.6	KOÇ	IC
TEKFEN	1981	1,396.0	TEKFEN	CC
EXSA	1973	1,360.0	SABANCI	IC
EDPA	1980	1,097.8	AKSU	TC
CAM	1976	1,031.0	İŞ BANK.	IC
MENTEŞE-OĞLU	1975	1,015.8	MENTEŞEOĞLU	GITC
ÇUKUROVA	1979	991.0	ÇUKUROVA	ISC
MEPA	1976	975.0	İŞ BANK.	IC
AKPA	1977	910.1	DINÇKÖK	TC
FEPAŞ	1983	866.9	FENİŞ	ISC
PENTA	1976	852.9	NOTAFFIL	—
İZDAŞ	1981	828.1	İZMİR DC	ISC
ÇOLAKOĞLU	1982	732.0	ÇOLAKOĞLU	ISC

SÜZER	1979	679.1	SÜZER	GITC
EPTAŞ	1983	619.9	METAŞ DC	ISC
BATI	1978	615.3	BİLGE	GITC
YAŞAR	1971	608.7	YAŞAR	IC
TEMEL	1974	554.8	STFA	CC
BORUSAN	1975	476.5	BORUSAN	ISC
EKİNCİLER	1978	439.7	EKİNCİLER DC	ISC
GSD	1986	328.2	GİYİM SAN.D.	TC
SODIMPEK	1986	280.4	RENAULT S.	GITC
OKAN	1983	273.8	OKAN	GITC
ERPEX	1976	247.9	ERCAN	IC
İMEKS	1974	245.6	DOĞUŞ	CC
EKSEL	1978	171.9	ECA	GITC

Sources: Turkish Foreign Trade Association.
[a] Year of establishment is indicated in brackets.
[b] Total export earnings during the 1980−88 period.
[c] Parent companies are classified on the basis of the following criteria:
    IC: Industrial Conglomerates
    CC: Construction Companies
    TC: Textile Companies
    GITC: General Industrial and Trading Companies
    ISC: Iron and Steel Corporations

References

Buchanan J., R. Tollison and G. Tullock,. 1980. *Toward a Theory Rent-Seeking Society*. Texas: Texas A & M University Press.

Buğra, A. 1988. "Political Sources of Uncertainty in Business Life in Turkey." Paper presented to the Conference on the Dynamics of States and Societies in the Middle East, Cairo.

Celâsun M. and D. Rodrik. 1988. *Debt Adjustment and Growth in Turkey*. Chicago: Chicago University Press for NBER.

Cumings, B. 1984. "The Origins and Development of the North East Asian Political Economy: Industrial Sectors, Product Cycles and Political Consequences." *International Organization* 38 (1).

Derviş, K. and S. Robinson. 1978. "The Foreign Exchange Gap Growth and Industrial Strategy in Turkey." *World Bank Staff Papers*. Washington, D.C.: The International Bank for Reconstruction and Development.

Deyo, F. 1987. *The Political Economy of New Asian Industrialism*. Ithaca, N.Y.: Cornell University Press.

Evans, P. 1987. "Predatory, Developmental and Other Apparatuses: A Comparative Analysis of the Third World State." Department of Sociology, University of New Mexico. Mimeo.

Hofheinz R. and K. Calder. 1982. *The East Asia Edge*. New York: Basic Books.

Dünya, March 3, 1989.

Johnson, C. 1982. *MITI and the Japanese Miracle*. Stanford, Calif.: Stanford University Press.

Katzenstein, P. 1977. *Between Power and Plenty*. Madison: University of Wisconsin Press.

Kojima, K. and T. Ozawa. 1984. *Japan's General Trading Companies Merchants of Economic Development*. Paris: OECD.

Kozlu, C. 1988. "A Study of the Sogo Shosha: Japanese Foreign Trade Companies as a Model of Development for Turkey." Ph.D diss., Department of Management, Bogazici University, Istanbul.

Krueger, A. O. 1974. *Foreign Trade Regimes and Economic Development: Turkey*. New York: National Bureau of Economic Research.

Little, I. M. D. 1982. *Economic Development: Theory Policy and International Relations*. New York: Basic Books.

Lueedde-Neurath, R. 1988. "State-intervention and Export-oriented Development in South Korea." in *Developmental States in East Asia*, edited by G. White. London: Macmillan Press.

Nas, T. and M. Odekon, eds. 1988. *Liberalization and the Turkish Economy*. Westport, Conn.: Greenwood Press.

Öniş, Z. and J. Riedel. 1989. "The Political Economy of Macroeconomic Policies, Crises, and Long-term Growth in Turkey." Paper presented to the World Bank Conference on Macroeconomic Policies, Crisis, and Growth in the Long-run, Mexico City.

Öniş, Z. and S. Özmucur. 1988a. "Supply Side Origins of Macroeconomic Crises in Turkey." Paper presented to the World Bank Conference on Macroeconomic Policies, Crisis and Growth in the Long-run, Madrid.

———. 1988b. "The Role of the Financial System in the Creation and Resolution of Macroeconomic Crises in Turkey." Paper presented to the World Bank Conference on Macroeconomic Policies, Crisis and Growth in the Long-run, Madrid.

Özakı, R. 1984. "How Japanese Industrial Policy Works." In *The Industrial Policy Debate*, edited by C. Johnson. San Francisco, Calif.: ICS Press.

Özel, M. 1988. *Dış Ticaret Sermaye Şirketleri: Japonya, Tayvăn, Guney Kore ve Türkiye*. (Foreign Trade Corporations: Japan, Taiwan, South Korea, and Turkey). Istanbul: Türktrade Yayinlari.

Riedel, J. 1988. "Macroeconomic Policies, Crises and Long-run Growth in Turkey: Analysis of Crises." Paper presented to the World Bank Conference on Macroeconomic Policies, Crisis, and Growth in the Long-run, Mexico City.

Rodrik, D. 1988. "Turkiye'nin Ihracat Patlamasinin Ne Kadari Hayali?" (What Portion of Turkish Export Boom is Fictional?) *Toplum ve Bilim* 42.

Samuels, R. 1987. *The Business of the Japanese State: Energy Markets in Comparative and Historical Perspective*. Ithaca, N.Y.: Cornell University Press.

Togan, S., H. Olgun, and H. Akder. 1988. *External Economic Relations of Turkey*. Istanbul: Turktrade Publication.

Wade, R. 1988. "State-intervention in 'Outward-looking' Development: Neoclassical Theory and Taiwanese Practice." in *Developmental States in East Asia*, edited by G. White. London: Macmillan Press.

Wade, R. and G. White. 1988. "Developmental States in East Asia: An Introduction." In *Developmental States in East Asia*, edited by G. White. London: Macmillan Press.

Waterbury, J. 1989. "Coalition Building, Export-led Growth and Public Sector in Turkey." Paper presented to the Middle East Studies Association Conference, Los Angeles, Calif.

White, G. 1988. *Developmental States in East Asia*. London: Macmillan Press.

Yaser, B. 1988. *A Comparative Analysis of Selected Financial Ratios of Private Manufacturing Firms in U.S.A. and Turkey, 1983–1984*. Istanbul: Istanbul Chamber of Industry Publication.

Yoshihara, K. 1982. *Sogo Shosha: The Vanguard of the Japanese Economy*. Oxford, England: Oxford University Press.

Yoshino, M. and T. Lifson. 1986. *The Invisible Link: Japan's Sogo Shosha and the Organization of Trade*. Cambridge: MIT Press.

5

Strategic Issues in Exchange Rate Liberalization: A Critical Evaluation of the Turkish Experience

Yaman Aşıkoğlu

Introduction

The experience of the Southern Cone countries and Turkey has revealed that exchange rate management plays a critical role in the success or failure of stabilization-liberalization programs. The importance of the exchange rate policy derives from the fact that the countries launching these programs face the dual problem of high inflation and an unsustainable external deficit. While the correction of external imbalances requires an exchange rate policy designed to offset the adverse effect of inflation on the competitiveness of the domestic economy, the resulting currency depreciation interferes with the disinflation objective through its impact on price formation and inflationary expectations.

Policymakers' approach to this dilemma has varied across countries and time. For example, Chile, Argentina, and Uruguay initially put the emphasis on correcting balance of payments difficulties. Accordingly, these countries adopted a regime of passive crawling peg geared to maintain the purchasing power parity of their currencies adjusted for changes in the terms of trade. Persistence of high inflation led all the three Southern Cone countries to change their policies in the late 1970s. Under the new regime, known as the *tablitta*, the domestic currency was depreciated at declining rates and the exchange rate was actively used as an anti-inflationary tool.

This policy of active downward crawling peg was in turn abandoned in 1982 because of its adverse effect on the external account through the process of overvaluation.[1] Policy authorities of several other countries, including Brazil, Israel, Peru, and Portugal swung between the orthodox exchange rate management (passive crawl) and attempt to disinflate through exchange rate management (active downward crawl). While the consensus view that emerged from the Southern Cone countries supports the orthodoxy of purchasing power parity rules, the inability of the countries taking this route to disinflate casts doubt over the effectiveness of these policies.

Plagued with problems of balance of payment difficulties and inflation, Turkey has not been immune to the policy dilemmas experienced elsewhere. Since the introduction of the stabilization and structural reform program in 1980, Turkey has been successful in reducing the external deficit but has not achieved the same progress in disinflation. The positive contribution of the new exchange rate policy to the correction of external imbalances is frequently acknowledged.[2] However, the potential role of exchange rate management in the unsatisfactory inflation performance is generally overlooked. This paper investigates the relationship between the exchange rate strategy being followed since 1980 and the recent macroeconomic performance of the Turkish economy with respect to inflation as well as the external account. In the following section, we briefly discuss the issues involved in the choice of an exchange rate regime in a developing country. Against this background, the next section provides a broad overview of the Turkish experience with exchange rate management. There will then be a critical evaluation of the exchange rate strategy followed in the post-1980 period. An assessment follows on the implementation of the new exchange rate policy, given the authorities' objective of continually depreciating the lira in real effective terms in order to protect and increase the competitiveness of exports. The issue is *then* approached from a broader perspective and addresses the question of the appropriate exchange rate strategy taking into account the interactions between exchange rate management, inflation, and the external account. Concluding comments follow in section six.

Issues in the Choice of an Exchange Rate Regime

Since the advent of generalized floating by industrial countries in 1973, an increasing number of developing countries, including Turkey, abandoned fixed exchange rate regimes and adopted various forms of flexible exchange rate arrangements. Issues involved in this transition have been the subject of extensive research. However, existing studies in the literature, surveyed by Williamson (1982) and Wickham (1985) do not lead to a consensus view regarding the appropriate exchange rate system in developing countries. Hence, determining a set of general principles that could be used by the authorities occupies a high priority in agenda for future research (Edwards and Ahmad 1986).

The selection of an exchange rate system involves a sequence of strategic choices. At the first stage, relative desirability of fixed and flexible rates are compared. If the latter is considered to be more appropriate, then the question to be addressed becomes: What would be the best way of achieving exchange rate flexibility? Here the choice is between market determined floating versus various methods of setting and periodically adjusting the value of the domestic currency.

There is a consensus on the benefits of having flexibility in exchange rates, mainly because of the emergence of severe balance of payments problems under a fixed rate system as a result of the negative effects on competitiveness of high domestic inflation rates. However, market-determined floating is generally ruled out as a realistic option because of the nature of financial markets in many developing countries (Black 1976; Branson and Katseli-Papaefstratiou 1981). Concerns about floating rates center around the potential volatility and instability of exchange rates due to the limited depth of financial markets, and the limited scope for, and high costs involved in, hedging against exchange rate risk in developing countries. This line of reasoning has recently been challenged by adoption of market-determined floating rates in fifteen developing country members of the IMF.[3]

Strategic choices to be made in the second stage depends on the form of exchange rate flexibility selected in the first stage. If the floating rate system is adopted, then the main issue is the institutional form that the foreign exchange market takes. The principal alternative would be a competitive model where the Central Bank conducts the market or an interbank system, which is operated by commercial banks and licensed foreign exchange dealers. If, on the other hand, the authorities opt for managed flexibility, then they face the challenging problem of selecting a rule for officially providing flexibility to the exchange rate.[4] Here there are two distinct and frequently confused issues. The first aspect of the policy is establishing a link between the domestic currency and an external standard, a unit to which to peg. The choice set includes pegging to a single currency or to a basket of currencies, including the special drawing rights (SDR) basket.[5] The second issue concerns the choice of a rule determining the magnitude and frequency (timing) of the changes in the value of the peg. A commonly used and widely recommended policy is the passive crawl or the relative purchasing power parity convention, according to which small and frequent adjustments are made to the value of the domestic currency on the basis of inflation at home and in major trading countries. The objective of this rule is to neutralize the effects of domestic inflation on external competitiveness and hence to preserve the constancy of some real exchange rate indicator at its initial value.[6]

Another well-known exchange rate policy, which was used by Argentina, Chile, and Uruguay during the second half of the 1970s, is the active crawling peg. In this case, exchange rate is actively used as an anti-inflationary tool. Based on the premise that the expected rate of currency depreciation is the main cause for inflationary expectations, the active crawling peg rule depreciates the domestic currency at declining rates according to a pre-announced timetable independently of the actual inflation performance.[7]

A Broad Overview of Exchange Rate Management in Turkey

PRE-1980 PERIOD

Turkey had a fixed exchange rate system and multiple currency practices with strict exchange controls until 1980. External adjustment was achieved through the use of reserves and curtailing imports through a highly protective trade regime. When the external imbalance reached an unsustainable level in 1970, the Turkish lira was devalued in sizable magnitudes. Inflationary consequences of a strong growth-oriented, inward-looking development strategy followed during the 1960s and most of the 1970s, coupled with fixed exchange rates, continuously eroded the competitiveness of the export sector.

The failure to cut the growth of absorption, overvaluation of currency, and antiexport biases in the trade regime led to a balance of payments crisis in 1977–78, the severity of which was magnified by the first oil price shock in 1973. The response of the authorities to the crisis was twofold. First, imports were substantially cut (more than one third in volume) in 1978 and 1979. Second, in two successive devaluations the dollar/lira exchange rate was depreciated first by 23 percent in March 1978 (from TL 19 per U.S.\$1 to TL 25 per U.S.\$1) and then by an additional 44 percent in June 1979 (to TL 47 per U.S.\$1). Table 5.1 displays the evolution of the dollar exchange rate of the Turkish

Table 5.1 Dollar Exchange Rate of the Turkish Lira

1st March 1978	25.00		1983.	Q1:	192.51
10th April 1979	26.50	(47.10)[a]		Q2:	210.81
10th May 1979	26.50	(42.10)[a]		Q3:	233.06
10th June 1979	47.10[b]			Q4:	258.83
25th January 1980	70.00	(55.00)[c]	1984.	Q1:	307.41
2nd April 1980	73.70	(57.90)[c]		Q2:	341.15
9th June 1980	78.00	(61.30)[c]		Q3:	385.87
4th August 1980	80.00	(62.87)[c]		Q4:	419.44
11th October 1980	82.70	(65.19)[c]	1985.	Q1:	468.23
26th October 1980	84.80	(72.50)[c]		Q2:	516.48
9th November 1980	87.95	(77.50)[c]		Q3:	536.02
10th December 1980	89.25	(78.66)[c]		Q4:	556.51
27th January 1981	91.90	(79.41)[c]	1986.	Q1:	598.51
5th February 1981	95.95	(83.38)[c]		Q2:	666.40
24th March 1981	95.65	(83.12)[c]		Q3:	676.87
15th April 1981	98.20			Q4:	733.95
May 1981	101.92[d]				
1981. Q1:	93.67		1987.	Q1:	761.05
1981. Q2:	101.90			Q2:	808.73
1981. Q3:	117.50			Q3:	887.07
1981. Q4:	127.13			Q4:	963.45
1982. Q1	140.83		1988.	Q1:	1,141.23
1982. Q2	151.54			Q2:	1,294.44
1982. Q3	169.83			Q3:	1,499.80
1982. Q4	180.86			Q4:	1,744.07

Source: Central Bank of Turkey, *Monthly Statistical and Evaluation Bulletins*.
[a] Premium rate for workers' remittances and tourism revenues.
[b] For exports of traditional agricultural goods and imports of petroleum and its products and fertilizer raw materials $ parity is kept at TL 35.00.
[c] For imports of fertilizers and agricultural pesticides.
[d] Since 1st May 1981, the exchange rate has been adjusted on a daily basis. Figures shown are averages of daily exchange rates.

lira since 1978.[8] However, the increased competitiveness was soon eroded by domestic inflation, which accelerated due to supply bottlenecks caused by import cuts and a lack of effective control on aggregate demand.

POST-1980 PERIOD

Exchange rate management changed fundamentally with the introduction of the new economic program in 1980. The new exchange rate policy not only brought stabilization measures such as the maintenance of a realistic real exchange rate, but also aimed at liberalizing the exchange and payments system. In accordance with the central orientation of the whole program, exchange rate management has been guided by increased reliance on market forces and with the objective that the exchange rate, like other prices in the economy, should reflect market conditions.

The main features of the new exchange rate policy are as follows. First, the lira was devalued by 33 percent in January 1980, followed by periodic and frequent adjustments to offset inflation differentials at home and in major industrial countries and to provide a competitive edge for exports. Since May 1981, the nominal exchange rate has been adjusted daily. Although the exchange rate policy during the post-1980 period has been broadly described as a passive crawl or a relative purchasing power parity rule,[9] it has, in fact, been a policy of continual real effective depreciation.[10] Between the end of 1979 and the end of 1988 the Turkish lira depreciated by 55 percent in real effective terms, at an average rate of 6.11 percent annually.[11]

In addition to these new stabilization features, important steps were also taken to liberalize the exchange rate system with the ultimate objective of making the lira convertible. The complex system of multiple exchange rates, which led to parallel foreign exchange markets and contained anti-export biases, was phased out by 1982. Furthermore, commercial banks were allowed to undertake foreign exchange operations, open foreign currency deposit accounts, and buy and sell foreign exchange at the rate that they set within a band around the Central Bank rate.[12] In addition, surrender requirements on export earnings were reduced.

Since August 1988, the exchange rate has been determined in the newly established foreign exchange market composed of the Central Bank and commercial banks.[13] The experience with the foreign exchange market is too recent to allow for a detailed analysis. However, it is safe to conclude that the exchange rate is still being determined according to the targets set by the policymakers.

A Critical Evaluation of the New Exchange Rate Policy Given Its Objective of Real Effective Depreciation

MACROECONOMIC PERFORMANCE OF THE TURKISH ECONOMY

Following the fall of the output level in 1979 and 1980, largely

Table 5.2 Selected Macroeconomic Indicators

	1980	1981	1982	1983	1984	1985	1986	1987	1988
				(Annual Percentage Change)					
Real GNP	-1.1	4.1	4.5	3.3	5.9	5.1	8.1	7.4	3.4
Exports	-0.8	47.0	24.9	9.1	20.4	11.3	-0.6	36.7	14.4
Imports	14.7	15.7	10.8	13.6	15.5	7.7	13.1	27.5	1.3
Real Effective Exchange Rate	-23.0	-13.3	-10.5	-3.1	-0.4	-0.7	-12.8	-6.7	-1.6
Consumer Price Index (1963 = 100)	101.4	33.9	28.3	30.8	47.3	44.9	35.2	59.7	75.8
Wholesale Price Index (1963 = 100)	107.2	36.8	25.2	30.6	52.0	40.0	26.7	48.4	59.3
M1	58.2	38.1	38.0	44.6	16.1	43.2	56.3	50.4	48.0
PSBR[a] (% of GNP)	-10.0	-5.4	-6.0	-5.2	-6.5	-4.9	-4.5	-8.3	
				($U.S. Billion)					
Current Account									
Balance	-3.4	-1.9	-0.9	-1.9	-1.4	-1.0	-1.5	-1.0	1.5
Exports	2.9	4.7	5.9	5.9	7.4	8.3	7.6	10.3	11.7
Imports	7.9	8.6	8.5	8.9	10.3	11.2	11.1	14.2	14.3

Sources: SPO, *Main Economic Indicators*, State Institute of Statistics, *Price Indices Monthly Bulletin*, Central Bank of Turkey, *Quarterly Bulletins*.

[a] Public sector borrowing requirements.

due to the lack of imported inputs, GNP growth resumed first at a moderate rate by Turkish standards and then accelerated to 8 percent in 1986 (see table 5.2). In 1987 real GNP expanded by 7.4 percent. The GNP growth slowed down to 3.4 percent in 1988. This recovery was led initially by the improvement of the foreign balance. For example, in 1982 foreign balance accounted for almost 60 percent of the GNP growth. Improvement in the foreign balance, in turn, was due to the impressive growth of exports, particularly until 1986. Stagnation of exports, together with the rise in imports, caused the contribution of the foreign balance to the GNP growth to be negative in 1986. Nevertheless, a very strong recovery of the domestic demand drove the GNP growth to 7.4 percent in 1987.

The success of the new program in improving the external balance and the output growth has been overshadowed by the persistence of high inflation, however. The Turkish economy has gone through three stages in the process of controlling inflation. In the 1980−82 period, inflation remarkably fell from a peak of 100 percent in 1980, to around 25 percent by the end of 1982. Removal of supply bottlenecks, easing of the domestic demand pressure, moderation of increases in import prices and agricultural support prices, and wage restraint, were among the most important factors underlying the deceleration of the inflation rate. However, in 1983, inflation accelerated rapidly and the economy entered the second stage, which lasted till the end of 1986. During this period, the authorities could not repeat their earlier success in disinflation but nevertheless were able to contain inflation rate to around 40 percent. Although the rate of inflation in 1986 was lower than the pre-1980 period, the gain in disinflation was, at best, moderate considering the favorable conditions such as the sharp fall in energy and commodity prices, the presence of unemployment, and the reduction of real wages. In the third phase, which started in 1987, inflation accelerated rapidly and authorities lost their grip over its evolution. Consequently, lowering inflation once again became the principal problem of the Turkish economy.

The time path of inflation can be traced through the changes in monetary and fiscal policies. The major reason behind the reacceleration of inflation in 1983 was the monetary expansion in the aftermath of the financial turbulence of the 1981−83 period.[14] The rise of the budget deficit in 1987, after a period of improvement from 1982 to 1986, together with an acceleration of monetary aggregates beginning in 1985, led to a sharp increase of the inflation rate since 1987.

Implementation of the New Exchange Rate Policy

The 1980–89 period can be divided into two subperiods from the perspective of exchange rate management. The one beginning in January 1980 and ending in May 1981, corresponds to the management of the macroeconomic crisis. Faced with an inflation rate exceeding 100 percent and a severe balance of payments crisis, the authorities assigned an overriding priority to preventing real appreciation of the Turkish lira. This was sought to be achieved by a 33-percent devaluation in January 1980, which was followed by a series of devaluations with smaller magnitudes. Figure 5.1 displays the evolution since 1980 of the indexes of the nominal and real effective exchange rates of the Turkish lira. Figure 5.2 presents only the time path of the real effective exchange rate (REER) index to better display its evolution. The data underlying these diagrams are presented in table 5.3, together with annual percentage changes in the REER. The January 1980 devaluation caused steep declines in both indexes. Although the subsequent price developments eroded some of the initial gain in the competitiveness, the Turkish lira depreciated by 23 percent in real effective terms in 1980 and by another 13 percent in 1981. Hence, the exchange rate strategy followed by the authorities enabled them to attain their objective of preventing overvaluation of the Turkish lira while they were combatting inflation through demand management policies.

The second stage of exchange rate management began in May 1981. Having lowered inflation to around 30 percent, authorities changed their method of preventing overvaluation of the lira. The new strategy applied daily adjustments to the exchange rate instead of relying on discrete devaluations. Although appreciation of the lira in real effective terms has been prevented since May 1981, the rate of real effective depreciation engineered by policymakers has significantly varied from one year to another (see table 5.3).

In 1982, for the third year in a row, the REER was depreciated by more than 8 percent per year. The rate of real depreciation was markedly lower in the subsequent three-year period. Concerns about accelerating inflation in 1984 led the authorities to tolerate a real appreciation for a prolonged period within the year, although the REER index closed the year slightly lower than its value at the end of the previous year. The policy of refraining from sizable real depreciation continued into 1985, but there was no instance of real appreciation within the year as was the case in 1984.

Concerns over the external account due to stagnating exports

Figure 5.1. Indices of the nominal and real effective exchange rate of the Turkish lira (1979 = 100)

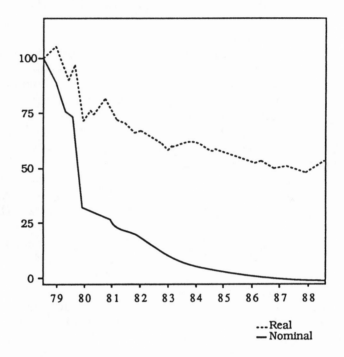

...Real
— Nominal

Figure 5.2. Real effective exchange rate index of the Turkish lira (1979 = 100)

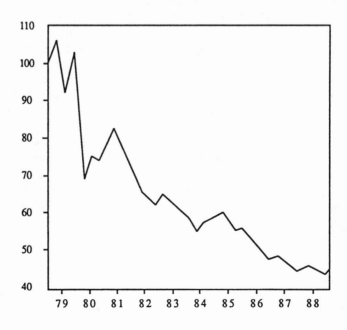

Table 5.3   Exchange Rate Developments

Period	Nominal Effective Exchange Rate	Real Effective Exchange Rate	% Change of REER[b] over the Previous Year
1979.1[a]	100.00	100.00	
1979.2	90.36	106.69	
1979.3	72.18	92.39	
1979.4	71.47	103.12	
1980.1	35.64	69.32	
1980.2	33.80	75.56	
1980.3	31.99	74.25	
1980.4	30.52	79.31	−23.09
1981.1	29.86	82.20	
1981.2	28.33	78.11	
1981.3	25.25	73.57	
1981.4	22.59	68.74	−13.33
1982.1	20.88	67.88	
1982.2	19.50	67.15	
1982.3	17.76	63.64	
1982.4	16.69	61.40	−10.55
1983.1	15.53	64.55	
1983.2	14.42	62.72	
1983.3	13.38	60.48	
1983.4	12.12	59.52	−3.06
1984.1	10.15	55.38	
1984.2	9.17	58.91	
1984.3	8.47	58.50	
1984.4	7.90	59.29	−0.40
1985.1	7.23	60.93	
1985.2	6.50	59.25	
1985.3	5.98	55.90	
1985.4	5.50	56.77	−0.68
1986.1	4.80	54.77	
1986.2	4.31	52.45	
1986.3	4.07	51.74	
1986.4	3.63	49.51	−12.79
1987.1	3.36	49.06	
1987.2	3.14	49.79	
1987.3	2.87	47.89	
1987.4	2.50	46.18	−6.73
1988.1	2.10	47.60	
1988.2	1.89	48.64	
1988.3	1.70	46.96	
1988.4	1.44	45.43	−1.60

Source: Central Bank of Turkey.
[a] Quarterly averages of monthly figures.
[b] Real effective exchange rate.

led the authorities to depreciate the lira in real effective terms by more than 13 percent in 1986. In 1987 the lira was depreciated by another 6.73 percent in order to compensate for the effect on the external account of the projected real growth differential of Turkey vis-à-vis its trading partners.

Beginning in 1988 we observe another slowing down in the rate of real depreciation because of the concerns over accelerating inflation. The 1.60-percent depreciation in 1988 is much less than the rate in the two preceding years, as well as the trend between 1980 and 1988. In 1989 the lira appreciated in real effective terms, by 6 percent, for the first time since 1980.

An observation other than changes in the rate of real depreciation from one year to another is the volatility of the REER within a given year. This can be demonstrated with the aid of monthly and quarterly data. Figures 5.3 and 5.4 display the annualized monthly and quarterly percentage changes in the REER index, respectively. The figures point out to substantial volatility in the REER on a monthly or a quarterly basis. Hence, annual depreciation of the REER was associated with months of real appreciation followed by months of real depreciation. Volatility of the REER was evident especially in the years of accelerating inflation (1983, 1984, 1987, and 1988). The uncertainty associated with real exchange rate volatility has from time to time been a major setback for policy-makers as the liberalization of foreign exchange transactions increasingly enabled market participants to take positions against the lira. In particular, the foreign exchange market experienced a severe turbulence in 1988 when inflation suddenly accelerated. The nominal exchange rates were not sufficiently adjusted so that the lira appreciated in real effective terms, leading to expectations of a discrete devaluation. Policy authorities introduced a set of policy measures in February 1988 in order to stop speculation and hoarding of foreign exchange.[15] The foreign exchange crisis, which was successfully calmed down by the Central Bank, demonstrates the difficulty of following the policy of real effective depreciation in the presence of high and accelerating inflation.

Exchange Rate Management as Part of the Overall Macroeconomic Policy

The conclusion of the preceding discussion is that the new exchange rate policy has very effectively protected and improved the price competitiveness of exports despite high domestic inflation. The

Figure 5.3. Monthly annualized percentage changes in the real effective exchange rate of the Turkish Lira.

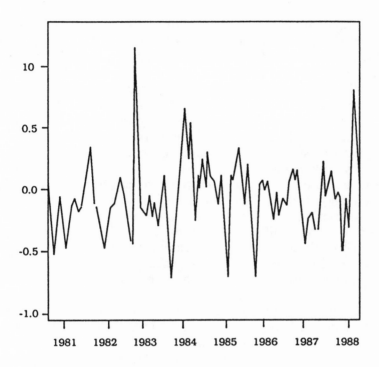

Figure 5.4. Quarterly annualized percentage changes in the real effective exchange rate index of the Turkish Lira.

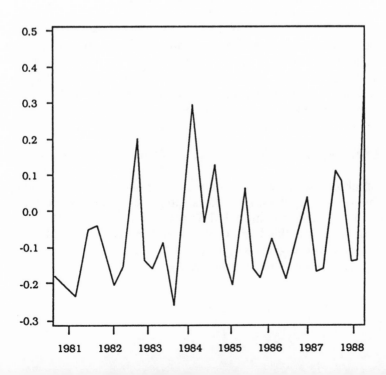

policy of continual real depreciation, together with direct and indirect subsidies, have been the key to an impressive growth of exports. Therefore, the exchange rate policy deserves credit for undoing the adverse effect of inflation on the competitive position of the Turkish economy. Maintaining competitiveness in the longer run requires an effective control over inflation, rather than shielding the external competitiveness from domestic inflation. Evaluating the exchange rate policy from this perspective casts doubt over its effectiveness due to the interaction between inflation and real currency depreciation.

The exchange rate inflation relation has been fundamentally altered since 1980. During the fixed exchange rate regime of the pre-1980 period, the direct contribution of exchange rates on inflation was not significant. However, the policy of fixed exchange rates indirectly led to the acceleration of inflation: overvaluation of the currency implied a growing need for external adjustment, and the reduction in the available foreign exchange resources caused serious supply bottlenecks.

Under the post-1980 policy of persistent real depreciation, the effect of the exchange rate management on inflation derives from several channels. First, the continual currency depreciation increases the cost of production and raises the inflation rate from the supply side. Second, such a policy stabilizes and increases the net exports component of aggregate demand. Hence, lowering inflation requires an effective control over the domestic part of total absorption. Unless restrictive fiscal and monetary policies contain and reduce the growth of domestic absorption, the exchange rate policy validates ongoing inflation through the demand side. Therefore, the policy of real effective depreciation may lead to loss of control over the inflationary process.[16] Finally, real depreciation raises the domestic currency cost of serving the foreign debt and increases the public sector's borrowing requirements since most of the foreign debt is the liability of the public sector.[17]

Exchange Rate Policy in an Optimization Framework[18]

We analyze the optimal exchange rate policy in Turkey using the methodology developed by the strategic approach to policy coordination.[19] Turkey is modeled as a small economy with two large trading partners: the United States and Europe. Considering that Germany is the biggest single national market for Turkey and developments in the German economy are, by and large, indicative of those in Europe, we concentrate on interactions between the United States, Germany, and Turkey. This framework enables us to discuss the exchange rate policy as one against the dollar and the Deutschemark (DM), in line with the Central Bank's practice of concentrating on the real effective exchange rate in terms of the U.S. dollar and the DM. Domestic output level, external account, as well as the rate of inflation, depend on the real U.S. dollar exchange rate of the Turkish lira, which is controlled by the authorities and by the terms of trade between the U.S. and Germany and by the output levels of the two foreign countries, which are determined as the outcome of the policy interactions between them.

In this context we analyze the optimal exchange rate strategy by postulating that the objective of the policymakers is to minimize deviations of inflation, output and external balance from their respective target values, subject to the reduced form of a three-country model describing the Turkish economy.[20] Because of the size differences between the home country and its trading partners, foreign variables, which are determined independently of the developments in the Turkish economy, affect the domestic economy through demand and supply channels. We compare and contrast the implications for the domestic macroeconomic performance of following the optimal rule and two alternative strategies: pegging to the dollar in real terms, and pegging to the real effective exchange rate index.[21]

As Turkey trades with both countries, we incorporate into the analysis two different terms of trade. However, the consistency between direct and cross-exchange rates (triangular arbitrage condition) implies that the TL/DM exchange rate is equal to the product of the $/DM and the TL/$ exchange rates. The significance of the exchange rate strategy derives from the following condition: since the $/DM exchange rate is determined as the outcome of the policy interactions between the U.S. and Germany, the domestic exchange rate rule for TL/$ (TL/DM) has an immediate effect on the TL/DM (TL/$) rate and hence on the macroeconomic performance through the effective exchange rate. The authorities can control the real effective exchange rate of the Turkish lira either by the real TL/DM exchange rate, or by the real TL/$ rate. Parallel to the Turkish experience we take the dollar as the intervention currency and hence the real dollar exchange rate (RDER) as the strategy variable.

Carrying out the optimization we derive the optimal rule for setting the level of the RDER, the inspection of which leads to the following conclusions: first, in its general form the optimal strategy is to set the RDER according to a feedback rule, which is a function of the real exchange rate between the two foreign currencies, foreign output levels, the underlying rate of domestic inflation, targets of the Turkish policymakers for output, inflation, and the trade account. A constant real TL/$ exchange rate (RDER) is optimal only in a polar case in which the real $/DM exchange rate as well as the foreign output levels remain unchanged, the inherited domestic inflation rate is equal to its target, and there is no change in the domestic targets for output and net exports. In this case the RDER should be kept at its initial level by depreciating the lira against the U.S. dollar according to the inflation differential. Since the real $/DM rate is unchanged in this case, the constant RDER rule is equivalent to the constant REER rule, no matter which weights are used to calculate the REER index.

Second, the rule of keeping the REER index constant coincides with the optimal strategy only if the relative weight given to inflation stabilization is zero and if there is no change in the foreign output levels and in the domestic targets for output and external balance. These results indicate that the policy of keeping either of the two indicators of the real exchange rate (RDER or REER) constant implies making restrictive assumptions on the external conditions and/or targeting a subset of macroeconomic variables. In particular, the desirability of these strategies stem from focusing only on the trade balance. Considering inflation as another variable to stabilize introduces a trade-off for policymakers, the nature of which changes with external developments. The interdependence between the external economic conditions and exchange rate management in Turkey is reflected in the functional dependence of the optimal RDER rule on the foreign variables because of their impact on the domestic variables that the authorities want to stabilize.[22] Therefore, the behavior of exchange rates in Turkey under the optimal policy is closely linked to the policy developments abroad.

Simulation Results

Using the optimization framework just outlined, simulation experiments are undertaken in order to provide numerical comparisons for the macroeconomic implications of alternative exchange rate strategies under several external circumstances. We consider four different scenarios for external developments. The first one assumes that both the U.S. and Germany have an inherited inflation rate of 15 percent and desire to lower it to 5 percent. The initial output levels are also assumed to equal their targets. In the second scenario the rates of core inflation and inflation targets are the same as in the first scenario but we assume the American fiscal policy to be more expansionary than Germany's. This experiment is a stylized characterization of policy developments during the 1982−85 period. The third scenario assumes that the U.S. and Germany are content with their inherited inflation of 5 percent but their output targets are revised up by 5 percent. This experiment, referred to as the joint expansion, assumes no change in fiscal positions relative to the base line.[23] Finally, the fourth scenario is similar to the third one except that the U.S. fiscal deficit is reduced.

The main result that follows from the simulation analyses is that the optimal RDER rule dominates the other two under all scenarios regardless of the relative weight attached to inflation.[24] However, the payoff to switching to the optimal rule from others increases with the importance of inflation in the macroeconomic loss function. Second, differences in loss levels obtained under three rules and the relative desirability of the optimal strategy are especially pronounced when the real exchange rate between the U.S. and Germany changes due to asymmetric fiscal positions and/or preferences in these countries (second and fourth scenarios). Third, the constant REER rule ranks between the constant RDER rule and the optimal rule. We also compare the alternative strategies according to the output and inflation stability that they provided.[25] The results reinforce the earlier conclusions. In general, the optimal rule is superior to the others in yielding smaller standard deviations for both output and inflation. The constant REER rule outperforms the constant RDER rule but is dominated by the optimal strategy.

Another result that emerges from simulations is that the relative weight given to stabilizing inflation introduces a trade-off between output and inflation stability within the optimal strategy. If this weight is zero, then the optimal rule manages to keep output and external account on their targets at the expense of rendering inflation volatile. As the authorities get more concerned about inflation, the optimal rule allows for higher volatility in output and the external account in order to achieve greater stability in inflation. Accordingly, the standard deviation of output/external account monotonically increases with the weight given to controlling inflation, whereas that of inflation declines.

Evaluation of Exchange Rate Management in Turkey

Comparison of the findings of the optimization framework with the exchange rate management in Turkey leads to several conclusions.

First, implementation of the exchange rate policy indicates that the strategy followed by the Central Bank resembles some form of a feedback rule rather than a passive crawl. The continual real effective depreciation of the lira together with changes in the rate of depreciation from one year to another are not consistent with a characterization of the exchange rate strategy followed in Turkey as a constant REER rule (passive crawl). Yet policy activism of the authorities in the form of taking feedback from the performance of the economy in setting the rate of depreciation should be distinguished from the active downward crawl strategy applied in the Southern Cone countries. Not only the Turkish authorities did not preannounce a table of decelerating rates of depreciations in an attempt to cut inflationary expectations, but also except for a brief period in 1984 they did not opt for using real appreciation as an anti-inflationary tool.

The second set of observations apply to the nature of the feedback rule that can be inferred from the experience of the post-1980 period. The Central Bank's use of the real effective exchange rate index in terms of the U.S. dollar and the DM rather than either of the two currencies as its policy instrument is consistent with the findings of the optimization framework. This indicates that the Central Bank takes account of relative exchange rate changes between the two foreign currencies. Also, as it was the case in 1987, policymakers have given explicit consideration to evolution of foreign output levels as the optimal strategy would suggest. However, whereas the optimal strategy would imply a feedback rule with respect to both inflation and the external account, the exchange rate policy in Turkey has been geared mostly toward the current account. On the other hand, in the years of accelerating inflation the policymakers slowed down the rate of real depreciation. A possible way to reconcile these observations with the feedback strategy is to argue that the weight given to controlling inflation relative to controlling external account has not always been uniform. In particular, a high weight seems to have been assigned in the years of accelerating inflation and otherwise the authorities have been predominantly concerned with the external equilibrium. This would not be a major issue if the rate of inflation were controlled by some other macroeconomic policy instrument. Under such a policy assignment, monetary and/or fiscal policy would be assigned to controlling inflation and the exchange rate policy would be given the task of stabilizing the real exchange rate around the value required by the external balance target. In the absence of the support of a consistent anti-inflationary program, the exchange rate policy has protected the competitiveness of exports but in general tolerated the inflationary consequences of the implied real depreciations. Therefore, the inflationary effects of the exchange rate policy have to be weighted against its contribution to export promotion.

In the face of high current inflation the authorities have several choices in formulating the exchange rate policy. An option would be to act within the framework of a feedback rule but to consistently assign a high weight to the inflation target. Although this suggestion seems to follow from the optimization framework, a detailed analysis of the situation rejects the proposition. The experience of the Southern Cone countries warns against attempting to disinflate through exchange rate policy and instead points out that disinflation should be achieved by controlling absorption. Assigning a higher weight to controlling inflation carries with it the risk of leading to overvaluation with detrimental effects on the external account. Hence, the desirability of a feedback rule is contingent upon a successful implementation of stabilization policies prior to using the rule. Otherwise, the feedback rule becomes a tool for disinflation rather than a method of stabilizing the REER around a level optimal from the point of view of both inflation and external account. An additional consideration in refraining from the feedback rule under the current conditions is the expectation formation process on which the rule is based. Inflation is assumed to evolve according to the discrepancy between demand and supply augmented by the core or underlying rate of inflation. Simulations take the latter as the rate inherited from the previous period. Although this is a realistic way of modeling inflation once it has been controlled by stabilization policies, inflation might evolve independently of demand and supply pressures and the current core rate during periods of accelerating inflation. Since presently Turkey has not eliminated the danger of having such an experience, the desirability of following a feedback rule derived from a model of core inflation cannot be argued unambiguously. Based on these considerations we propose the implementation of a stabilization policy package to be followed by an exchange rate policy in the form of a feedback rule.

Conclusions and Policy Implications

The liberalization program in Turkey has addressed the dual problem of high inflation and an unsustainable external deficit. The impressive growth of exports and a strong recovery of output in the post-1980 period are the two areas that the liberalization program has been credited with. The results obtained in the inflation front overshadows these achievements. In as early as 1980 it was noted that the most difficult task was to lower inflation and yet, without success in this respect, it would be difficult to achieve a viable external balance and sustainable economic growth over the longer run.[26] The persistence of high inflation since 1980 has confirmed this prediction.

The central orientation of the exchange rate policy has been continuous depreciation of the lira in real effective terms in order to protect and improve the external competitiveness of the Turkish economy. The present paper concludes that the exchange rate policy has been successful in preventing overvaluation of the domestic currency and in engineering persistent real depreciation despite the complications experienced in implementing such a strategy in inflationary circumstances. However, the desirability of continuous real depreciation becomes questionable when the exchange rate policy is viewed as part of the overall macroeconomic management. The optimization framework reviewed in this paper suggests that the appropriate strategy would be to follow a feedback rule by which the real effective exchange rate is altered, taking account of the domestic inflation and external account targets as well as the evolution of foreign output levels and the relative exchange rate changes between the major trading partners. Evaluation of the exchange rate policy from this perspective suggests that a form of feedback policy was in effect, yet the actual strategy differed from the feedback rule discussed in this paper with respect to the way inflation was handled. However, the main drawback of the exchange rate policy is the authorities' insisting on using the policy of persistent real depreciation for external account purposes (with occasional feedback from inflation side) long after they lost the support of an anti-inflationary stabilization policy.

My main policy implication is that the overriding priority should be given to lowering inflation through a stabilization package of restrictive demand policies. During the process of disinflation the authorities should follow passive crawl in order not to put extra burden on the demand policies through persistent real depreciation. Export promotion should be increasingly based on improving nonprice competitiveness of Turkish exports. This, in turn, should be achieved through investment incentives to the export-oriented sectors.

Notes

1. See Corbo and de Melo (1987) for a review of exchange rate policies in the Southern Cone countries, and Dornbusch (1982) for the experience of Argentina and a discussion of theoretical issues associated with active exchange rate management.

2. For example, see OECD (1988).

3. See Quirk et al. (1987) for a comprehensive study on the experience of developing countries with market-determined floating exchange rates.

4. See Adams and Gros (1986) and Howard (1987) for an evaluation of real exchange rate rules.

5. In the case of a basket peg, an additional consideration arises with respect to the weights to be used in the construction of the basket. The popular alternatives are elasticity weights, import weights, and export weights, or weights based on total trade. For analyses of optimal currency baskets, see Lipschitz and Sundararajan (1980 and 1982), Connolly and Yousef (1982), and Connolly (1983).

6. For a more detailed discussion of crawling peg see Williamson (1982). See Blejer and Leiderman (1981) for the analysis of crawling peg in Brazil. It should be noted that theoretically, the passive crawl does not preclude the possibility of changing the value of the real exchange rate indicator that the rule tries to preserve when there is a persisting need to facilitate the external adjustment.

7. See Mantel and Martirena-Mantel (1982) for a theoretical analysis of the active crawling peg. Mathieson (1976) addresses the question of optimal crawling peg. Edison and Marquez (1986) apply the optimal control theory to analyze optimal crawling peg in Venezuela.

8. As part of the multiple currency practices, the lira was devalued to TL 47 per U.S.$1 for workers' remittances and tourist receipts on April 10, 1979. On June 10, 1979, the exchange rate became TL 35 per U.S.$1 for agricultural exports and imports of oil chemicals, etc. For further details see table 5.1.

9. See Kopits (1987) for such characterization of the exchange rate policy in Turkey.

10. "In fact, so long as the current account is in deficit a real devaluation of the lira is aimed at in order to improve price competitiveness of exports" (OECD 1987: 18).

11. The calculations are based on the real effective exchange rate series provided by the Central Bank of Turkey.

12. The band was initially set at +/− 8 percent, removed in July 1985, and reinstated at +/− 1 percent in 1986.

13. Equilibrium exchange rate is determined at the end of the daily sessions conducted by the Central Bank. For transactions up to $50,000 banks are required to buy and sell foreign exchange within a band around the equilibrium rate. For larger transactions, banks are free to set their own rates.

14. Following the financial crisis of the 1981−82 period, monetary authorities increased the growth of money supply in order to prevent a major crisis in the banking system.

15. The policy package included measures to tighten credit and changes in surrender requirements for the foreign exchange earnings of exporters.

16. See Adams and Gros (1986) for a detailed analysis of this point.

17. This point has recently been emphasized by Rodrik (1988). See also OECD (1988).

18. In this paper we present the main findings of the framework developed in Aşıkoğlu (1988).

19. See Buiter and Marston (1985), Hamada (1985), and Fischer (1988) as general references to the literature on policy coordination.

20. Macedo (1986) utilized a similar macroeconomic framework of developed and developing countries to analyze the West African Monetary Union.

21. Several other studies have addressed the issue of optimal exchange rate strategy in developing countries [see, e.g., Lipschitz and Sundararajan 1980, 1982; Connolly and Yousef 1982; Connolly 1982, 1983]. The analysis of this paper differs from the earlier studies in its strategic approach, in its focus on the aggregate demand-aggregate supply framework as opposed to the commodity arbitrage as the inflation-generating process, and in the macroeconomic objectives that it considers. Furthermore, our emphasis is on the determination of the level of the peg whereas much of the existing literature addresses the problem of constructing an exchange rate index appropriate for the objective of the policymakers.

22. In particular, inflation and output targets and the core rates of inflation in the foreign countries affect the RDER because of their impact on the foreign output levels. The relative fiscal positions of foreign countries and differences in their macroeconomic objectives and underlying inflation rates enter into the optimal RDER rule since they determine the real dollar-DM exchange rate.

23. This experiment is qualitatively similar to the IMF's baseline scenario in Adams and Gros (1986).

24. Thus, in game-theoretical terminology, the optimal exchange rate rule is the dominating strategy.

25. The volatility of output and external account, as measured by their standard deviations, are monotonic transformations of each other. Hence, for brevity the following discussion focuses on the standard deviation of output only.

26. See OECD (1980), esp. p. 29.

References

Adams, C. and D. Gros. 1986. "The Consequences of Real Exchange Rate Rules for Inflation." *IMF Staff Papers* 33:439–76.

Aşıkoğlu, Y. 1988. "Macroeconomic Consequences of Alternative Exchange Rate Strategies." City University of New York. Mimeo.

Black, S. W. 1976. "Exchange Rate Policies for Less Developed Countries in a World of Floating Rates." Essays in International Finance 119, Princeton University.

Blejer, M. and L. Leiderman. 1981. "A Monetary Approach to the Crawling Peg System: Theory and Evidence." *Journal of Political Economy* 89:132–51.

Branson, W. H. and L. T. Katseli-Papaefstratiou. 1981. "Exchange Rate Policy in Developing Countries." In *The World Economic Order: Past and Prospects*, edited by S. Grossman and E. Lundberg, 391–419. London: Macmillan Press.

Buiter, W. H. and R. C. Marston. 1985. *International Economic Policy Coordination*. New York: Cambridge University Press.

Connolly, M. 1983. "Optimum Currency Pegs for Latin America." *Journal of Money, Credit and Banking* 56–72.

———. 1982. "The Choice of an Optimum Currency Peg for a Small, Open Country." *Journal of International Money and Finance* 1:153–64.

Connolly, M. and A. Yousef. 1982. "Optimum Currency Pegs for Arab Countries." In *The International Monetary System: Choices for the Future*, edited by M. Connolly. New York: Praeger Press.

Corbo, V. and J. de Melo. 1987. "Lessons from the Southern Cone Policy Reforms." *The World Bank Research Observer* 2:111–43.

Dornbusch, R. 1982. "Stabilization Policies in Developing Countries: What Have We Learned?" *World Development* 10:701–8.

Edison, H. J. and J. Marquez. 1986. "Optimal Crawling Peg in Venezuela." *Journal of Economic Dynamics and Control* 10:201–4.

Edwards, S. and L. Ahmad, eds. 1986. *Economic Adjustment and Exchange Rates in Developing Countries*. Chicago: University of Chicago Press.

Fischer, S. 1988. "International Macroeconomic Policy Coordination." In *International Economic Cooperation*, edited by M. Feldstein. Chicago: University of Chicago Press.

Hamada, K. 1985. *The Political Economy of International Monetary Interdependence*. Cambridge: MIT Press.

Howard, D. R. 1987. "Exchange Rate Regimes and Macroeconomic Stabilization in a Developing Country." International Finance Discussion Papers 314.

Kopits, G. 1987. *Structural Reform, Stabilization, and Growth in Turkey*. IMF Occasional Paper 52. Washington, D.C.: IMF.

Lipschitz, L. and V. Sundararajan. 1980. "The Optimal Basket in a World of Generalized Floating." *IMF Staff Papers* 25:80–100.

———. 1982. "The Optimal Currency Basket in a World of Generalized Floating with Price Uncertainty." In *The International Monetary System: Choices for the Future*, edited by M. Connolly, 121–34. New York: Praeger Press.

Macedo, J. B. 1986. "Collective Pegging to a Single Currency: The West African Monetary Union." In *Economic Adjustment and Exchange Rates in Developing Countries*, edited by S. Edwards and L. Ahmad. Chicago: University of Chicago Press.

Mantel, R. and A. M. Martirena-Mantel. 1982. "Exchange Rate Policies in a Small Open Economy: The Active Crawling Peg." *Journal of International Economics* 13:301–20.

Mathieson, D. J. 1976. "Is there an Optimal Crawl?" *Journal of International Economics* 6:183–202.

OECD. 1988. *Economic Surveys: Turkey*. Paris: OECD.

———. 1987. *Economic Surveys: Turkey*. Paris: OECD.

———. 1980. *Economic Surveys: Turkey*. Paris: OECD.

Quirk, P. J., B. V. Christensen, K. M. Huh, and T. Sasaki. 1987. "Floating Exchange Rates in Developing Countries: Experience with Auction and Interbank Markets." IMF Occasional Paper 53.

Rodrik, D. 1988. "Some Policy Dilemmas in Turkish Macroeconomic Management." Paper prepared for the conference on Turkey's Economic Development in the 1980s, Harvard University, April.

Wickham, P. 1985. "The Choice of Exchage Rate Regime in Developing Countries: A Survey of the Literature." *IMF Staff Papers* 32:248–88.

Williamson, J. 1982. "A Survey of the Literature on the Optimal Peg." *Journal of Development Economics* 11:39–61.

6

Economic Stabilization and Structural Adjustment in Turkey: Evidence from Macroeconomic Accounts

Patrick Conway

Introduction

In Turkey, as in a majority of highly indebted developing countries, government policy has been restructured in recent years to finance and ultimately eliminate large external payments requirements. These policy initiatives can be broadly categorized as short-run *stabilization policies* to reduce imports and attain current account balance and longer-run *structural adjustment policies* to maintain this external balance while fostering positive and noninflationary economic growth. From the perspective of developing countries the stabilization policy is seen as a necessary but painful temporary prescription, while structural adjustment to sustainable economic growth is the goal of forward-looking and permanent policies.[1]

Stabilization policies are macroeconomic policies (e.g., reduction in government budget deficits or reduction in money supply growth) designed to achieve short-run macroeconomic effects through aggregate demand management; they are thus fairly easily assessed. Structural adjustment policies are less easily evaluated. They are microeconomic and relative-price based in nature, as indicated by the following excerpt from Thomas (1988: 3):

> Domestic policy changes ... have involved incentives for resource reallocation, inducements for savings and investment, redirection of public investment priorities, and often a variety of sector-level reforms.

Nevertheless, they are designed to have a sustained positive macroeconomic impact through a supply-side improvement of the productive economy. Given this goal, it is natural to look to the macroeconomic balances for evidence of structural adjustment.

Turkey provides an excellent example of both stabilization and structural adjustment policies in the period since 1979. Stabilization policies were implemented in the crisis years 1978–80. Since 1980, Turkey has become a leading example of the introduction and implementation of structural adjustment reforms. It was one of the first to receive structural adjustment lending from the World Bank in early 1980, and during the period 1980–87 received 8 separate adjustment loans totaling $2.5 billion from the World Bank.[2] In addition, the IMF made available 2 SDR billion in standby arrangements during the period 1978–85.[3] In Conway (1987) I enumerate the wide range of structural reforms undertaken by the Turkish government during this period, including reforms of trade policy, financial-sector regulation, public enterprise operations, and public investment decision-making.

How successful have these policies been in both their short and long-term goals? Two positive results are the rapid growth rates in exports and in real GNP. Commodity exports quadrupled in dollar value over the period 1981–88, while the average annual growth rate in GNP was 5.2 percent. As recently as 1986, GNP grew at an 8.1 percent annual rate. However, the current account and inflation performance are less positive aspects of this adjustment period. The annual inflation rate is below its crisis peak of 107 percent in 1980 but has remained stubbornly high: the average annual rate for 1981–88 was 40 percent. The current account as a percentage of GNP averaged a deficit of 2.5 percent through 1987, then became a 2.1-percent surplus in 1988. As a result, Turkey's external debt rose as a percent of GNP from 27 percent in the crisis year 1980, to 53 percent in 1988.

Given this mixed record, it is easy to agree with Kopits (1987) that "while the Turkish experience is widely seen as a successful case of economic liberalization and stabilization, the adjustment process is not yet complete." Investigation of the macroeconomic performance through national accounts, government finance, and balance of payments data demonstrates that this is in fact the case. I will argue that the difficulties that remain are less a product of the structural adjustment process than of an insufficiently pursued stabilization policy. These difficulties introduce instability into the Turkish adjustment process and threaten the long-run viability of that program.

I organize my analysis around the investment/saving identity for an open economy. A country that is a candidate for stabilization and structural adjustment policies is one with significant reliance on foreign saving to finance national expenditures: by definition, then, a country with significant national dissaving. Stabilization policies are those designed to reduce this dissaving to acceptable levels. Structural adjustment policies are adopted to improve the sectoral allocation of resources and should have the effect of redistributing this acceptable level of dissaving to sectors with comparative advantage. There is an inevitable tension between stabilization and structural adjustment for indebted countries in that structural adjustment is more rapidly achieved and readily implemented during periods of positive economic growth. Turkey has been successful in maintaining positive GNP growth through the process; this, however, has led to continued public-sector dissaving that may have endangered the sustainability of these structural reforms.

In the next section I present the saving/investment balance in Turkey in terms of foreign, private, and public saving. This exercise demonstrates that the structural adjustment process has had its successes in reallocating resources to productive sectors, most notably in its encouragement of export promotion and private saving. The stabilization policy was less successful, however, in bringing about a reduction in public dissaving — either when originally implemented in 1978–79 or during the structural adjustment period of the 1980s. In the third section these trends are examined for separate subperiods of structural adjustment: an initial period 1981–84 and a subsequent adjustment period 1985–88. The final section summarizes the conclusions of this study and suggests extensions of this research.

Calculating the Extent of Turkish Structural Adjustment

Structural adjustment policy has become necessary because of the reduced availability of international financing for developing countries.[4] Since this financing represented foreign saving that funded developing-country expenditures, structural adjustment policies will be successful if they increase private and public saving within the economy. The national expenditure identity provides a framework for such an evaluation. Total GNP must equal the sum of private consumption (C), public consumption (G_c), private investment (I_p), government investment (I_g), and net exports of goods and nonfactor services (TB).

$$(6.1) \qquad GNP = C + I_p + I_g + G_c + TB$$

If public revenues are denoted R, we can transform (6.1) into a statement about public, private, and foreign saving.

(6.2) $[GNP - C - R - I_p] + [R - G_c - I_g] = TB$

Although this does not yet include many of the complexities of the Turkish economy, it does illustrate the interplay of private, public and foreign saving. The first bracketed term in (6.2) is a measure of private saving, while the second bracketed term measures public saving. TB is a measure of dissaving by foreigners.

Stabilization and structural adjustment policies become necessary when insufficient foreign saving is available; private and public saving must then be increased to compensate. Stabilization policy acts through reducing the expenditure components of the two bracketed terms — G_c and I_g directly, while C and I_p indirectly through its recessionary effects. Structural adjustment policies, by contrast, seek to improve public and private saving through expanding GNP and R. This expansion will be due to the static gains of reallocating resources to comparative-advantage sectors as well as to the dynamic gains from more efficient investments.

There are additional features of the Turkish economy that must be included in this decomposition: international factor service payments (e.g., remittances and payments on foreign debt), revenues and expenditures of state economic enterprises (SEEs) and extra-budgetary funds (EBF), public-private transfer programs, and public service of existing domestic and international debt.[5] With these additions (6.1) can be reinterpreted such that the sum of net private saving (PS) and net public saving (GS) must equal net dissaving by foreigners as measured by a surplus of the current account (B) of the balance of payments.

(6.3) $PS + GS = B$

There are three subperiods of the post-1973 economic history of Turkey. The first is the period prior to crisis, stabilization, and structural adjustment: I call this the *base* subperiod 1974–77. The second is the subperiod of *stabilization*, or import-compression, of 1978–79. The third is the *structural-adjustment* subperiod beginning in 1980 but more completely implemented in 1981–88. I will take the base subperiod as a standard for comparison, and will examine average macroeconomic performance in the other subperiods for evidence of success in stabilization or structural adjustment.[6]

Success of the joint stabilization-structural adjustment program is indicated by a reduction in net saving by foreigners (a reduction in the current account deficit) and by increased public-and private-sector saving. Saving behavior has been quite volatile for Turkey for the period 1974–88. Table 6.1 combines national account and government budgetary information to illustrate the evolution of these aggregates. Performance aggregated by subperiod is given in the lower part of the table.

The current account (B) remained in deficit throughout the 1974–87 period until turning to surplus in 1988. The current account deficit averaged 4.47 percent of GNP during the base subperiod, while the stabilization policies of the import-compression years led to a reduced deficit of on average 1.77 percent of GNP. During the structural-adjustment subperiod 1981–88 the deficit averaged 1.82 percent of GNP, although the annual deficit figures indicate a reduction over that subperiod. Turkey has clearly been able to attract foreign saving to finance international purchases even during its stabilization and structural adjustment episodes, but the postcrisis deficits have been much smaller on average than those of the base subperiod.

This reduction on average in the current account deficit indicates a partial success of the combined policy, and must correspond to an increase on average in private and public net saving. As the third column of table 6.1 illustrates, net private saving as a percentage of GNP improved markedly during the import compression subperiod. In the base subperiod it was negative on average as private expenditures exceeded private income, but improved to an average of 3.74 percent of GNP during the import compression period. This positive trend was partially reversed during the structural-adjustment subperiod with net saving of 1.7 percent of GNP on average, but the most recent years indicate a strong private-saving performance. The stabilization policy thus had its immediate desired effect, but not until 1987–88 was there evidence that the structural-adjustment program was equally effective in promoting saving. Net public saving followed a less satisfactory path as illustrated in the fourth column of table 6.1. In the base subperiod public dissaving (expenditure over income) averaged 4.21 percent of GNP. During the import-compression subperiod public dissaving *worsened* to a deficit of 5.5 percent of GNP. During the structural-adjustment subperiod there was a reduction in public dissaving to an average of 3.52 percent, or slightly below that of the base subperiod. The stabilization policy thus did not have its desired direct effect on government expenditure, and the structural adjustment period indicates that the saving imbalance is being reduced only slowly.

The dynamic of adjustment to the stabilization/structural adjustment policy has thus been complex. During the import-compression subperiod the necessary expenditure reduction fell upon the pri-

Table 6.1 National Income and Product Identity:
Turkey (% of Current-Value GNP)

Year	B	PS	GS
1974	−2.15	1.22	−3.37
1975	−4.43	−1.20	−3.23
1976	−4.81	−1.28	−3.53
1977	−6.47	0.22	−6.69
1978	−2.19	2.05	−4.24
1979	−1.34	5.43	−6.77
1980	−5.04	1.20	−6.24
1981	−2.83	1.74	−4.57
1982	−1.55	1.46	−3.01
1983	−3.57	−0.96	−2.61
1984	−2.81	1.17	−3.98
1985	−1.90	0.44	−2.34
1986	−2.60	0.85	−3.45
1987	−1.44	4.56	−6.00
1988	2.08	4.28[a]	−2.19[a]
Subperiod Averages:			
1974−77	−4.47	−0.26	−4.21
1978−79	−1.77	3.74	−5.50
1981−88	−1.82	1.69	−3.52

Source: The Appendix.
[a] Provisional figures.

vate sector. The increased saving in that sector outweighed the increase in public dissaving and led to an improved external balance. During the structural-adjustment subperiod a relaxation of import-compression policies and the private reallocation of resources in response to relative-price incentives has led to a reduction in private saving. There has been an insufficient reduction in public dissaving, though, and the external balance has worsened in consequence when compared to the import-compression era. The record for 1988 suggests an improvement in the public-saving picture, but this should be viewed with caution: 1988 figures other than those of the current account are only preliminary estimates.

FOREIGN SAVING

Turkish current-account performance is decomposed into its components in table 6.2. The second column of that table restates

Table 6.2   Components of the Current Account Surplus (B) (% of Current-Value GNP)

Year	B	TB	PTR	FI	OTR	OS
1974	−2.15	−6.36	4.64	−0.33	0.09	−0.19
1975	−4.43	−8.09	3.53	−0.33	0.03	0.44
1976	−4.81	−7.01	2.33	−0.51	0.04	0.35
1977	−6.47	−8.03	2.02	−1.18	0.02	0.68
1978	−2.19	−3.66	1.85	−1.28	0.00	0.90
1979	−1.34	−4.00	2.40	−1.27	0.00	1.54
1980	−5.04	−7.82	3.55	−1.15	0.03	0.35
1981	−2.83	−5.63	4.22	−2.02	0.03	0.57
1982	−1.55	−3.42	3.98	−2.73	0.20	0.41
1983	−3.57	−3.87	2.95	−2.81	0.46	−0.30
1984	−2.81	−3.67	3.61	−3.17	0.46	−0.04
1985	−1.90	−2.73	3.22	−3.29	0.44	0.46
1986	−2.60	−2.66	2.76	−3.63	0.42	0.51
1987	−1.44	−1.31	2.93	−3.67	0.52	0.10
1988	2.08	2.98	2.41	−3.88	0.50	0.07
Subperiod Averages:						
1974−77	−4.47	−7.37	3.13	−0.59	0.05	0.32
1978−79	−1.77	−3.83	2.12	−1.28	0.00	1.22
1981−88	−1.82	−2.54	3.26	−3.15	0.38	0.23

Source: The Appendix.
Notes:
TB: Balance of trade in goods and nonfactor services.
PTR: Net private remittance flows.
FI: Net interest payments to foreigners. These are calculated after debt relief and rescheduling reductions.
OTR: Net official transfer flows.
OS: Net other factor services.
B = TB + PTR + OTR + OS − FI

the current account (foreign saving) percentages of table 6.1. The four following columns represent the components that sum to the value of B. These identify two striking trends in Turkey's external balance. First, there has been a notable improvement in the deficit in trade of goods and nonfactor services, although until 1988 the deficit remained a substantial percent of GNP. This is certainly a success of the structural-adjustment policy, as the export sectors have been strongly stimulated through real exchange rate depreciation, trade liberalization measures and export subsidies. The continuation of the TB deficit until 1988 indicates however that imports also grew apace, perhaps indicating an insufficiently strict stabilization policy. The contribution of remittance receipts to the current account has also improved slightly in the structural-adjustment period with the introduction of foreign-exchange denominated deposits in Turkey. Second, net interest payments to foreigners climbed sharply as a share of GNP. These net interest payments provide a steadily growing counterweight to the improvements made in the goods and services accounts.

PUBLIC SAVING

The net public-saving position represents the excess of revenues over expenditures by the public sector. This sector includes not only central government transactions but also the "departments" of local governments, SEEs, revolving fund agencies, and extra-budgetary funds. These generate interdepartmental transfers as well as revenues and expenditures.

We can, by analogy to the private household, speak of the disposable income of the public sector (DPY). This is defined as the aggregated revenues of all public-sector departments minus all net transfers from the government to private or foreign residents minus net interest payments to domestic and foreign residents. Table 6.3 presents Turkey's DPY as well as a number of its important components, including consolidated central government revenue (R), the after-tax but preinvestment income of the SEEs (π), official transfers from abroad (OTR), and net interest payments to foreigners (FI).[7] The residual items in DPY are summarized in the other income (OPY) and include the revenues of extrabudgetary funds (EBF) and local governments as positive elements and domestic interest payments as negative elements.

DPY has fallen by nearly 2 percent of GNP on average in the transition from the base to the structural-adjustment subperiod. There have been two identifiable causes: a fall in central government revenue and a 2.4-percent-share increase in the cost of servicing foreign debt.[8] One "point of light" in the historical record is the structural success in reversing the losses incurred by SEEs: these contributed an average of 1.8 percent of GNP to DPY during the 1980s while having been a drain of nearly equal proportions during the 1970s. Note, however, that these measured gains and losses of SEEs do not include capital expenditures.

DPY is a major component of the public-saving balance. Table 6.4 presents this balance decomposed into receipts (DPY) and

Table 6.3   Components of Disposable Public Income (% of Current-Value GNP)

	DPY	R	π	FI	OTR	OPY
1974	18.40	16.79	0.33	−0.33	0.09	1.53
1975	20.90	20.12	−0.62	−0.33	0.03	1.69
1976	20.60	21.30	−2.31	−0.51	0.04	2.09
1977	19.70	21.49	−3.96	−1.18	0.02	3.32
1978	18.60	24.14	−3.89	−1.28	0.00	−0.37
1979	16.10	23.84	−3.09	−1.27	0.00	−3.38
1980	17.50	20.61	−0.52	−1.15	0.03	−1.47
1981	19.30	21.34	0.12	−2.02	0.03	−0.16
1982	19.70	19.43	1.00	−2.73	0.20	1.81
1983	17.40	20.03	0.46	−2.81	0.46	−0.74
1984	14.96	15.27	3.43	−3.17	0.46	−1.03
1985	17.34	16.25	2.59	−3.29	0.44	1.35
1986	19.05	17.18	3.49	−3.63	0.42	1.59
1987	16.67	17.28	3.24	−3.67	0.52	−0.69
1988[a]	16.66	15.54	3.79	−3.88	0.50	0.71
Subperiod Averages:						
1974−77	19.90	19.93	−1.64	−0.59	0.05	2.16
1978−79	17.35	23.99	−3.49	−1.28	0.00	−1.88
1981−88	17.96	18.25	1.85	−2.94	0.34	0.47

Source: The Appendix.
[a] Provisional figures.
Notes:
$DPY = R + \pi + OTR - FI + Other$
R: Consolidated government revenues.
FI: Total domestic interest payments on foreign debt.
OTR: Net official transfers.
π: After-tax income of SEEs plus depreciation and provisions.
  This does not include investment expenditures by SEEs.
  OPY: Other net public income.

expenditures. These expenditures are the government investment (I_g) and government consumption (G_c) figures drawn from the national accounts. Public dissaving has been reduced during the structural-adjustment period despite the fall in the share of DPY in GNP. This is almost entirely due to the even larger fall in the share of government consumption. Government investment has maintained a relatively constant share of GNP when compared with the base subperiod although it has risen in comparison with the import-compression subperiod.

Table 6.4 Net Public Saving (% of Current-Value GNP)

Year	GS	DPY	G_c	I_g
1974	−3.37	18.40	11.00	10.77
1975	−3.23	20.90	11.93	12.21
1976	−3.53	20.60	12.53	11.60
1977	−6.69	19.70	13.32	13.07
1978	−4.24	18.60	13.37	9.47
1979	−6.77	16.10	13.37	9.50
1980	−6.24	17.50	12.27	11.47
1981	−4.57	19.30	10.68	13.19
1982	−3.01	19.70	10.75	11.96
1983	−2.61	17.40	10.18	9.83
1984	−3.98	14.96	8.82	10.12
1985	−2.34	17.34	8.24	11.44
1986	−3.45	19.05	8.45	14.04
1987	−6.00	16.67	8.58	14.09
1988[a]	−2.19	16.66	8.56	10.29
Subperiod Averages:				
1974−77	−4.21	19.90	12.20	11.91
1978−79	−5.50	17.35	13.37	9.48
1981−84	−3.54	17.84	10.11	11.27
1985−88	−3.49	17.43	8.46	12.47

Source: The Appendix.
[a] Provisional figures
G_c: Government consumption.
I_g: Government investment (inclusive of stock changes).
$GS = DPY - G_c - I_g$
Note: GS does not correspond exactly with calculations of the public
 sector borrowing requirement. It is based upon expenditure figures
 from the national income and from product accounts, and in addition, excludes revaluation of SEE inventory and net payables
 incurred.

The stabilization policy of the import-compression subperiod
was unsuccessful in public-sector expenditures. Rather than the
desired reduction in G_c there was a large increase; the expenditure
reduction fell upon I_g. There was in addition the substantial drop
in DPY during this period, due to SEE losses and foreign interest
payments among others. It was only in the structural-adjustment
period that government consumption was reduced; this delayed
stabilization feature offset an increase in I_g and allowed an improvement in public saving.

Table 6.5   Public Sector Budget Surpluses (% of Current-Value GNP)

	LGO	SEE	CGO	EBF	TOTAL
1984	0.19	−4.53	−2.89	0.59	−6.64
1985	0.24	−4.52	−1.33	0.77	−4.84
1986	−0.08	−4.10	−2.83	2.16	−4.86
1987	−0.49	−4.75	−3.59	0.91	−7.93
1988[a]	−0.53	−3.24	−3.94	1.76	−5.96

[a] Provisional figures

LGO: Local government revenues minus expenditures.

SEE: State Economic Enterprises after-tax income minus investment expenditures plus depreciation plus other financial provisions.

CGO: Consolidated central government budget surplus.

EBF: Special and extrabudgetary funds surplus.

Notes: These percentages differ from those presented by OECD (1990) in that nontax transfers between public-sector entities are excluded. If there is a discrepancy in the value of the transfer, the figure given in the central government budget is used.

The total budget deficit in this table is an alternative measure of public dissaving. It differs from those in the other tables in that there is no use of public spending figures from the national accounts — all figures are drawn directly from the departmental budgets. There are substantial discrepancies between the two sources as these figures make clear.

This aggregate examination of public saving masks a number of important trends in "departmental" saving within the public sector. These trends are illustrated by examination of departmental budget surpluses. Comparable statistics are not available for the entire period under study here, but I report the public sector borrowing requirement in table 6.5 for the period 1984−88.[9]

These statistics include revenues as well as current and capital expenditures by each department of the public sector. The public-sector dissaving is centered (as it has always been in recent history) in the deficits of the SEEs and of the central government. In table 6.5 these deficits are stated without the customary transfers from central government to SEEs and thus underscore the deficitary nature of SEE operations. Despite the movement toward surplus in preinvestment income of the SEEs, the investments undertaken create a budgetary deficit. The other noteworthy feature of the departmental budgets is the growing importance of extrabudgetary funds in the public-sector accounting. Sequestering of funds in these "off-budget" accounts tends to reduce the government's accountability to the legislature, as Waterbury notes in chapter 3 of this volume. This may be the reason the EBF accounts are now required (with some exceptions) to transfer 30 percent of revenues of the central government.[10] These funds have become a quite important source of revenue to the public sector; according to OECD (1990) EBF revenues were equal to 30 percent of the central government's consolidated revenues in 1988. Their expenditures are consequently quite large to generate a surplus of only 1.76 percent of GNP.

PRIVATE SAVING

Net private saving has followed a pattern consistent with the imposition of stabilization and structural adjustment policies during the period under consideration. This adjustment is decomposed in table 6.6. Net private saving was negative on average during the 1970s. It became strongly positive at 3.74 percent of GNP during the stabilization subperiod as saving was forced on the private sector through the import compression policies. Net saving then declined to 1.69 percent of GNP for the structural adjustment period. There were two dominant trends causing the shift to positive net saving during the import-compression period: increases in net private saving from domestic sources (S_γ) and reductions in private investment (I_p). During the structural-adjustment subperiod the reduction in private saving relative to the stabilization subperiod is almost completely due to a revival of private investment. As I note in Conway (1990), this revival to a large extent took the form of residential investment. The trend in S_γ is further strikingly positive — from a value of 9.36 percent in 1981, to 17.58 percent in 1988 — during the structural-adjustment period.

The value of PS is the residual in these calculations, and it is thus treacherous to put great store in any single reported value or to blame volatility on inconsistent government policy. However, the downturn in 1983 corresponds well to the consumption spree in the aftermath of the 1982 crisis in the brokerage industry.[11] The upturn in private saving in 1987−88 could be due to the increasing incidence of the "inflation tax" during the runup to the recent high inflation rates.

The Structural Adjustment Period in Greater Detail

The tension between stabilization and structural-adjustment policies

Table 6.6   Net Private Saving (% of Current-Value GNP)

Year	PS	S_y	I_p
1974	1.22	11.17	9.95
1975	−1.20	9.05	10.25
1976	−1.28	11.85	13.13
1977	0.22	12.10	11.88
1978	2.05	11.10	9.05
1979	5.43	14.19	8.77
1980	1.20	11.12	9.91
1981	1.74	10.04	8.31
1982	1.46	9.82	8.36
1983	−0.96	8.77	9.73
1984	1.17	10.76	9.59
1985	0.44	9.87	9.44
1986	0.85	11.66	10.81
1987	4.56	16.79	12.23
1988	4.28	17.61	13.33
Subperiod Averages:			
1974−77	−0.26	11.04	11.30
1978−79	3.74	12.64	8.91
1981−88	1.69	11.91	10.23

Source: The Appendix.
[a] Provisional figures.
Notes:
S_y: Private net saving from domestic sources.
$S_y = GNP + PTR − C − (DPY − OTR + FI)$
I_p: Private gross national investment (including stock changes).
$PS = S_y − I_p$

serves as a common thread pulling together the fabric of the preceding discussion. Despite notable successes in structural adjustment the Turkish economy remains far from its goal of external balance. Furthermore, only in the provisional figures of 1988 is there an indication that the government has been able to intermediate a net saving transfer from the private sector to finance its own dissaving; this is, however, a precondition for a sustainable structural adjustment. Table 6.7 provides a closer look at the fabric of adjustment by decomposing the structural-adjustment subperiod into an initial period (SA_1) of 1981−84 and a subsequent period (SA_2) of 1985−88.[12] The base subperiod value is calculated as the

Table 6.7 Relative Changes in the Structural Adjustment Period (% of Current-Value GNP)

Net Saving	Base Value	Change in SA_1	Change in SA_2
B	−4.47	1.78	3.51
PS	−0.26	1.11	2.79
GS	−4.21	0.67	0.72

Source: The Appendix.
Notes:
Base period: Four-year average for 1974−77.
Change in SA_1: Four-year average for 1981−84 minus base period average.
Change in SA_2: Four-year average for 1985−88 minus base period average.

average for 1974−77. Changes in SA_i is the change in the saving balance on average between the base subperiod and either SA_1 or SA_2. Improvements in economic efficiency due to structural adjustment have both static and dynamic effects on the macro-economy, so that the two periods should demonstrate immediate and continuing improvements in the three balances.

The figures for the base subperiod indicate the situation of the prereform economy. A deficit on the current account financed public dissaving, with private saving and investment in rough balance. The objective of the stabilization and structural adjustment policies was then to bring down the twin deficits while maintaining the rough balance in private accounts.

The structural-adjustment subperiods were characterized by striking improvement in the private and foreign saving balances with modest improvement in public saving. There were on average roughly equal improvements in the current account during SA_1 and SA_2, although the economy remained on average a net borrower from the rest of the world. This borrowing through the assumption of short-term international debt provides a destabilizing element to the adjustment process as indicated earlier by the growth in external debt as well as debt service payments to foreigners. The adjustment in private saving due to both stabilization and structural adjustment policies is in evidence during both structural adjustment periods, with the greater adjustment during SA_2 an indicator that some of the gains from structural adjustment have been dynamic efficiency gains as opposed to the static gains from stabilization policies.

The government saving improvement during the structural-adjustment subperiod has been quite modest, and almost totally centered in the initial SA_1 period. The continuation of such government dissaving introduces an important internal imbalance, with the discouraging inflation performance in Turkey a likely consequence. The present analysis does not examine the importance of inflation in the private saving performance, but Rodrik (1990) provides evidence that the "inflation tax" component of private saving is an important means for intermediation of the public deficit. Monetary economists like Friedman and Cagan have demonstrated that such inflation taxes are not sustainable — the inflation rate necessary to sustain such private saving edges into hyperinflation.

Conclusions

Stabilization and structural-adjustment policies must work hand-in-hand to be successful in the short term and sustainable in the long term. The historical record for Turkey suggests that a comprehensive structural-adjustment policy has been coupled with insufficient attention to stabilization, with the result that the desired balance of public and private net saving has not consistently been achieved. Turkey has been able to finance this saving shortfall through foreign borrowing, but that policy is a potentially destabilizing one due to the rapidly rising burden of servicing international debt. Recent provisional figures suggest an end to this national saving shortfall in 1988, and such success if duplicated, would indicate an end to the aggregate imbalance. It would leave, however, a persistent imbalance between public and private sector saving that could as well become destabilizing.

Turkey is not alone in this inattention to the necessary stabilization policies. There is a tension between stabilization and structural-adjustment policies, since structural adjustment is easier in a growing economy while stabilization typically requires economic recession. This tension is resolved in many indebted countries through simultaneously implementing relative-price reforms (trade liberalization, financial liberalization, and real depreciation), while expanding domestic expenditure. The resulting economy will have hallmarks of structural adjustment, but will also have made insufficient effort to eradicate the fundamental saving/investment imbalance in the national economy. The insufficiency of this effort can have extremely negative consequences in the future as interest payments from the government to both private and foreign savers destabilize the public-sector budget — a difficulty the United States as well is grappling with!

The analysis of this chapter has uncovered a number of interesting trends in Turkish macroeconomic performance. It could be extended profitably in (at least) two directions. First, if constant-value statistics are available, a further decomposition could be made between real and valuation effects in the observed structural adjustment. Balassa (1981), Mitra (1981), and more recently Celâsun and Rodrik (1989) have outlined such decompositions. These calculations are done using current values, and thus include both volume and relative price changes. The use of constant-value data would provide results corrected for relative price changes. Second, further research on the public saving/investment balance would be quite useful in making more precise the public sector role in financial and goods markets. Since 1984 in Turkey there has been a proliferation of extra budgetary funds designed to move selected self-contained programs "off budget." For example, the Mass Housing Fund was set up to provide financing for residential construction. The PPF is designed to oversee state enterprises slated for privatization. Both of these funds gain revenues from special taxes and are not included in the consolidated government budget. An effort by the SPO to unify these accounts would make future research in this area much more complete and useful.

Notes

1. The perceived temporary nature of stabilization policies is perhaps due to their frequent use in IMF standby agreements. These agreements insist upon immediate adherence to stabilization targets, but IMF disbursement of funds occurs relatively quickly — thus, stabilization targets are not required past that time. Two useful volumes on stabilization policies are Cline and Weintraub (1981) and Williamson (1983). Structural adjustment policies have been best documented and analyzed in World Bank research. Thomas (1988) provides a useful overview of this work.

2. These data are drawn from Nicholas (1988). Turkey received five structural adjustment loans (SALs) between 1980 and 1984, and three sectoral adjustment loans (SECALs) subsequently. Only Jamaica has received as many such loans, and no country has received more.

3. See Kopits (1987: 1–3).

4. It is important to note, however, that Turkey has been remarkably successful in the 1980–88 period in attracting international financing. During 1984 and 1985, for example, Turkey's trade in goods, services, and net private transfers was in deficit by, on average, 18 percent of export value. The Baker Plan countries, by contrast, were able to incur similar deficits of only 1 percent of export value on average. These figures were drawn from the Central Bank of the Republic of Turkey (1985) and IMF (1986).

5. I break this equation into public and private components by adding and subtracting total revenues of the central government, local government and EBFs (R) and SEE aftet-tax income plus depreciation and other provisions (π). The SEEs are thus treated as a component of the public sector.

$$TB = (GNP - \pi - R - C - I_p) + (R + \pi - I_g - G_c)$$

SEE capital expenditure is included in I_g.

GNP is a measure of the value of final goods and services produced by the nation in one year. As a result it excludes transfers. It also excludes interest payments on government debt. These can be incorporated in stages. First, unilateral transfers with the rest of the world and net interest payments to foreigners are added to both sides. The left-hand side then become the current account B.

$$B = [PTR + DI + DT + (GNP - C) - (\pi + R) - I_p]$$
$$+ [(R + \pi) - I_g - G_c + OTR - FI - DI - DT]$$

Official transfers (OTR) are net government receipts from abroad. Private transfers (PTR) are private sources of income from abroad. The net payment of interest to foreigners (FI) is assigned as a government expense to reflect the nature of the international debt as predominantly public and publicly guaranteed. [In 1984, private unguaranteed debt represented 2.4 percent of total long-term debt as reported by the World Bank (1988).] Government interest payments to domestic holders of its debt (DI) and other transfers (DT) are transfers from the public to private sector.

This expression is simplified by the definition of public-sector disposable income (DPY).

$$DPY = R + \pi + OTR - FI - DI - DT$$

DPY represents the government's purchasing power of final goods and services.

$$B = [GNP + PTR - C - I_p - (DPY - OTR + FI)] + [DPY - I_g - G_c]$$
$$B = PS + GS$$

The bracketed right-hand side terms are denoted PS and GS, respectively, to represent private and government saving denominated in Turkish lira. In what follows PS is found as a residual, given that the data on current-account and government budget transactions are more readily available.

6. There is room for debate on the appropriate base period for Turkey. The 1974–77 period is one of consistent government policies reflecting the preform incentives, and is chosen for that reason. A case could also be made for the use of 1978–80, since that was the period immediately preceding the reforms. It was, however, characterized by such chaotic economic policy and internal unrest that the economy's performance could not be considered a product of the preform incentives.

7. The series for DPY prior to 1984 was drawn from Celâsun and Rodrik (1989). For 1984–88 I constructed a series from the data provided in OECD (1990). This series was quite different in 1984, but of similar magnitude in the other overlapping years of 1985–86.

8. The Turkish government introduced a value-added tax in 1985 that has been successful in bringing in additional tax revenue. As this tax regime becomes more broadly based Nicholas (1988) suggests that the poor consolidated government revenue position will improve.

9. These calculations are drawn from the tables in OECD (1990). The total public sector borrowing requirement differs from that reported there because of my efforts to make consistent the size of transfers between departments of the government.

10. This innovation is reported in OECD (1990: 69).

11. I'm grateful to an anonymous referee for this insight.

12. This indicator of performance is improved by the exclusion of the figures for 1980. I chose to exclude 1980 from consideration under the structural adjustment program for two reasons. Civil unrest was such that economic statistics may well not adequately reflect policy effectiveness. Also, the lag in the implementation of policies announced in 1980 makes 1981 the first true test of those policies.

Appendix

DATA SOURCES FOR TURKEY

National accounts variables (GNP, C, I_p, I_g, and G_c) are taken from national income and product accounts reported in SPO (1985), in Celâsun and Rodrik (1989), and in OECD (1990). The balance of goods and nonfactor services (TB), foreign interest payments (FI), and unilateral transfers (OTR and PTR) are taken from balance of payments statistics reported by the Central Bank of the Republic of Turkey (1987) and OECD (1990). Other services (OS) is derived as a residual. The current account deficit in dollar terms is taken from Celâsun and Rodrik (1989, table A14) and from OECD (1990) and adjusted to remove debt relief from interest payments.

The SPO provides a time series of public disposable income, or DPY, which corresponds to the sum $(R + \pi) + OTR - FI - DI - DT$. R is general government revenue (including EBFs and local governments) and π is the after-tax and before-investment income of SEEs inclusive of depreciation and other provisions. These are taken from World Bank statistics and from OECD (1990). Other net revenues (OPY) in the decomposition of DPY is derived as a residual.

National account and balance of payments figures for 1988 are final, while all others are provisional.

References

Balassa, B. 1981. "Adjustment to External Shocks in Developing Economies." World Bank Working Paper 472.

Celâsun, M. and D. Rodrik. 1989. "Debt, Adjustment and Growth: Turkey." In *Developing Country Debt and Economic Performance*, edited by J. Sachs and S. Collins. Chicago: University of Chicago and NBER.

Central Bank of the Republic of Turkey. 1987. *Annual Report*. Ankara, Turkey: Central Bank.

———. 1985. *Annual Report*. Ankara, Turkey: Central Bank of the Republic of Turkey.

Chenery, H. and M. Syrquin. 1975. *Patterns of Development, 1950–1970*. London: Oxford University Press.

Cline, W. and S. Weintraub, eds. 1981. *Economic Stabilization in Developing Countries*. Washington, D.C.: Brookings Institution.

Conway, P. 1990. "The Record on Turkish Private Investment." In *The Political Economy of Turkey: Debt, Adjustment and Sustainability*, edited by T. Arıcanlı and D. Rodrik. London: Macmillan Publishing Co.

———. 1987. *Economic Shocks and Structural Adjustments*. Amsterdam: North Holland.

IMF. 1986. *World Economic Outlook*. Washington, D.C.: IMF.

Kopits, G. 1987. *Structural Reform, Stabilization and Growth in Turkey*. IMF Occasional Paper 52. Washington, D.C.: IMF.

Mitra, P. 1981. *An Analysis of Adjustment in Developing Countries*. World Bank Development Research Department Working Paper.

Nicholas, P. 1988. "The World Bank's Lending for Adjustment." World Bank Discussion Paper 34.

OECD. 1990. *Economic Surveys: Turkey*. Paris: OECD.

Rodrik, D. 1990. "Premature Liberalization, Incomplete Stabilization: The Özal Decade in Turkey." Unpublished paper.

SPO. 1985. *V. Beş Yıllık Plan Destek Çalışmaları*. (Support Studies for the Fifth Five Year Plan). Ankara, Turkey: SPO.

Thomas, V. 1988. "Issues in Adjustment Lending." World Bank PPR Working Paper WPS2.

Waterbury, J. 1990. "Export-Led Growth and the Center-Right Coalition in Turkey." Chapter 3 in this volume.

Williamson, J., ed. 1983. *IMF Conditionality*. Cambridge: MIT Press.

World Bank. 1988. *World Debt Tables*. Washington, D.C.: World Bank.

7

The Effects of Liberalization on Traded and Nontraded Goods Sectors: The Case of Turkey

Merih Uçtum

Introduction

Economic liberalization programs involve deregulation, opening up of the domestic economy, and elimination of restrictions and distortions in the economy.[1] The literature on various country experiences with stabilization and liberalization programs has grown in the past few years. The welfare implications of liberalization programs are surveyed in Edwards and van Wijnbergen (1986) and Rodrik (1987). Country specific studies are conducted by Diaz-Alejandro (1981), Hanson and de Melo (1983), Wogard (1983), and Zahler (1983). Corbo and de Melo (1987) underline the fact that inconsistent domestic stabilization policies and external shocks can adversely affect the results of liberalization reforms. This issue is investigated by Khan and Zahler (1985) in a simulation analysis. The sequence of reforms are discussed by McKinnon (1982), Frenkel (1982), Khan and Zahler (1983), and surveyed by Edwards (1984). A collection of papers in Nas and Odekon (1988) provides a comprehensive review of the liberalization policies implemented in Turkey since 1980. However, all of these studies emphasize the short-term effects of the structural reforms, disregarding long-term issues such as the investment process and its implications for domestic physical capital formation and resource allocation.[2]

This paper focuses on the long-run effects of liberalization policies in the context of a two-sector macroeconomic model.[3] In the short run, the economy allocates its resources between tradable and nontradable commodities. The point where the economy is located on the short-run transformation curve depends on the relative prices of these two commodities measured in terms of the real exchange rate, i.e., the ratio of the price of the traded good to the price of the nontraded good. In the long run the transformation curve shifts outward due to capital accumulation. External surplus is determined by the discrepancy between the production and absorption of tradables, implying that a balance of payments surplus can be achieved and sustained by creating and maintaining a positive wedge between the supply and demand of tradables.

Viewed from this perspective, liberalization programs have two distinct effects on resource allocation. The short-run effect involves a movement along the transformation curve, which results in increased productions in, and reduced consumption of, tradable goods. The method to achieve this is through the depreciation of the real exchange rate. In the long run, the transformation curve shifts outward so that the increased production of tradables can be sustained. This is achieved by increasing the rate of capital accumulation in the tradables relative to the nontradables.

The rest of the chapter discusses the extent to which these objectives have been achieved in Turkey. It focuses on the composition of the gross domestic product (GDP) and the pattern of investment in the postreform period. It is argued that although the short-run objective has been satisfied, the authorities failed to achieve the long-run objective because of reduced private investment in both sectors.

The Pattern of Resource Allocation in Pre- and Postliberalization Period

THE EVOLUTION OF THE GDP

Table 7.1 describes the sectoral composition of the GDP during two subperiods. Panel A gives the growth figures of different sectors of the GDP, whereas Panel B displays the evolution of the production of tradables relative to nontradables.[4] The figures show that the program as a whole has been successful. The growth rate of GDP rose by approximately 20 percent between 1972 and 1979 and 1980 and 1988.

When sectors are classified into tradable and nontradable categories, it appears that both have expanded (see table 7.1, Panel B). The percentage change in growth rate of tradables (37.2 percent) has been proportionately larger than that of nontradables (17.9 percent). The growth of the former was mainly due to expansion in industry, whereas in the latter the expansion was driven by trans-

Table 7.1   Indicators of Sectoral Composition of GDP

	Prereform: 1972−79	Postreform: 1980−88
Panel A: Growth of GDP by Sector (Sample Means of Annual Percentage Changes)		
Agriculture	2.16	3.70
Industry	7.13	9.06
Construction	6.39	3.19
Wholesale and Retail Trade	6.83	9.10
Transport and Communication	5.97	16.20
Financial Institutions	7.30	7.44
Housing	6.27	4.89
Services	5.03	6.28
Government, Health, and Education	6.03	4.56
GDP (total)	5.90	7.16
Panel B: Growth of the Tradable and Nontradable Goods and that of *Their Share in GDP* (Sample Means of Annual Percentage Changes)		
GDP_T	4.65	6.38
GDP_N	6.26	7.38

Source: The author's calculations are based on GDP and investment data
        by SPO and State Institute of Statistics.
Notes: The subscripts T and N stand for the traded goods sector and the
        nontraded goods sector, respectively. Industry (manufacturing,
        mining, and energy) and agriculture are aggregated into the traded
        goods sector. The nontraded goods sector is composed of whole-
        sale and retail trade, private professions and services, govern-
        ment, health and education, ownership of dwellings, financial
        institutions, and transport and communications. All figures are in
        constant 1968 prices.

portation and communication and wholesale and retail trade.
However, an examination of figure 7.1 indicates that the success of
liberalization is not due to a rise in the share of the tradables sector,
which is necessary for the restructuring of the economy, but rather
it is due to the reversal of the downward trend of the traded to
nontraded goods production that was set in the earlier period. The
figure shows a declining ratio of the traded to nontraded goods
production between 1976 and 1979. It remained almost constant during the first year of liberalization, and steadily increased thereafter

Figure 7.1. The Ratio of traded to nontraded goods production.

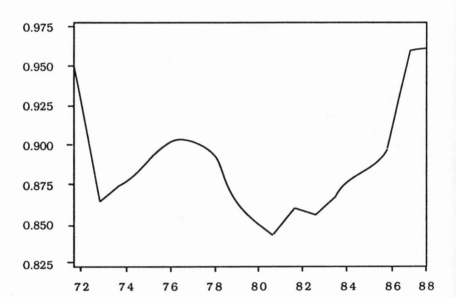

reaching a plateau in 1987. Undoubtedly, the exchange rate policy, together with export promotion incentives, should be credited for this expansion in the traded goods sector. However, a close examination of the evolution and composition of fixed capital formation casts doubt over the durability of this export-led growth.

The Evolution of Investment

Table 7.2 displays the change in investment in various categories.[5] Total investment as a percentage of the GDP peaked at 27 percent in 1976, and continuously fell thereafter until 1984. The rate of decline slowed down between 1980 and 1984 and then picked up in 1985 and 1986. Yet, the investment/GDP ratio in the postliberalization period (20.66 percent) remained below its pre-1980 value (20.70 percent).

The ratio of private sector investment in traded goods to that in

Table 7.2   Comparison of Various Investment Ratios,
1972−1979 and 1980−1988

	Pre-reform: 1972−79	Post-reform: 1980−88
I/GDP	20.70	20.66
I_T/GDP	11.42	12.45
$I^{P_N^R}/GDP$	5.82	4.21
$I^{P_T^R}/GDP$	5.12	4.53
$I^{P_N^U}/GDP$	3.46	4.00
$I^{P_T^U}/GDP$	6.31	7.93
I_T/I	55.35	51.21
$I^{P_T^R}/I^{PR}$	46.84	42.34
$I^{P_N^R}/I^{PR}$	53.16	57.66
$I^{P_T^U}/I^{PU}$	64.62	57.55
$I^{P_N^U}/I^{PU}$	35.38	47.45
I^{PR}/I^{PU}	1.11	0.75
$I^{P_T^R}/I^{P_T^U}$	0.81	0.57
$I^{P_N^R}/I^{P_N^U}$	1.68	1.05

Source: The author's calculations are based on GDP and
investment data by SPO and State Institute of
Statistics.
Notes: The superscripts PR and PU denote private and
public sector, respectively. Traded goods investment is composed of investment in agriculture,
mining and quarrying, manufacturing, and energy
and tourism. Nontraded goods investment consists
of investment in housing, education, health,
transportation, and communication, and other
investment. All figures are in constant 1968 prices.

nontraded goods fell in the post-1980 period except in 1980 and
1984. The corresponding ratio for the public sector also declined
during the same period except in 1982 (see fig. 7.2). This reflects
the withdrawal of the public sector from the traded goods industries
in order to create room for private sector expansion. However, the
latter could not fill the gap, and the shares of both private and
public sector traded goods investment in their sectoral totals fell
from 46.84 and 64.62 percents in 1972−79, to 42.34 and 57.55
percents in 1980−88, respectively. Consequently, the relative weight
of investment in traded goods declined after 1980. The share of
total traded goods investment in total investment fell from 55.35
percent to 51.21 percent and its share in GDP increased from 11.42

Figure 7.2. Ratios of traded and nontraded investment in private
and public sectors.

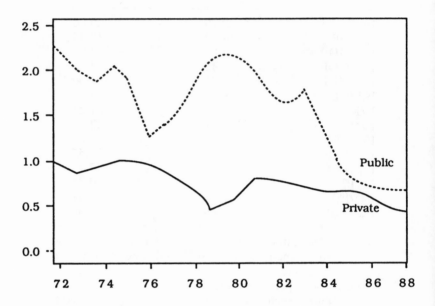

percent to 12.45 percent (see table 7.2 and fig. 7.3). Private investment in the nontraded and traded goods sectors declined in terms
of total GDP from 5.82 to 4.21 and 5.12 to 4.53, respectively,
while the same figures increased for the public sector from 3.46 to
4.00 and 6.31 to 7.93.

The last three lines of table 7.2 display the change in the relative
importance of public and private sectors in tradables and nontradables investment as well as total investment. The ratio of private
investment to public investment declined from 1.11 to 0.75. The
increase of the relative importance of the public sector is evident in
both tradables and nontradables although a greater decline of the
private sector is observed in nontradables.

The Political Economy of Resource Allocation

The liberalization program in Turkey had two aims: (1) achieving

Figure 7.3.   Investment in traded and nontraded goods sectors as percentage of GDP.

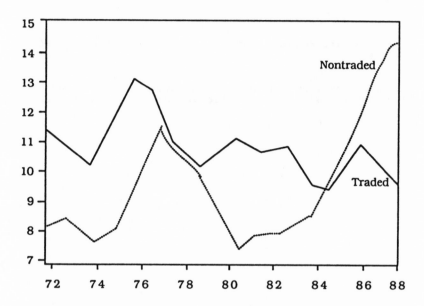

an export-led growth and (2) reducing the weight of the public sector in the economic activity. The achievements of the program can be summarized in terms of a two-dimensional diagram reflecting the objectives of the political authority (see fig. 7.4). The relative importance of the private to public sector in capital formation is represented by the horizontal axis. The origin of the diagram is unity indicating equal shares of private and public investment. Points to the right (left) of the origin represent greater weight of private (public) sector relative to the public (private). The relative importance of investment in tradables versus nontradables is measured by the vertical axis. The prereform period is represented by point A, whereas postreform by point B. The coordinates of these points are obtained from table 7.2.

The prereform period is characterized by a relatively larger share of private to public sector investment (in the order of 1.11) and a relatively larger share of tradables with respect to nontradables (in the order of 1.24). Starting from the initial point A, the objective

Figure 7.4. The Sectoral Evolution of the Relative Share of Investment[a].

[a]The relative size of investment in tradables to nontradables is calculated by using data in Table 4.2 and the following formula:

$$I_T/I_N = (I_T/GDP)/\{(I-I_T)/GDP\}$$

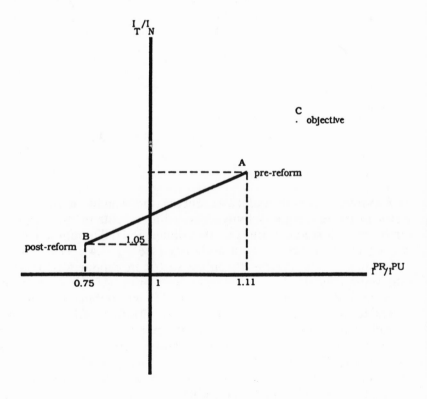

of the program was to move the economy in the northeast direction to point C. In contrast to its stated objective, the liberalization program has moved the Turkish economy in the southwest direction toward point B, indicating a relatively lower weight of the private sector in capital accumulation (0.75) and a lower ratio of investment in tradables (1.05).

Judged from this perspective, the liberalization program has ended up with a serious bottleneck. Although the production of tradables could be mobilized in the short run as indicated by the GDP data, the possibility of maintaining this short-run resource reallocation is severely handicapped.

Several explanations can be put forward for this pattern. First, to maintain an increasing private investment in the traded goods sector, a permanent relative price improvement is necessary. In this respect, authorities were successful in depreciating the real exchange rate in a persistent manner. Second, private firms must be encouraged to undertake long-term projects. However, this condition has not been met in a satisfactory way. In Turkey, the climate for business was not conducive to investing in tradables mainly for two reasons. (1) The cost of investing increased. After the financial liberalization, the transition from a negative real interest rate economy to one with positive real interest rates left corporations with two options: to borrow from banks or issue securities that compete with alternative assets such as bank deposits and government bonds. Either way the cost of financing was high. Financial liberalization removed ceilings on deposit rates and banks put a high spread on these in determining the loan rates (see Aydoğan 1990). On the other hand, private sector securities could not compete with treasury securities because these had been made more attractive than corporate securities in terms of yields as well as terms.[6] (2) Investment in nontradables, especially in housing became attractive. From the supply side, the government has consistently put a strong emphasis on construction and housing, and encouraged economic activities in this sector through the Office of Public Housing. From the demand side, housing is still an important form of investment as a means of hedge from inflation.

As argued by Corbo and de Melo (1987), the speed of the reform should be consistent with the *rate* individuals and institutions can adjust. Authorities can attain their objectives if investment increases and industry expands simultaneously with the liberalization of the economy. When financial liberalization was introduced in Turkey, corporations had very high debt-equity ratios and relied mostly on bank loans as the main form of financing. The speed of liberalization has been higher than the adjustment of corporate financing pattern toward lower leverage ratios. This discrepancy of adjustment has been partially responsible for the series of bankruptcies, which in turn increased the perceived risk in investment.[7]

Conclusion

This chapter has analyzed, from a long-term perspective, the performance of the liberalization program adopted in Turkey. The main conclusion is that the program has not been successful in achieving its stated long-run objectives. The objective of export-led growth was generally satisfied in the short-run, and the downward trend in the traded to nontraded goods production was reversed mainly through real depreciation. However, the program failed to induce the private capital accumulation in the tradables sector, which is necessary for a long-lasting solution to the current account problem. The relative importance of the private to public sector in the economic activity has not changed in the desired direction because of the withdrawal of the private sector from capital accumulation process in the economy. One explanation for the lack of success is that the liberalization attempts have coincided with the stabilization program implemented simultaneously, which had a contracting effect on the economy. A closer examination of the lessons from the experience of South American countries also supports the view that the optimal sequence to be pursued is to stabilize the economy before liberalizing it. It would be too unrealistic to expect the Turkish economy to perform in a very different way from its predecessors.

Notes

1. Another major aspect of these policies is the differences between the external and internal reforms. External reforms imply opening up domestic financial and/or goods markets to international markets by removing controls and barriers. Internal reforms entail freeing those domestic markets where prices are rigid. An example for this would be a domestic financial market with interest rate ceilings and credit rationing or a financial market with interest rate ceilings and credit rationing or a rigid labor market. It has been argued that there is an optimal sequence in the implementation of internal and external liberalization and that liberalization should start in those markets where prices tend to be least responsive. Accordingly, the internal reform should precede the trade account liberalization, which in turn should precede the freeing of domestic financial markets followed by capital account liberalization.

2. The topic of investment in developing countries has been analyzed by Blejer and Khan (1984) and Tun and Wong (1982), but has not been treated within the context of liberalization.

3. The technical aspects of which are elaborated in Uçtum (1989).

4. The calculations of the GDP produced in the traded and nontraded goods sectors are based on the GDP data published by the SPO, Main Economic Indicators, and the State Institute of Statistics, Price Indices Monthly Bulletin.

5. The calculations of investment in traded and nontraded goods sectors are based on the investment data published by the SPO and the OECD (1987, 1988).

6. See Ersel (1990) for the relative attractiveness of private and public securities as well as for a review of financial liberalization in Turkey. The negative impact of developments in public finance for private cost of capital has been analyzed in detail by Rodrik (1988).

7. Recent research by Aşıkoğlu and Ercan (1990) has indicated that the rise in financial expenses and the deterioration of liquidity ratios have been the major factors in corporate bankruptcies.

References

Aşıkoğlu, Y. and M. Ercan. 1990. "Predicting Corporate Bankruptcy in Turkey during the Post-Liberalization Period." City University of New York. Mimeo.

Aydoğan, K. 1990. "The Competitive Structure of the Turkish Banking Industry." Bilkent University, Ankara. Mimeo.

Blejer, M. and M. S. Khan. 1984. "Private Investment in Developing Countries." *Finance and Development* 21:26–29.

Corbo, V. and J. de Melo. 1987. "Lessons from the Southern Cone Policy Reforms." *The World Bank Research Observer* 2:111–43.

Diaz-Alejandro, C. 1981. "Southern Cone Stabilization Plans." In *Economic Stabilization in Developing Countries*, edited by W. Cline and S. Weintraub, 119–47. Washington, D.C.: Brookings Institution.

Edwards, S. 1984. "The Order of Liberalization of the External Account in Developing Countries." Essays in International Finance 156, Princeton University, December.

Edwards, S. and S. van Wijnbergen. 1986. "The Welfare Effects of Trade and Capital Market Liberalization." *International Economic Review* 27(1):141–48.

Edwards, S. and L. Ahmad, eds. 1986. *Economics Adjustment and Exchange Rates in Developing Countries*. Chicago: University of Chicago Press.

Ersel, H. 1990. "Monetary Policy in a Changing Financial Environment: The Recent Experience in Monetary Programming." Central Bank of the Republc of Turkey. Mimeo.

Frenkel, J. A. 1982. "The Order of Economic Liberalization: Lessons from Chile and Argentina." In *Economic Policy in a World at Change*, edited by K. Brunner and A. H. Meltzer, 119–201. Carnegie-Rochester Conference Series on Public Policy 17. Amsterdam: North Holland.

Hanson, J. A. and J. de Melo. 1983. "The Uruguayan Experience with Liberalization and Stabilization, 1974–1981." *Journal of Inter-American Studies and World Affairs* 25:477–508.

Khan, M. S. and R. Zahler. 1985. "Trade and Financial Liberalization Given External Shocks and Inconsistent Domestic Policies." *IMF Staff Paper* (March) 22–55.

———. 1983. "The Macroeconomic Effects of Changes in Barriers to Trade and Capital Flows: A Simulation Analysis." *IMF Staff Papers* (June) 223–82.

McKinnon, R. I. 1982. "The Order of Economic Liberalization: Lessons from Chile and Argentina." In *Economic Policy in a World of Change*, edited by K. Brunner and A. H. Meltzer, 159–85. Carnegie-Rochester Conference Series on Public Policy 17. Amsterdam: North-Holland.

Nas, T. and M. Odekon, eds. 1988. *Liberalization and the Turkish Economy*. Westport, Conn.: Greenwood Press.

OECD. 1988. *Economic Surveys: Turkey*. Paris: OECD.

———. 1987. *Economic Surveys: Turkey*. Paris: OECD.

Rodrik, D. 1987. "Trade and Capital-Account Liberalization in a Keynesion Economy." *Journal of International Economics* 23:113–29.

Rodrik, D. 1988. "Some Policy Dilemmas in Turkish Macroeconomic Management." Paper prepared for the conference on Turkey's Economic Development in the 1980s, Harvard University. April.

Tun, W. U. and C. Wong. 1982. "Determinants of Private Investment in Developing Countries." *Journal of Development Studies* 19:19–36.

Uçtum, M. 1989. "Capital Account Liberalization and Investment." University of Laval, Quebec. Discussion Paper 8907.

Wogart, J. P. 1983. "Combining Price Stabilization with Trade and Financial Liberalization Policies: the Argentina Experience, 1976–81." *Journal of Interamerican Studies and World Affairs* 25:445–76.

Zahler, R. 1983. "Recent Southern Cone Liberalization Reforms and Stabilization Policies: The Chilean Case, 1974–82." *Journal of Interamerican Studies and World Affairs* 25:509–62.

8

Turkish Liberalization: From the Perspectives of Manufacturing Firms

Mehmet Odekon

Introduction

The performance of the Turkish economy in the 1980s has been impressive. The initial deceleration in the rate of inflation, the achievements in the external balance, and the various attempts to transform the highly regulated, inward-looking, and debt-ridden economy into an open, market-oriented economy rendered Turkey an exemplary developing country for a good part of the 1980s.[1] Since 1989, however, the Turkish economy has fallen below the achievements of the 1981−87 period. This worsening of the economy is reflected in the eroding political powers of the governing party and of its charismatic leader, Turgut Özal. Some argue that the liberalization program in Turkey like those in Latin America, had limited favorable effects and that these were confined to the external sector of the economy.[2] Moreover, it could be argued that even these effects have been exaggerated since some exogenous developments, such as the Iran-Iraq War, may have contributed substantially to the success of the export sector.

The structural changes proposed in many of the liberalization packages are mainly directed to firms, in the hope that they would achieve specialization and efficiency in production. Given this framework, it may, then, be the case that the limited success of liberalization has been the result of firms' failure to respond to the proposed macropolicies in the expected manner, or the policies' inability to channel the firms in the right direction. Hence, a proper approach to the analysis of liberalization policies calls for an investigation of firms' perceptions of, and responses to, those broader macropolicies associated with the overall liberalization scheme.

This study begins with a discussion of the post-1980 performance

Table 8.1 Selected Indicators of Macroeconomic Performance of Turkish Economy, 1977–1988

	1977–79	1981–87	1980	1981	1982	1983	1984	1985	1986	1987	1988
Output Growth[1]	2.1	5.5	-1.1	4.2	4.5	3.3	5.9	5.1	8.1	7.4	3.4
Inflation Rate[2]	43.7	38.0	110.2	36.6	30.8	31.9	48.4	45.0	34.6	38.9	68.8
Trade deficit/Exports	1.4	0.5	1.6	.8	.5	.5	.4	.4	.4	.3	.2**
Credit Expansion[3,4]	44.9	55.3	83.7	49.1	46.2	38.6	77.2	62.6	54.4	59.0	56.5***
Credit to Gov't[3,5]	63.1	59.3	101.4	24.0	45.3	27.7	138.4	66.3	52.4	61.1	69.6***
Monetary Expansion[3,6]	43.9	52.6	66.9	89.0	50.2	27.9	59.3	57.1	43.0	41.7	42.4***

Source: IMF, International Financial Statistics (IFS), various issues.
Notes:
[1] Real GNP growth.
[2] CPI inflation.
[3] Percent annual change.
[4] IFS, Line 32.
[5] IFS, Lines 32 and 32bx.
[6] IFS, Lines 34 and 35.
** First three quarters.

of the Turkish economy emphasizing two unique features of the 1980 reform program: interest rate liberalization and exchange rate adjustment. From here the analysis turns to the results of a cross-sectional survey of firms' perceptions of, and reactions to, the liberalization policy reforms.

Macroeconomic Performance

Foreign exchange shortages, balance of payments problems, and the resulting debt crisis of the 1977–79 subperiod were the main reasons behind the deep recession in the Turkish economy in 1980. Despite the recession, however, the remarkable success in the external sector in the post-1981 period was reflected by a sharp decline in the trade deficit/export ratio, which first increased to 1.6 in 1980 and then steadily declined thereafter (see table 8.1). In addition, the sluggish growth in real GNP experienced in the late 1970s and the drop in 1980 was replaced by a marked turnaround during the 1981–87 period. While the growth rate peaked in 1986 to an impressive 8.1 percent, it did not have a positive effect on the unemployment rate. The official unemployment rate of 11.5 percent in 1980 dropped only to about 10 percent in 1988.[3] The persistence of high unemployment has been partly attributed to the initially contractionary macropolicies and to the adverse effects of liberalization programs on employment. In the latter case, liberalization policies favored large-scale export oriented firms with relatively capital-intensive production techniques, which do not increase employment.[4]

The Turkish authorities have successfully combatted the high inflation rate, lowering it from 110.2 percent in 1980, to 30.8 percent in 1982, mainly by controlling the credit expansion in the economy. However, the inability or perhaps the unwillingness of the policymakers to maintain a low credit expansion ceiling, especially in appropriating credits to the public sector and in monetizing the public debt, were the main causes for the rise of the inflation rate to about 75 percent in 1988.

These developments in the economy were the outcome of the various measures put into effect since January 24, 1980. In essence, the program promoted liberalization in foreign and domestic sectors by eliminating all price and nonprice barriers in factor and commodity markets, and introduced measures to improve the functioning of the free-market mechanism. From among these policy measures, the adjustments in the value of the TL and the attempts to deregulate financial markets and interest rates are the primary features of the Turkish reforms. The adjustments in the value of the TL rendered Turkish exportables competitive in the world markets, and deregulation of interest rates was expected to stimulate saving, discourage consumption, and stabilize domestic prices.

Initially, the authorities adjusted the value of the TL vis-à-vis the U.S. dollar on a periodic basis with cross-rates accordingly aligned. This series of adjustments started in January 1980 with a massive devaluation of the TL by approximately 140 percent in nominal and 30 percent in real terms (see table 8.A1 in the Appendix). In May 1981, the Central Bank began to adjust the parity on a daily basis. This persistent approach of the monetary authorities with regard to the real depreciation of the TL was also aided by the reluctance of foreign capital to flow into Turkey.

The interest rate policies lacked the consistency of the exchange rate policies and followed a stop-and-go pattern (see Appendix, table 8.A2). The lending and deposit rates remained regulated until mid-1980, when they were liberalized in mid-June of that year. Two years later, following the historic brokers' crisis, interest rate liberalization came to a halt.[5] However, the damage was done. High nominal and real lending rates had already adversely affected private investment and raised costs of production, with only marginal favorable effects on saving. This stop-and-go approach to interest rate and financial markets' liberalization has been perhaps the most uncertain and unfavorable aspect of the liberalization program. The uncertainty was felt by the firms, in particular by those that were accustomed to negative real borrowing rates and hence to cheap external sources of finance. As the following survey results display, firms were strongly and adversely affected by the interest rate liberalization.

The Survey

A mail survey of manufacturing firms in Turkey was conducted in late 1988 and early 1989 to find out how they perceived the post-1980 reforms. The survey (Corbo and de Melo, 1985) was used to collect information on their perceptions of policy reforms and on the ways they adjusted to the macropolicies.[6]

Similar studies have been undertaken by the World Bank in Chile, Uruguay, and Argentina.[7] The findings of these studies show that firms have, in general, welcomed the removal of price and nonprice distortions in the domestic and foreign sectors of the economy and responded to the reforms by attempting to improve their efficiency by either laying off labor or by reducing product variety or both. As a result, firms have improved their competitiveness at home and abroad. However, in all these countries unemployment rose. On the other hand, the appreciation of the domestic currencies and the rise in the real interest rates were aspects of the liberalization program firms listed consistently as unfavorable. Both of these developments were perceived as increasing risk and uncertainty in the economy.

The present study has two related objectives. The first is to determine those aspects of the reforms Turkish firms consider to be favorable and unfavorable. The second objective is to assess whether these perceptions differ across firms with various specific characteristics, such as their sales volume, degree of openness, or form of ownership.

Favorable Changes

Table 8.2 lists the favorable aspects of the reforms in a descending order according to mean scores.[8] The abolition of tariff and non-tariff barriers seem to be one of the most favorable aspects of the liberalization program. Despite the well-publicized export orientation of the program, firms consistently rank the liberalization of the import regime higher than that of the export regime.[9] This result reflects their dependence on raw material and machinery and equipment imports in the pre-1980 import substitution period.

The decrease in labor costs is perceived to be another favorable aspect of the policy reforms. In 1980, the Turkish labor movement was brought to an abrupt halt. Unions and strikes were outlawed and wages were set by the Supreme Arbitration Board. This weakening of the labor movement resulted by an average annual decrease of 1.6 percent in real wages during 1980–88.[10]

Table 8.2   Favorable Aspects of Policy Reforms

	Mean Score
Increased ease in importing raw materials	2.9
Increased ease in importing machinery and equipment	2.8
Increase in export possibilities	2.8
Decrease in labor costs	2.4
Increased ease in the relations with the state	2.3

Institutional changes introduced with the reform package were also looked upon favorably. These changes ranged from the creation of new policy coordinating committees and ministries, such as the Economic Affairs High Coordination Council, to reducing state involvement and bureaucratic regulations in the economy. These institutional reforms have substantially facilitated the day-to-day functioning of the firms.

Table 8.3 gives the distribution of firms that ranked the favorable variables as either "important" or "very important."[11] For instance, all the textile firms in the sample agree that the post-1980 reforms have favorably affected raw material and machinery imports (PRAWIMP and PMACIMP), have increased export possibilities (PXPOSS), and have eased relations with the state (PSTATE). Only a single textile firm has indicated that the decrease in labor costs is perceived as a favorable change. This favorable response on the part of textile firms is somewhat surprising, especially within the context of the widely held belief that liberalization reforms redistribute incentives from traditional industries, like food and textiles, to newly emerging export industries by eliminating the existing antiexport bias.[12] However, if one considers the fact that the firms in the sample are among those that survived the bankruptcy wave of the mid-1980s, the result is expected. These "survivors" depended on the imports of such important raw materials as chemicals and dyes. In addition, they have traditionally been in export activities. Hence, it is not surprising that they express strong positive perception of the reforms.

Firms, irrespective of their industrial classification, consistently perceive easing import and export restrictions as favorable changes. In "metal" and "machinery" categories, three additional variables emerge as important. They are "ease in acquiring foreign patents and know-how," "increase in firms' profitability," and "ease in labor relations." Apparently firms regard acquisition of foreign know-how and modernization of the production technology as an important part of their adjustment. Even though they welcome the banning of labor unions and strikes, the firms, particularly in metal industries, do not perceive the decrease in labor costs as a significant positive change. Rather, they regard the tax reforms introduced since 1980 as factors that contributed to the increase in their profitability.

It is worth noting that firms have not cited other variables, such as fixed and working capital financing, domestic resource use, and output price, as favorably affected by the reforms. As we will see in this section, these are variables that were perceived as unfavorably affected by the policy changes.

Table 8.3 Industrial Distribution of the Favorable Aspects of Policy Reforms

	Textile	Paper Printing	Chemicals	Rubber Plastic	Glass	Metal	Machinery	Electronics	Transportation Motor Vehicle
PFIXCAP[a]	1	1	2	1	1	1	2	1	3
PWORKCAP	1	2	2	–	1	1	1	2	3
PMACIMP	3	1	6	1	3	5	3	1	4
PDRESUSE	2	–	2	–	2	1	2	1	3
PRAWIMP	3	1	4	1	2	4	2	2	5
PPRICE	1	1	2	1	1	2	2	1	3
PXPOSS	3	2	6	2	–	4	3	2	5
PSTATE	3	–	4	1	1	3	3	2	4
PDCOMP	–	–	1	–	2	–	1	1	1
PCRCOST	2	–	1	–	1	2	–	1	4
PPATENT	–	–	1	–	1	4	3	–	3
PPROFIT	1	1	1	–	1	3	3	1	3
PLABREL	2	2	–	–	2	4	3	1	2
PLABCOST	1	–	–	–	1	–	2	–	1
No. of Firms	3	3	8	2	3	5	3	3	7

[a] A glossary for abbreviations is in table 8.A6 in the Appendix.

Table 8.4 presents the distribution of firms according to such characteristics as ownership, affiliation, and size. The figures in the table are the number of firms that ranked the left column variables as "important" or "very important." The last row gives the total number of firms in each column. An asterisk indicates that the difference between the proportions of firms with different characteristics is statistically significant at least at the 10-percent level. The comparisons are to be made between the column with the asterisk and the one to the left of it.[13]

Even though firms consistently assign high rankings to rank ease in imports of machinery and raw materials and increase in export possibilities, table 8.4 displays that they differ in their perceptions of other variables when broken down by various characteristics. For example, firms owned by shareholders regard "financial" variables significantly more important than family corporations. The proportion of firms owned by shareholders that perceive ease in fixed and working capital financing and liberalization of output price as favorable is statistically different from the proportion of family-owned companies. The latter group, in contrast, regards the increase in profits and the improvement in labor relations as important favorable changes. It could be that family-owned corporations are more labor intensive and hence more concerned with labor relations.

A noteworthy finding is that multinational firms rank import-related variables relatively higher. This result supports the hypothesis that multinationals have generally been import-substituting industries and depended on raw material imports.

In spite of the fact that most firms cite the rise in export possibilities as favorable, the proportion of companies that are part of a holding company or are larger according to their sales, and rank the rise in export possibilities high, is significantly different. This finding is in support of the view that the liberalization program is biased in favor of larger firms in promoting exports.

Firms with large export ratios, on the other hand, favor the effects of the policies on domestic resource use, labor relations, and domestic competition. These three factors contribute to improved competitiveness of large export firms. A rise in domestic resource use suggests that domestic resources are substituted for imports, thus allowing firms to shield themselves against the devaluation-induced rise in the cost of imported raw materials. The decrease in labor's power benefits these larger firms disproportionately, since a larger share of unionized labor is employed by them. Hence, they welcome the changes in labor legislature. The decrease in domestic competition strengthens these export firms further at home as well as abroad.

Table 8.4 Distribution of the Favorable Aspects of Policy Reforms according to Firms's Characteristics

	Multinational Corp.	Family Corp.	Owned by Shareholders	Part of Holding		Part of Finance Group		Sales		Export Ratio	
				Yes	No	Yes	No	Small	Large	Small	Large
PFIXCAP[a]	1	8	9*	17	6*	5	18	11	12	10	13
PWORKCAP	1	10	9*	16	9	5	19	15	10	9	16
PMACIMP	4	22	10	22	19	6	34	24	17	12	29
PDRESUSE	2	8	4	12	8	3	16	8	12*	10	10*
PRAWIMP	5	22	9	23	18	5	35	21	20	14	27
PPRICE	–	10	9*	17	7	6	18*	12	12	9	15
PXPOSS	2	20	11	30	12*	5	37	20	22*	18	24
PSTATE	1	14	10*	19	12	5	26	16	15	12	19
PDCOMP	1	4	–	5	3	2	5	6	2	–	8*
PCRCOST	–	9	4	12	6	3	14	11	7	5	13
PPATENT	1	11	7	13	7	3	16	10	10	9	11
PPROFIT	–	14*	7	16	10	3	22	14	12	11	15
PLABREL	–	14*	7	14	11	4	20	12	13	11	14*
PLABCOST	–	7	2	8	2	3	6*	8	2	3	7
No. of Firms	5	32	14	36	26	8	53	35	27	20	42

[a] A glossary for abbreviations is in table 8.A6 in the Appendix.

Table 8.5   Unfavorable Aspects of Policy Reforms

	Mean Score
Rise in the cost of credit	3.7
Rise in the cost of working capital	3.3
Rise in the cost of fixed capital	3.1
Rise in the cost of raw materials exceeding the rise in the output price	2.4
Rise in the cost of production as a result of the VAT	2.3

Unfavorable Changes

The mean scores on important unfavorable changes in table 8.5 show the developments in the financial system as being the major source of dissatisfaction for the firms. The rising cost of credit and the cost of fixed and working capital are major concerns among most firms regardless of size, openness, activity, and ownership. The two other unfavorable changes emphasized in the survey are the rising cost of imports resulting from the frequent adjustments in the value of the TL and the adverse effects of the 10-to-12-percent (VAT). Both of these factors are perceived as raising the cost of production. In other words, these adverse effects of the liberalization program are perceived as output reducing.

The negative effects of the rise in the cost of firms' financial requirements, i.e., credit, fixed, and working capital, is agreed upon by all firms in table 8.6. In addition, firms in metal industries list the increase in foreign competition (NFCOMP) and the subsequent decline in export revenues (NXREV) as unfavorable outcomes of liberalization policies. Therefore, three out of five "metal" firms in the survey complain of the increase in imperfect competition (NXIMPC) in the export sector, presumably referring to the disproportional export incentives given to the larger firms.

Table 8.7 reveals additional information on survey results. Family corporations in the sample, which are relatively smaller companies, point out the negative effects of the policies on labor costs (NLABCOST) and the rise in imperfect competition in the export sector (NXIMPC). Nine out of 32 family corporations refer to the decrease in export earnings (NXREV), whereas none of the multinational corporations rank it as "important." Firms that are part of

Table 8.6 Industrial Distribution of the Unfavorable Aspects of the Policy Reforms

	Textile	Paper Printing	Chemicals	Rubber Plastic	Glass	Metal	Machinery	Electronics	Transportation Motor Vehicle
NFIXCAP[a]	2	3	4	2	1	5	2	1	5
NWORKCAP	2	3	5	2	1	5	3	3	6
NCRCOST	2	3	8	2	2	5	3	3	7
NLABCOST	1	–	–	–	2	3	1	1	2
NDEPEN	–	–	1	–	–	1	–	1	1
NFCOMP	–	1	2	1	–	4	2	2	2
NXREV	1	–	–	–	–	3	2	2	2
NPCONT	–	–	2	–	1	–	1	–	1
NVAT	1	1	1	1	2	3	1	–	3
NIXMPC	1	–	3	–	1	3	3	2	3
NPRAW	1	1	4	2	2	5	2	1	5
No. of Firms	3	3	8	2	3	5	3	3	7

[a] A glossary for abbreviations is in table 8.A6 in the Appendix

Table 8.7 Distribution of the Unfavorable Aspects of Policy Reforms according to Firms' Characteristics

	Multinational Corp.	Family Corp.	Owned by Shareholders	Part of Holding Yes	No	Part of Finance Group Yes	No	Sales Small	Large	Export Ratio Small	Large
NFIXCAP[a]	3	20	13*	27	16	6	37	21	22*	16	27
NWORKCAP	4	24	12	31	18	5	33	26	23	17	32
NCRCOST	5	27	14	36	21*	8	48	31	26	19	38
NLABCOST	1	10	2	7	9	4	11*	13	3*	4	12
NDEPEN	1	4	2	6	2	3	5*	3	5	3	5
NFCOMP	2	7	6*	12	6	2	18	10	10	9	11
NXREV	–	9	2	12	2*	1	13	10	4	3	11
NPCONT	1	4	3	6	4	3	6*	4	6	3	7
NVAT	1	10	8	14	6	2	17	9	11	11	9*
NIXMPC	2	16	6	17	10	1	25*	16	11	10	17
NPRAW	3	20	8	23	16	5	33	19	20	16	23*
No. of Firms	5	32	14	36	26	8	53	35	27	20	42

[a] A glossary for abbreviations is in table 8.A6 in the Appendix

a holding company list the loss in export earnings as a significant adverse effect of the liberalization program and lay blame to the rise in imperfect competition in the export sector. Small firms, broken down by sales and export ratio, unfavorably regard the liberalization of the import regime since the latter increased foreign competition.

The results of both positive and negative effects of the policy reforms bring out the fact that the liberalization program favored the large firms. In addition, in response to an open-ended question, firms repeatedly cite the uncertain economic environment that the stop-and-go approach to financial liberalization in general has created.

Firms' Adjustments

Most of the adjustments, particularly in production, pricing, marketing and labor practices, and investment and financial decisions, are made in response to the increasingly competitive economic environment.[14] With the 1980 coup having taken care of labor problems, firms have tried to restore their profitability and to position themselves in a rapidly growing economy by improving product quality, adopting new marketing strategies, and taking measures to become more price-competitive. New investment, in general, has taken the form of replacement investment.

Areas of firms' adjustments ranked according to mean scores are listed in table 8.8. Apparently, the not-so-successful financial liberalization attempts and the resulting high cost of borrowing has inevitably led firms to give additional consideration to financial management. This is especially the case for firms in industries like metal, machinery, and electronics (see table 8.9). The same firms are also actively seeking to decrease their debt and to raise their net worth to decrease their dependency on financial markets. Changing their marketing strategies is an important aspect of adjustment for all textile and glass manufacturers, whereas the two producers of rubber and plastic are not concerned with marketing strategy at all. Even though most firms claim to have their product quality improved, companies in "chemical" and "rubber and plastic" activities do not mention any attempt to alter their product quality.

In table 8.10, firms classified as large according to their sales, significantly differ from smaller ones in their adjustments. They have relied more on adjustments in marketing strategy, improvements in product quality, changes in inventory system to comply with the new tax law, and on consolidating their product line. It

Table 8.8   Areas of Firms' Adjustments

	Mean Score
Change in financial management	2.9
Change in marketing strategy	2.7
Change in pricing policy	2.6
Rise in investment	2.6
Change in product quality	2.4

is worth noting that firms generally are not introducing new products into their existing product mix. They are taking advantage of the liberalized import regime and replacing obsolete machinery and equipment. One can argue that the foreign exchange crises of the previous decade have barred firms from undertaking this long overdue replacement investment.

Smaller export firms, on the other hand, have relied on price changes significantly more than large firms to increase their competitiveness in the world markets.

Conclusions

Several conclusions emerge from the study. The first and most important one is that liberalization policies have strongly favored larger firms over the smaller ones. This finding partly explains the persistent unemployment mentioned before. When large firms replaced their obsolete machinery and equipment and modernized to meet the standards of international markets, capital was substituted for labor. These presumably capital intensive, export-oriented firms were then not able to absorb the labor released from the shrinking import-competing industries. Thus, unemployment rose and remained high in the entire period of liberalization signaling a more fundamental rather than a temporary adjustment problem. Policy authorities have to acknowledge this persistence of high unemployment and take measures to provide incentives for investment in labor-intensive and small-scale activities.

Other adverse effects of liberalization relate to its financial aspects. The rise in the real lending rates but also the real depreciation of the TL and the value added tax have all contributed to the high and persistent inflation in Turkey. Even though the rise in domestic and foreign competition may have dampened the price increases, firms have shifted the rise in production cost to consumers in the form of higher prices. On the other hand, the rise

Table 8.9 Industrial Distribution of Firms' Adjustments

	Textile	Paper Printing	Chemicals	Rubber Plastic	Glass	Metal	Machinery	Electronics	Transportation Motor Vehicle
CHFINAN[a]	2	1	3	2	2	4	3	3	5
CHMARK	3	2	2	—	3	3	2	2	4
CHPRICE	2	2	2	1	3	4	2	1	5
CHINV	3	1	2	—	2	3	1	3	5
CHPRQL	2	1	—	—	2	4	2	2	4
CHPROD	2	1	1	—	1	1	1	2	4
CHINVEN	1	1	1	—	1	—	—	—	2
CHPRVOL	—	—	—	—	—	—	1	—	—
CHDEBT	1	1	2	1	2	2	3	2	2
CHWORTH	1	1	3	1	2	3	2	2	4
No. of Firms	3	3	8	2	3	5	3	3	7

[a] A glossary for abbreviations is in table 8.A6 in the Appendix

Table 8.10 Distribution of Firms' Adjustments according to Their Characteristics

	Multinational Corp.	Family Corp.	Owned by Shareholders	Part of Holding		Part of Finance Group		Sales		Export Ratio	
				Yes	No	Yes	No	Small	Large	Small	Large
CHFINAN[a]	3	23	9	26	18	6	37	25	18	13	31
CHMARK	3	17	9	19	16	5	29	16	19*	13	22
CHPRICE	2	19	11	21	15	4	31	21	15	16	20*
CHINV	2	16	8	15	15	5	24	17	13	10	20
CHPRQL	1	14	9	21	10	6	24	14	17*	11	20
CHPROD	–	7	8	10	8	2	15	1	2	2	7
CHINVEN	1	5	3	9	3	3	9	2	10	9	3
CHPRVOL	–	3	3	7	1	2	6	1	7	4	4
CHDEBT	1	11	4	15	7	2	19	12	10	8	14
CHWORTH	1	14	7	16	12	4	23	15	13	10	18
No. of Firms	5	32	14	36	26	8	53	35	27	20	42

[a] A glossary for abbreviations is in table 8.A6 in the Appendix

in aggregate demand, resulting from the expansion of credit to the public sector, has contributed to the building-up of inflationary pressures. Instead of taking measures to curb their deficits, authorities offered state-owned enterprises for privatization. To attract customers, the relatively profitable enterprises were the first ones to be offered to the public with share prices below the market price. This meant further losses in revenues and more public borrowing, not to mention the speculative atmosphere that this form of privatization created.

In spite of these adverse effects and with the exception of financial reforms, firms, in general, favor liberalization. However, it should be mentioned that faltering financial liberalization attempts have led some firms in the sample to question the credibility of the policy reforms. These firms admit that they had postponed any adjustment for about one to two years in the early 1980s to see the impact of the financial reforms. Fortunately, however, only few firms share this view.

Firms' adjustments to policy reforms have generally been as expected. Improvements in product quality and marketing strategies, in financial management, as well as relying more on competitive pricing were all expected adjustments. Hence, one may conclude that firms must have perceived the policy reforms as long-run phenomena, a necessary condition for the success of the liberalization program. In this respect, in spite of all its ills, the program as a whole is considered a success.

Acknowledgments

I would like to thank T. Nas, R. Rotheim, and T. Koechlin for their helpful comments on an earlier version of this paper; Arman Oruç for his computer assistance; and Skidmore College for financial support.

Notes

1. For a detailed analysis of the Turkish liberalization policies see Şenses (1988).
2. For a comparative study see Kopits (1987) and Odekon (1988).
3. See OECD (1990).
4. See Odekon (1988: 31)
5. The brokers' crisis refers to a wave of failures experienced by brokerage houses in 1982, culminating in June 1982 with the bankruptcy of the largest brokerage firm in the country.
6. A questionnaire was sent out to 168 industrial firms in Turkey in November 1988. The 62 completed surveys amount to a return rate of 36.9 percent. The

basic characteristics of the firms are listed in the Appendix, tables 8.A4, 8.A5, and 8.A6.

7. See Corbo and Sanchez (1985). Mezzera and de Melo (1985), and Petrei and de Melo (1985).

8. The range of responses run from 0 (not relevant) to 4 (very important) with a somewhat arbitrary cutoff point of 2.3, a mean score between important and somewhat important changes. Thus, only those variables ranked 2.3 and above are included in tables 8.2, 8.5, and 8.8.

9. The Spearman rank correlation coefficient of .2606 between the variables "ease in importing raw materials" and "increase in export possibilities" is significant at 5 percent. The average ranking of "ease in importing raw materials" and "ease in importing machinery and equipment" against "increase in export possibilities" yields a similar result with a Spearman rank correlation coefficient of .2092, significant at 5 percent.

10. Calculated from OECD Economic Surveys-Turkey, various issues.

11. Only 37 firms have provided information to distribute them according to SITC.

12. See Şenses (1988: 19).

13. The statistics used to test the difference between two population means is $(ps1 - ps2)/sqr[(pb(1 - pb)(1/n1 + 1/n2))]$, where $ps1$ and $ps2$ are sample proportions, $n1$ and $n2$ are sample populations, and $pb = (x1 + x2)/(n1 + n2)$, $x1$ and $x2$ being sample size.

14. In response to a set of questions on the comparison of pre- and post-1980 competitive economic environment, firms consistently ranked post-1980 as being more competitive, specifically in relation to product quality and marketing. The Spearman rank correlation coefficients of .4449 and .2879 are significant at 5 percent, respectively.

Appendix

Table 8.A1   Nominal and Real Exchange Rates, 1980–1988

Year	Nominal Exchange Rate	Change in Nominal Exchange Rate (%)	Real Exchange Rate[a]	Change in Real Exchange Rate (%)
1980	76.04	144.66	14.57	30.41
1981	111.22	46.27	17.17	17.89
1982	162.55	46.15	20.63	20.14
1983	225.46	38.70	22.62	9.65
1984	366.68	62.64	25.99	14.90
1985	521.98	42.35	26.62	2.41
1986	674.51	29.22	26.16	−1.74
1987	857.20	27.09	24.63	−5.85
1988	1,422.30	65.92	——	——

Source: IMF, International Financial Statistics, 1988 Yearbook.

[a] Real Exchange Rate = Nominal Exchange Rate (CPI/CPI), where CPI is that of industrial countries, calculated from index numbers for CPI and CPI (1985 = 100).

Table 8.A2 Nominal and Real Deposit and Lending Rates, 1980–1988

| | Nominal | | Inflation | Real | |
	Deposit	Lending	Rate	Deposit	Lending
1980	10.0	25.67	110.2	−100.2	−84.53
1981	28.5	35.58	36.6	−8.1	−1.02
1982	45.0	36.00	30.8	14.2	5.20
1983	51.9	35.50	32.9	19.0	2.60
1984	54.3	52.33	48.4	5.9	3.93
1985	49.2	53.50	45.2	4.2	8.50
1986	41.9	52.63	34.6	7.3	18.03
1987	35.4	50.00	38.9	−3.5	11.10
1988	45.0[a]	54.00[b]	68.8	−23.8	−14.80

Source: IMF, International Financial Statistics, various issues.
[a] First quarter of 1988 (OECD 1987–88: 45)
[b] February 1988 (OECD 1987–88: 46)

Table 8.A3 Industry Distribution of the Firms in the Sample

	Frequency
Textile Products	3
Paper Products and Printing	3
Chemicals	8
Rubber and Plastic	2
Glass Products	3
Metal Industries	5
Industrial Machinery	3
Electronics and Electrical Equipment	3
Transportation and Motor Vehicles	7
Others	8
No Answer	17
Total	62

Table 8.A4 Ownership and Other Characteristics of the Firms in the Sample

	Frequency
Multinational	5
Family Corporation	29
Public Partnership	3
Owned by Shareholders	14
Other	2

No Answer	9
Other Characteristics:	
No. of Firms part of a Holding	36
No. of Firms part of a Financial Group	8

Table 8.A5   Size Distribution of Firms in the Sample

	Frequency
According to Sales	
Large (more than TL 35 billion)	35
Small (less than TL 35 billion)	27
According to Export Ratio	
Large (more than 17%)	42
Small (less than 17%)	20

Table 8.A6   Glossary of Abbreviations

PFIXCAP:	Ease in fixed capital financing
PWORKCAP:	Ease in working capital financing
PMACIMP:	Ease in importing machinery
PDRESUSE:	Rise in domestic resource use
PRAWIMP:	Ease in raw material imports
PPRICE:	Liberalization of the product prices
PXPOSS:	Increase in export possibilities
PSTATE:	Ease in relations with state
PDCOMP:	Decrease in domestic competition
PCRCOST:	Decrease in cost of credit
PPATENT:	Ease in acquiring foreign patents and know-how
PPROFIT:	Increase in firms' profitability
PLABREL:	Ease in labor relations
PLABCOST:	Decrease in labor cost
NFIXCAP:	Rise in cost of fixed capital financing
NWORKCAP:	Rise in cost of working capital financing
NCRCOST:	Rise in cost of credit
NLABCOST:	Rise in labor cost exceeding the rise in price
NDEPEN:	Rise in dependency on imports
NFCOMP:	Rise in foreign competition
NXREV:	Fall in export earnings
NPCONT:	Rise in price controls
NPRAW:	Rise in raw material prices
NVAT:	Negative effect of value-added tax on price

NXIMPC:	Rise in imperfect competition in export sector
CHFINAN:	Adjustment in financial management
CHMARK:	Adjustment in marketing strategies
CHPRICE:	Adjustment in pricing policy
CHINV:	Adjustment in investment
CHPRQL:	Adjustment in product quality
CHPROD:	Adjustment in product mix
CHINVEN:	Adjustment in inventory system
CHPRVOL:	Consolidation of product line
CHDEBT:	Decrease in firms' debt
CHWORTH:	Increase in firms' net worth

References

Corbo, V. and J. de Melo, eds. 1985. *Scrambling for Survival*. World Bank Staff Working Papers 764. Washington, D.C.: World Bank.

Corbo, V. and J. M. Sanchez. 1985. "Adjustments by Industrial Firms in Chile during 1974–82." In *Scrambling for Survival*, edited by V. Corbo and J. de Melo, 83–118. Washington, D.C.: World Bank.

Kopits, G. 1987. *Structural Reform, Stabilization and Growth in Turkey*. IMF Occasional Paper 52. Washington, D.C.: IMF.

Mezzera, J. and J. de Melo. 1985. "Adjustments by Industrial Firms in Uruguay during 1974–82." In *Scrambling for Survival*, edited by V. Corbo and J. de Melo, 153–210. Washington, D.C.: World Bank.

Odekon, M. 1988. "Liberalization and the Turkish Economy: A Comparative Analysis." In *Liberalization and the Turkish Economy*, edited by T. Nas and M. Odekon, 29–46. Westport, Conn.: Greenwood Press.

OECD. Economic Surveys-Turkey, various issues. Paris: OECD.

Petrei, H. and J. de Melo. 1985. "Adjustments by Industrial Firms in Argentina during 1976–81." In *Scrambling for Survival*, edited by V. Corbo and J. de Melo, 25–84. Washington, D.C.: World Bank.

Şenses, F. 1988. "An Overview of Recent Turkish Experience with Economic Stabilization and Liberalization." In *Liberalization and the Turkish Economy*, edited by T. Nas and M. Odekon, 9–28. Westport, Conn.: Greenwood Press.

9

Arbitrage and Return for Political Risk in Turkey in the 1980s

Doğan Tırtıroğlu and Ercan Tırtıroğlu

Introduction

Turkey has been a politically risky environment for potential investors for many years. The country suffered turmoil, and has been the scene of military interventions in the past several decades. An account of the political risk issues in Turkey covering a long period until the early 1980s is given in Erdilek (1985). Our purpose in this chapter is to consider the question of a return for political risk in Turkey in the 1980s. We rely on the model proposed in Aliber (1978), which aims at identifying political risk and exchange risk based on interest rate comparisons across borders. Introducing an arbitrage viewpoint in addition, we focus on the 1984–87 period.

According to Aliber (1978: 46), "Interest rates on similar assets available in various countries differ because investors demand a payment for carrying political risk." He also points out that the interest rate on U.S. dollars in Moscow, in İstanbul, in London, and in Paris, ... should be exactly the same as the interest rate on U.S. dollars in New York if no political risk existed.[1] In other words, no banker in any country would be willing to offer an additional risk premium on similar U.S. dollars accounts in the absence of political risk since such a differential represents an arbitrage possibility for the investors.

Profit or loss on an investment in the form of foreign currency held in a bank account may come from (1) exchange rate (parity) fluctuations; i.e., currency value appreciations or depreciations; and/or (2) interest earned (rental return).

Parity fluctuations are uncertain movements, and they may result in a profit or loss, while interest earned can be viewed as a guaranteed return. Thus, the parity fluctuations represent the "exchange risk" that an investor has to confront while the differences in interest

rates across countries are linked to the "political risk," which
constitutes the basis of the main theme of this discussion.

We can think of the investment in foreign currency (held in a
bank account) as being similar to an investment in common stocks,
where the investor has a similar uncertainty arising from the stock
price fluctuations. Moreover, the investor is entitled to a dividend
if the company decides to pay it which, once announced, is a
guaranteed return on investment similar to the interest earned of
foreign currency — with the exception that dividend announcement
is stochastic.

The stock price changes occur fundamentally as a response to
some overall economy-wide factors. On the other hand, dividend
payments provide some firm-specific information about the firm's
condition. By analogy, then, we can posit that (1) exchange rate
fluctuations occur as a result of international economic forces; and
(2) the interest paid on foreign currency in some country provides
information specifically about that country.

Following (2), we argue that interest rates on foreign currency
accounts should reveal relevant information about the conditions
prevailing in a country.

Exchange risk, which is not examined in this work, can be studied
using asset pricing models (e.g., Capital Asset Pricing Model).[2]
This is so because foreign currency is an asset.

A fundamental assumption of asset pricing models in financial
economics is that there are no frictions in the financial markets.
Such frictions include taxes, bankruptcy costs, and information
availability. In the international context, however, national borders
come up as an additional element of friction. Since in the absence
of national borders country-specific political risk would not exist as
an issue of comparative return, the fact that they do exist (as an
element of friction) is our reason for studying return for political
risk with an arbitrage viewpoint.

In pricing foreign currency, an assumption of absence of borders
would mean that political risk does not exist across international
markets, and that the return differentials in interest rates on similar
foreign currency accounts in different markets provide arbitrage
possibilities. If there exists any rate differential in such a frictionless
market, this information would be available to every investor at no
cost by virtue of no frictions in these markets. Therefore, such a
situation will definitely distort the market equilibrium since there
will be an infinite demand for such an account, which will dominate
all other similar accounts in international markets. The ever-
increasing demand will eventually lead to a decrease in the interest

rate, bringing all interest rates on these accounts to the same level across the nations involved.

The existence of national borders raises the political risk issue as we pointed out. Our approach to political risk suggests that the interest rate differentials on similar U.S. dollars accounts in İstanbul and in New York represent the return for this political risk component in Turkey, and to some extent, the degree or strength of the friction. We argue that the differentials do not provide arbitrage possibilities; that they are simply a way of compensating the political risk pertinent to a country; and that equilibrium in foreign currency markets is possible even in the presence of interest rate differentials.[3]

The year 1984 is an important turning point in Turkish politics and economics: the military government was replaced by an elected government headed by Turgut Özal. The then-newly formed government of Özal initiated some major economic liberalization measures that were, in fact, determined to a large extent by some legal and political changes.[4] One such change that had a relevant and significant set of ramifications was the removal of the legal barriers hampering the foreign exchange transactions. Following this removal, the Turkish banks became a more active member of the international banking community, beginning to actively operate in Euro-currency markets (*Supplement to Euromoney*, April 1985 and December 1986). This is particularly important for our purposes in this chapter, since the participation of the Turkish banks in the Euro-currency markets facilitates the use of Aliber's model as it leads to the availability of the data for comparing Turkey with other countries.

It is clear that the liberalization movement in Turkey, which provided banks with a new challenge of joining the Euro-currency markets and enabled them to become more active members of the international banking community has also provided us with a unique opportunity to obtain a measure of return commensurate with the political risk pertaining to Turkey. Now that the Turkish banks operate with U.S. dollar accounts, we may be able to compare the interest rates between similar İstanbul dollars and New York dollar accounts, and gain some insight as to the level of the political risk. We would like to point out at the outset that the removal of the Turkish legal barriers previously hampering the foreign exchange related activities is in itself a positive signal to the international markets since, as we discussed, it is now possible to obtain some political risk-return measurement in Turkey. Naturally, providing this information should have more value than not providing it.

The next section gives a discussion of the Aliber's model. We then focus on the 1984–87 period, which is the period that is of primary interest in this chapter. We conclude with a discussion.

Aliber's Model

The existence of offshore (e.g., Euro-dollar) markets is an important prerequisite for making cross-country comparisons in the assessment of political risk. Aliber (1978: 47) gives the following explanation:

> The growth of the Euro-currency and Euro-bond markets facilitates a sharper evaluation of political risk on similar financial assets issued in various centres. These markets involve the issue of liabilities in various centres — principally London, Zurich, Frankfurt, Luxembourg, and Singapore — denominated in currencies other than that of the country in which the transaction occurs. For example, many banks in London — the London branches of U.S. and of Swiss banks as well as British banks — issue deposits denominated in U.S. dollars; these deposits share the exchange risk attribute of dollar deposits issued in the United States but not their political risk attribute. Dollar deposits issued in London, like sterling deposits produced there, are primarily within the regulatory jurisdiction of the British banking authorities. The growth of offshore financial markets is a response to government regulation of financial transactions in domestic financial markets. Transactions are less extensively regulated in the offshore market than in the domestic markets; offshore deposits are not subject to interest rate ceilings, and banks generally are not required to hold reserves against their external currency deposits. Indeed, if offshore transactions are significantly regulated they become non-competitive and so the transactions would be shifted to the centres which are freer of regulation.

An investor, for example, with a dollar deposit in London would be concerned with political risk because British authorities may apply exchange controls, as opposed to regulation of domestic markets, to London dollar deposits, which might delay or prevent the shift of dollar funds from Britain.

Aliber suggests, moreover, that investor attitude toward riskiness of particular assets can be inferred from the interest rates available on these assets. Using these arguments as his starting point, Aliber develops a model based on cross-country interest rate comparisons involving New York dollar and London sterling, London dollar and London mark, New York and London dollars, and London and Zurich dollars.[5]

The comparison between New York and London dollars involves

the risk that the British authorities might apply controls to the movements of funds denominated in a foreign currency from a domestic financial to a foreign center.

Investors are concerned with the political risk since they undertake the risk that their funds might be "frozen" or imposed some exchange controls. Therefore, these investors continually evaluate the benefits and costs of dollar deposits in London, Zurich, Madrid, São Paulo, and Moscow to avoid the host government's regulations on foreign currency transactions. Because bureaucratic traditions of São Paulo and Moscow are perceived to be much stronger than other financial centers, we see that these two centers do not attract many investors. Aliber (1978: 50) notes that "the major centers of offshore banking are London, Zurich, Luxembourg, and Singapore is not an accident, for the authorities in these countries have established traditions of minimal interference of financial transactions."

It is useful to note that Aliber's usage of the term *risk* is quite general. One can refine this usage by making a distinction between risk and uncertainty. Rescher (1989) examines this distinction and points out that 1) risk arises when the probability of occurrence of a given state of nature is not known, but it can be assessed; and 2) uncertainty arises when it is not even possible to ascertain the probability distribution of different states.

Istanbul's efforts to become a major financial center are quite obvious. However, the traditions of the Turkish government have not been complementary with such efforts since there have been extensive interference in the markets by previous governments resulting in inconsistencies in the stabilization efforts. Thus, investors have been very cautious in evaluating a commitment in Turkey.

The 1984—1987 Period

Turkish military forces were in control of the government during the 1980—83 period. Their primary objective was to control the turmoil in the country. Thus, we observe this period as a transition from a chaotic environment of the 1970s, to a stable environment of the mid-and late 1980s. Therefore, the political risk and return is not an issue for the 1980—83 period as this was a period of controlling a small-scale civil war; or healing the wounds; and most importantly, of creating a politically sound environment for the governments that would follow the military rule.

We can now turn our attention to the 1984—87 period in which we can employ cross-country interest rate differentials on U.S.

Table 9.1   Interest Rate Comparisons by Different Accounts

Year	Istanbul $	New York $	Differential
a) Savings Accounts %			
1984	7.27	5.50	1.77
1985	7.00	5.50	1.50
1986	7.00	5.34	1.66
1987	7.00	5.19	1.81
b) Time Deposits for 6 months %			
1984	9.55	10.29	−0.74
1985	8.43	8.29	0.14
1986	7.50	6.64	0.86
1987	7.50	6.59	0.91
c) Time Deposits for 1 year %			
1984	9.70	10.75	−1.05
1985	8.89	8.85	0.04
1986	7.75	7.00	0.75
1987	7.75	6.87	0.88

Sources: Federal Reserve Bank Bulletins (1984−87) and authors' survey.
Interest rates in Turkey belonged to the rates offered by Turkiye
İş Bankası, Aş (Turkish Business Bank, Inc.); the largest
commercial bank in Turkey.
Notes: Interest rates are nominal rates and weighted average annual
figures for every account type for both countries.

dollar accounts in İstanbul and in New York to measure the political
risk and return trade-offs. Table 9.1 displays the average annual
rates on U.S. dollar accounts in İstanbul and in New York for
different types of accounts and the corresponding interest rate
differentials by year. A more rigorous examination of rate differentials can be achieved by some statistical techniques. This
requires more data than currently available. Therefore, we confine
our work to a descriptive analysis.

An interesting result is that there is a positive return differential
on similar dollar accounts in Turkey with an exception in 1984.
(This exception is clearly observable in table 9.4 where we have
reorganized table 9.1. We will mention this exception later in the
chapter.) Another interesting result is that the rate differentials on
all accounts show an increasing trend from one year to another.
We may interpret this as an ongoing process of risk reassess-
ments and corresponding return adjustments. The increases might
represent the government's willingness to provide more incentives

Table 9.2   Direct Foreign Investment in Turkey
($ U.S. Million)

Year	Authorized	Actual	Realization Rate %
1980	97	53	55
1981	337	60	18
1982	167	55	33
1183	103	87	84
1984	377[a]	113	30
1985	135	98	73
1986	190	125	66

Source: Erdilek (1986) and OECD (1988).
[a] 201 of this total is for a single tourism project proposed by a Syrian investor.

to foreign investors to invest more in Turkey. We can see this behavior in a better way by examining the direct foreign investment (DFI) in Turkey (see table 9.2).[6] The realization rates fluctuate widely and are not close to 100 percent. This indicates foreign investors' cautious evaluations. Moreover, these investors should feel that the return on projects in Turkey is not commensurate with the political risks involved. There should be other international markets where this trade-off is more fruitful.

Considering the distinction between political risk and uncertainty mentioned at the end of the previous section, perhaps a different interpretation of the results appearing in these tables would also be of interest. It might be that, despite the liberalization reform — which is expected to reduce the political risk — the low realization rates of direct foreign investments in Turkey is an indication of continued political uncertainty perceived by investors.

The low realization rates of DFI might be attributed more to political uncertainty than to political risk. Having experienced inconsistent stabilization policies on several occasions in the past, perhaps the foreign investors have been less responsive to the liberalization reform than one would expect (see Erdilek 1985; and other chapters in this volume for an account of inconsistent stabilization policies of the past).

It is conceivable that continued endorsement of the liberalization movement by future governments (which may have ideological differences) would hopefully change the perceptions of instability and uncertainty.

Table 9.3   Workers' Remittances
($ U.S. Million)

Year	Amount
1975	1,312.4
1976	982.7
1977	981.9
1978	983.1
1979	1,696.4
1980	2,070.9
1981	2,490.0
1982	2,140.0
1983	1,513.0
1984	1,807.0
1985	1,714.0
1986	1,614.0

Source: OECD (1988).

An interesting and important group of investors for the Turkish markets is the Turkish workers in Europe. Their remittances have not increased in response to these interest rate differentials (see table 9.3). This behavior represents their awareness of political risk, which is not compensated by the extra return differentials. This might be taken as a piece of evidence of workers' lack of confidence in the Turkish markets.[7,8]

Migrant Turkish workers have a major stake in Turkey. It has been found that the political risk is a major concern for them, and that they represent perhaps the largest investor group in Turkey (see Swamy 1981). Swamy points out that the efforts and incentives of the Turkish authorities to attract the workers' remittances are not as important to the workers as an environment of confidence in the safety and liquidity of assets they hold in the stability and security of the host country's environment. Such behavior is quite understandable if we are to consider the fear due to a possibility of losing hard-earned income saved miles away from home, and often, away from loved ones. Not unexpectedly, these people have close family ties and business relations in Turkey. Therefore, they have ample access to qualitative and informal information about Turkey that other investors do not. Thus, to other rational investors, the behavior of the Turkish workers may be a good source of information signaling the political prospects in Turkey. By observing

Table 9.4   Interest Rate Comparisons by Year

	Account	Differential
1984		
	Savings	1.77
	6-Month	−0.74
	1-Year	−1.05
1985		
	Savings	1.50
	6-Month	0.14
	1-Year	0.04
1986		
	Savings	1.66
	6-Month	0.86
	1-Year	0.75
1987		
	Savings	1.81
	6-Month	0.91
	1-Year	0.88

Source: Table 6.1.

the behavior of Turkish workers, these investors may be able to develop some initial judgments about the political risk in Turkey.

As we mentioned earlier, table 9.4, which provides us with some more light, is a reorganization of table 9.1. The year 1984 was the first year that the Turkish banks were allowed to open foreign currency accounts. The negative returns on time deposits in 1984 represent the lack of experience on the part of Turkish banks in the international markets and in dealing with foreign currency.[9] This situation is corrected in the following years. Another interesting result from this table is that the interest rate differentials on savings accounts are significantly higher than those on other time deposit accounts. The savings differential in 1984 is positive, whereas the time deposit differentials are negative. We interpret this finding as a rush for liquidity for foreign currency reserves. The liberalization measures also relaxed import procedures. Therefore, there has been an increase in imports, as well. The effects of this is that it enhances the need for foreign currency reserves, and for liquidity.

Conclusion

Our major remark is that Turkey has provided the international investors with information that was not available before. Therefore, the country's political standing is no more a black box that should undergo evaluations behind closed doors. It is subject to international investment communities' scrutiny (similar to stock market scrutiny of companies and their top managers) through the information available from the banking sector. This is a major plus for the country in the 1980s. *Institutional Investor*'s annual country credit ratings in the 1980s have indicated that Turkey was one of the rapidly and progressively improving countries in country-credit ratings in a list maintained for more than 100 countries. This positive development is good news, but the same ratings have some not so good news, too: rated 47th in March 1987, a rise from being 51st in September 1986, Turkey had a credit rating of 39.7, which was still below the global average rating of 40.0 pertaining to March 1987. This means that the country has to do more to maintain the confidence built in the 1980s and attract more investors. Thus, political risk is still an important element in Turkey that the international investors are cautious about. The wide fluctuations in the realization rates of DFI also confirm this cautious behavior.

We conclude by stating that the liberalization was a first step for opening doors to the international community. Further measures should foster the spirit of liberalization framework from a political risk and return viewpoint.

Acknowledgments

We would like to thank Drs. Selim S. İlter and Gaffer Ağaoğlu for their valuable support. We also acknowledge the valuable comments of an anonymous referee, particularly regarding the distinction between political risk and political uncertainty. We also thank the editors for their encouragement and support.

Notes

1. The liberalization program was actually a follow-up of Özal's economic policies of the 1980–82 period during which he was the economic advisor to the military-backed government of B. Ulusu, a former admiral and commander in chief of the Turkish Naval Forces.

2. There is an international version of Capital Asset Pricing Model. See Copeland and Weston (1989: 810).

3. We do not mean that arbitrage is not possible. If the differential is large enough, arbitrage can occur. Moreover, arbitrage is a much broader issue. We adopt a narrow and unidirectional version of arbitrage. It is, for example, conceivable for a Turkish investor to realize arbitrage possibilities in other countries given the assumption of no frictions across borders.

4. The member countries of the EC have agreed on the gradual unification of Europe by removing borders and other elements of political and national frictions. Our hypothesis predicts a gradual convergence of interest rates on similar foreign currency accounts into a uniform rate cross-sectionally as the frictions become less influential. Turkey's possible full membership in the EC is therefore expected to have a significant impact on rate differentials and political risk assessments.

5. These cities are used in a symbolic manner, such that each represents the corresponding country.

6. Erdilek (1986) examines DFI in Turkey in an interesting article.

7. Some researchers examine the workers' companies in Turkey as a source of economic growth (see Gitmez 1979; Swamy 1981). As argued in the media, some of these people prefer to invest in Europe rather than to remit to or invest in Turkey ["İşçiydiler, Patron Oldular" ("Were once employees, now they are bosses.") 1987].

8. A more reliable basis of investigating the behavior of the Turkish workers can be achieved through rate comparisons between German mark accounts in Bonn and German mark accounts in Istanbul. The account types in these two countries do not allow for a sound comparison. But the workers have the option of converting their savings into dollars in Europe before remitting those savings. This way they may benefit from the rate differentials that exist between Istanbul dollar accounts and New York dollar accounts. The workers would do so if they feel that return for political risk (i.e., rate differential) is large enough to justify to undertake the risk.

9. For example, most banks have few employees who know a foreign language. See *Banks' Association of Turkey* (1987).

References

Aliber, R. Z. 1978. *Exchange Risk and Corporate International Finance*. New York: John Wiley & Sons.

Banks' Association of Turkey. 1987. *Banks in Turkey, 1986*. Ankara, Turkey: Ayyıldız Matbaası.

Copeland, T. E. and F. J. Weston. 1989. *Financial Theory and Corporate Policy*. Reading, Mass.: Addison-Wesley Publishing Co.

"Country Credit Ratings." *Institutional Investor*. 1980–87.

Erdilek, A. 1986. "Turkey's New Open-Door Policy of DFI: A Critical Analysis of Problems and Prospects." *METU Studies in Development* 13(1–2):171–91.

———. 1985. "The Dynamics of the Foreign Direct Investment Environment in Turkey: Political Risks in the Past and the Present." In *Political Risks in International Business, New Directions for Research, Management and Public Policy*, edited by T. L. Brewer. New York: Praeger Publishers.

Federal Reserve Bulletins. 1984–87.

Gitmez, A. S. 1979. *Dışgöç Öyküsü* (Immigration Stories). Ankara, Turkey: Maya Matbaacılık-Yayıncılık Ltd. Şti.

"İşçiydiler, Patron Oldular" (Were Once Employees, Now They are Bosses). *Hürriyet Gazetesi*. 30 January 1987.

OECD. 1987. *Economic Surveys: Turkey*. Paris: OECD.

Rescher, N. 1989. *RISK: A Philosophical Introduction to the Theory of Risk Evaluation and Management*. Washington, D.C.: University Press of America.

Supplement to Euromoney. 1986. "Turkish Banking and Finance: The Markets Mature," December.

————. 1985. "The New Challenge for Corporate Turkey," April.

Swamy, G. 1981. "International Migrant Workers' Remittances: Issues and Prospects." World Bank Staff Working Paper 481.

References

Adams, C. and D. Gros. 1986. "The Consequences of Real Exchange Rate Rules for Inflation." IMF *Staff Papers* 33:439−76.

Ahmad, F. 1985. "The Transition to Democracy in Turkey." In *Third World Quarterly* 211−26.

———. 1977. *The Turkish Experiment in Democracy, 1950−1975*. London: Hurst & Co.

Akyüz, Y. 1988. "Financial System and Policies in Turkey in the 1980s." Paper presented for the conference on Turkey's Economic Development in the 1980s: Changing Strategies and Prospects for the Next Decade, Harvard University.

Aliber, R. Z. 1978. *Exchange Risk and Corporate International Finance*. New York: John Wiley & Sons.

Ames, B. 1987. *Political Survival: Politicians and Public Policy in Latin America*. Berkeley: University of California Press.

Anand, R., A. Chibba, and S. van Wijnbergen. 1988. "External Balance and Sustainable Growth in Turkey: Can They Be Reconciled?" Paper presented at the conference on Turkey's Economic Development in the 1980s, Harvard University, April.

Arat, Y. 1987. "Social Change and the 1983 Political Elite in Turkey." Unpublished mimeo.

Arıcanlı, T. and D. Rodrik, eds. 1990. *The Political Economy of Turkey: Debt, Adjustment and Sustainability*. London: Macmillan Publishing Co.

Aşıkoğlu, Y. 1988. "Macroeconomic Consequences of Alternative Exchange Rate Strategies." City University of New York. Mimeo.

Aşıkoğlu Y. and M. Ercan. 1990. "Predicting Corporate Bankruptcy in Turkey during the Post-Liberalization Period." City University of New York. Mimeo.

Aydoğan, K. 1990. "The Competitive Structure of the Turkish Banking Industry." Bilkent University, Ankara. Mimeo.

Balassa, B. 1983. "Outward Orientation and Exchange Rate Policy in Developing Countries: The Turkish Experience." *Middle East Journal* 37(3).

———. 1981. "Adjustment to External Shocks in Developing Economies." World Bank Working Paper 472.

Banks' Association of Turkey. 1987. *Banks in Turkey, 1986*. Ankara, Turkey: Ayyıldız Matbaası.

Baysan, T. and C. Blitzer. 1988. "Turkey's Trade Liberalization in the 1980s and Prospects for Sustainability." Paper presented at the conference on Turkey's Economic Development in the 1980s, Harvard University, April.

Bianchi, R. 1984. *Interest Groups and Political Development in Turkey*. Princeton, N.J.: Princeton University Press.

Birand, M. A. 1984. *12 Eylül: Saat 04.00.* (September 12: 4 a.m.) İstanbul: Karacan Yayınları.

Black, S. W. 1976. "Exchange Rate Policies for Less Developed Countries in a World of Floating Rates." *Essays in International Finance* 119, Princeton University.

Blejer, M. and M. S. Khan. 1984. "Private Investment in Developing Countries." *Finance and Development* 21:26−29.

Blejer M. and L. Leiderman. 1981. "A Monetary Approach to the Crawling Peg System: Theory and Evidence." *Journal of Political Economy* 89:132−51.

Boratav, K. 1988. "Inter-Class and Intra-Class Relations of Distribution Under 'Structural Adjustment': Turkey during the 1980s." Paper presented for the conference on the Political Economy of Turkey in the 1980s, Harvard University, April.

————. 1986. "Import Substitution and Income Distribution under a Populist Regime: The Case of Turkey." *Development Policy Review* 4:117−39.

Boratav, K. and O. Türel. 1988. "Notes on the Current Development Problems and Growth Prospects of the Turkish Economy." *New Perspectives on Turkey* 2(1):37−50.

Branson, W. H. and L. T. Katseli-Papaefstratiou. 1981. "Exchange Rate Policy in Developing Countries." In *The World Economic Order: Past and Prospects*, edited by S. Grossman and E. Lundberg, 391−419. London: Macmillan Press.

Bruno, M. 1979. "Stabilization and Stagflation in a Semi-industrialized Economy." In *International Economic Policy: Theory and Evidence*, edited by R. Dornbusch and J. Frenkel, 270−91. Baltimore, M.: Johns Hopkins University Press.

Buchanan J., R. Tollison and G. Tullock. 1980. *Toward a Theory Rent-Seeking Society*. Texas: Texas A & M University Press.

Buffie, E. F. 1984. "Financial Repression, the New Structuralists, and Stabilization Policy in Semi-industrial Economies." *Journal of Development Economics* 14(3):305−22.

Buğra, A. 1988. "Political Sources of Uncertainty in Business Life in Turkey." Paper presented for the Conference on the Dynamics of States and Societies in the Middle East, Cairo.

Buiter, W. H. and R. C. Marston. 1985. *International Economic Policy Coordination*. New York: Cambridge University Press.

Calder, K. 1988. *Crisis and Compensation: Public Policy and Political Stability in Japan, 1949−1986*. Princeton, N.J.: Princeton University Press.

Çavdar, T. 1988. "Erken Seçim'in Düşündürdükleri" (Thoughts on Early Elections). *Mülkiyeliler Birliği Dergisi* 23(91):3−7.

Celâsun, M. 1988. "Turkey: Fiscal Aspects of Adjustment in the 1980s." Conference on Turkey's Development in the 1980s, Harvard University, April.

————. 1986. "Income Distribution and Domestic Terms of Trade in Turkey." *METU Studies in Development*. Special issue on the Turkish economy, 1977−84. 13(122):193−216.

Celâsun, M. and D. Rodrik. 1989. "Debt, Adjustment and Growth: Turkey." In *Developing Country Debt and Economic Performance*, edited by J. Sachs and S. Collins. Chicago: University of Chicago and NBER.

————. 1988. *Debt Adjustment and Growth in Turkey*. Chicago: Chicago University Press for NBER.

————. 1987. *Debt, Adjustment and Growth: Turkey*. NBER Project on Developing Country Debt. Preliminary draft.

Central Bank of the Republic of Turkey. *Annual Report*. Various issues. Ankara: Central Bank.

————. 1987. *Annual Report*. Ankara, Turkey: Central Bank.

————. 1985. *Annual Report*. Ankara, Turkey: Central Bank.

Chenery, H. and M. Syrquin. 1975. *Patterns of Development, 1950–1970*. London: Oxford University Press.

Cline, W. and S. Weintraub, eds. 1981. *Economic Stabilization in Developing Countries*. Washington, D.C.: Brookings Institution.

Connolly, M. 1983. "Optimium Currency Pegs for Latin America." *Journal of Money, Credit and Banking* 56–72.

————. 1982. "The Choice of an Optimum Currency Peg for a Small, Open Country." *Journal of International Money and Finance* 1:153–64.

Conolly, M. and A. Yousef. 1982. "Optimum Currency Pegs for Arab Countries." In *The International Monetary System: Choices for the Future*, edited by M. Connolly. New York: Praeger Publishers.

Conway, P. 1990. "The Record on Turkish Private Investment." In *The Political Economy of Turkey: Debt, Adjustment, and Sustainability*, edited by T. Aricanli and D. Rodrik. London: Macmillan Publishing Co.

————. "1988. The Impact of Recent Trade Liberalization Policies in Turkey." In *Liberalization and the Turkish Economy*, edited by T. Nas and M. Odekon, 47–67. Westport, Conn.: Greenwood Press.

————. 1987. *Economic Shocks and Structural Adjustments: Turkey after 1973*. Amsterdam: North Holland.

Cooper, R. 1971. "Currency Devaluation in Developing Countries." *Princeton Essays in International Finance* 86:3–31.

Copeland, T. E. and F. J. Weston. 1989. *Financial Theory and Corporate Policy*. Reading, Mass.: Addison-Wesley.

Corbo, V. and J. de Melo. 1987. "Lessons from the Southern Cone Policy Reforms." *The World Bank Research Observer* 2:111–43.

————. and J. de Melo, eds. 1985. *Scrambling for Survival*. World Bank Staff Working Papers 764. Washington, D.C.: World Bank.

Corbo, V. and J. M. Sanchez. 1985. "Adjustments by Industrial Firms in Chile during 1974–82." In *Scrambling for Survival*, edited by V. Corbo and J. de Melo, 83–118. Washington, D.C.: World Bank.

Coşan, F. M. and H. Ersel. 1987. "Turkish Financial System: Its Evolution and Performance, 1980–1986." *Inflation and Capital Markets*. Ankara, Turkey: Capital Market Board Publications.

"Country Credit Ratings." *Institutional Investor*. 1980–87.

Cumhuriyet, March 28, 1989.

Cumings, B. 1984. "The Origins and Development of the North East Asian Political Economy: Industrial Sectors, Product Cycles and Political Consequences." *International Organization* 38(1).

Dateline, June 18, 1988.

————, May 21, 1988.

Derviş, K. and S. Robinson. 1978. "The Foreign Exchange Gap Growth and Industrial Strategy in Turkey." *World Bank Staff Papers*. Washington, D.C.: IBRD.

Deyo, F. 1987. *The Political Economy of New Asian Industrialism*. Ithaca, N.Y.: Cornell University Press.

Diaz-Alejandro, C. 1981. "Southern Cone Stabilization Plans." In *Economic Stabilization in Developing Countries*, edited by W. Cline and S. Weintraub, 119–47. Washington, D.C.: Brookings Institution.

Dodd, C. H. 1983. *The Crisis of Turkish Democracy*. Walkington, England: Eothen Press.

Doğan, Y. 1985. *Dar Sokakta Siyaset (1980–1983)* (Politics in the Alley). İstanbul: Tekin Yayınevi.

Dornbusch, R. 1982. "Stabilization Policies in Developing Countries: What Have We Learned?" *World Development* 10:701–8.

Dünya, March 3, 1989.

Ebiri, K. 1980. "Turkish Apertura." *METU Studies in Development* 7(3–4): 209–54.

Economic and Social Studies Conference Board. 1969. *State Economic Enterprises*. Istanbul: Economic and Social Studies Conference Board.

Edison, H. J. and J. Marquez. 1986. "Optimal Crawling Peg in Venezuela." *Journal of Economic Dynamics and Control* 10: 201–4.

Edwards, S. 1984. "The Order of Liberalization of the External Account in Developing Countries." Essays in International Finance 156, Princeton University, December.

Edwards, S. and L. Ahmad, eds. 1986. *Economic Adjustment and Exchange Rates in Developing Countries*. Chicago: University of Chicago Press.

Edwards, S. and S. van Wijnbergen. 1986. "The Welfare Effects of Trade and Capital Market Liberalization." *International Economic Review* 27(1):141–48.

Elkin, S. L. 1985. "Between Liberalism and Capitalism: An Introduction to the Democratic State." In *The Democratic State*, edited by R. Benjamin and S. L. Elkin, 1–17. Lawrence: University of Kansas Press.

Erdilek, A. 1988. "The Role of Foreign Investment in the Liberalization of the Turkish Economy." In *Liberalization and the Turkish Economy*, edited by T. Nas and M. Odekon, 141–59. Westport, Conn.: Greenwood Press.

———. 1986. "Turkey's New Open-Door Policy of DFI: A Critical Analysis of Problems and Prospects." *METU Studies in Development* 13(1–2), 171–91.

———. 1985. "The Dynamics of the Foreign Direct Investment Environment in Turkey: Political Risks in the Past and the Present." In *Political Risks in International Business, New Directions for Research, Management and Public Policy*, edited by T. L. Brewer. New York: Praeger Publishers.

Ergüder, Ü. 1988. "Post-1980 Politics and Parties in Turkey." In *Perspectives on Democracy in Turkey*, edited by E. Özbudun, 115–45. Ankara: Turkish Political Science Association.

Ergüder, Ü and R. I. Hofferbert. 1987. "Restoration of Democracy in Turkey? Political Reforms and the Elections of 1983." In *Elections in the Middle East: Implications of Recent Trends*, edited by Linda Layne, 19–46. Boulder, Colo.: Westview Press.

Ekzen, A. 1981. "Kamu Iktisadi Kuruluşlarinin Yeniden Düzenlenmesi Yaklaşim-lari ve Dördüncü Beş Yillik Plan'in Politikalar" (Approaches to the Reorganization of the State Economic Entreprises and the Policies of the Fourth Plan). *METU Studies in Development.* Special issue. 227–60.

Ersel, H. 1990. "Monetary Policy in a Changing Financial Environment: The Recent Experience in Monetary Programming." Central Bank of the Republic of Turkey. Mimeo.

Ersel, H. and G. Sak. 1987. "Ownership Structure of Public Corporations in Turkey." *Yapı Kredi Economic Review* I(2).

Ertan, I. 1969. "The Problem of the Reorganization of State Economic Enterprises." *State Economic Enterprises* 133–69. Istanbul: Economic and Social Studies Conference Board.

Evans, P. 1987. "Predatory, Developmental and Other Apparatuses: A Comparative Analysis of the Third World State." Department of Sociology, University of New Mexico. Mimeo.

Federal Reserve Bulletins. 1984–87.

Fischer, S. 1988. "International Macroeconomic Policy Coordination." In *International Economic Cooperation*, edited by M. Feldstein. Chicago: University of Chicago Press.

Frenkel, J. A. 1982. "The Order of Economic Liberalization: Lessons from Chile and Argentina." In *Economic Policy in a World at Change*, edited by K. Brunner and A. H. Meltzer, 119–201. Carnegie-Rochester Conference Series on Public Policy 17. Amsterdam: North Holland.

Gitmez, A. S. 1979. *Dışgöç Öyküsü.* (Immigration Stories). Ankara: Maya Matbaacılık-Yayıncılık Ltd. Şti.

Gürol, M. A. 1989. "Privatization and Labor Relations in Turkish State Economic Enterprises." Wharton School, Philadelphia. Unpublished monograph.

Hale, W. 1981. *The Political and Economic Development of Turkey.* New York: St. Martin's Press.

Hamada, K. 1985. *The Political Economy of International Monetary Interdependence.* Cambridge: MIT Press.

Hanson, J. A. and J. de Melo. 1983. "The Uruguayan Experience with Liberalization and Stabilization, 1974–1981." *Journal of Inter-American Studies and World Affairs* 25:477–508.

Harris, G. S. 1985. *Turkey: Coping with Crisis.* Boulder, Colo.: Westview Press.

Helliwell, J. 1988. "Comparative Macroeconomics of Stagflation." *Journal of Economic Literature* 26:1–28.

Heper, M. 1985. *The State Tradition in Turkey.* Walkington, England: Eothen Press.

Heper, M. and A. Evin, eds. 1988. *State, Democracy, and the Military: Turkey in the 1980s.* New York: Walter de Gruyter.

Hofheinz, R. and K. Calder. 1982. *The East Asia Edge.* New York: Basic Books.

Howard, D. R. 1987. "Exchange Rate Regimes and Macroeconomic Stabilization in a Developing Country." International Finance Discussion Papers 314.

IMF. 1986. *World Economic Outlook.* Washington, D.C.: IMF.

"Işçiydiler, Patron Oldular." (Were Once Employees, Now they are Bosses). *Hürriyet Gazetesi.* 30 January 1987.

Johnson, C. 1982. *MITI and the Japanese Miracle.* Stanford, Calif.: Stanford University Press.

Karataş, C. 1989. "Privatization in the U.K. and Turkey." University of Bradford. Unpublished paper.

———. 1986. "Public Economic Enterprises in Turkey: Reform Proposals, Pricing and Investment Policies." *METU Studies in Development* 13:135–69.

Karpat, Kemal. 1988. "Turkish Democracy at Impasse: Ideology, Party Politics, and the Third Military Intervention." *International Journal of Turkish Studies* (Spring-Summer) 1–43.

Katzenstein, P. 1977. *Between Power and Plenty.* Madison: University of Wisconsin Press.

Kaufman, R. 1979. "Industrial Change and Authoritarian Rule in Latin America: A Concrete Review of the Bureaucratic Authoritarian Model." In *The New Authoritarianism in Latin America,* edited by D. Collier, 189. Princeton, N.J.: Princeton University Press.

Kazgan, G. 1985. *Ekonomide Dışa Açık Büyüme.* (Outward-looking Growth). İstanbul: Altın Kitaplar.

Kepenek, Y. 1983. *Türkiye Ekonomisi.* (Turkish Economy). Ankara,: Orta Doğu Teknik Universitesi.

Keyder, Ç. 1987. *State and Class in Turkey: A Study in Capitalist Development.* Lodon: Verso.

———. 1984. "İthal İkameci Sanayileşme ve Çelişkileri" (Import Substituting Industrialization and its Inconsistencies). In *Krizin Gelişimi ve Türkiye'nin Alternatif Sorunu,* edited by K. Boratav, Ç. Keyder, and Ş. Pamuk, 13–35. İstanbul: Kaynak Yayınları.

Khan, M. S. and R. Zahler. 1985. "Trade and Financial Liberalization Given External Shocks and Inconsistent Domestic Policies." *IMF Staff Paper* (March) 22–55.

———. 1983. "The Macroeconomic Effects of Changes in Barriers to Trade and Capital Flows: A Simulation Analysis." *IMF Staff Papers* (June) 223–82.

Kojima, K. and T. Ozawa. 1984. *Japan's General Trading Companies Merchants of Economic Development.* Paris: OECD.

Kopits, G. 1987. *Structural Reform, Stabilization and Growth in Turkey.* IMF Occasional Paper 52. Washington, D.C.: IMF.

Kozlu, C. 1988. "A Study of the Sogo Shosha: Japanese Foreign Trade Companies as a Model of Development for Turkey. Ph.D diss.," Department of Management, Boğaziçi University, Istanbul.

Krueger, A. O. 1974. *Foreign Trade Regimes and Economic Development: Turkey.* New York: National Bureau of Economic Research.

Krugman, P. and L. Taylor. 1978. "Contractionary Effects of Devaluation." *Journal of International Economics* 8:445–56.

Lim, J. 1987. "The New Structuralist Critique of the Monetarist Theory of Inflation." *Journal of Development Economics* 25:45–61.

Lipschitz, L. and V. Sundararajan. 1982. "The Optimal Currency Basket in a World of Generalized Floating with Price Uncertainty." In *The International Monetary System: Choices for the Future,* edited by M. Connolly, 121–34. New York: Praeger Publishers.

———. 1980. "The Optimal Basket in a World of Generalized Floating." *IMF Staff Papers* 25:80–100.

Little, I. M. D. 1982. *Economic Development: Theory Policy and International Relations.* New York: Basic Books.

Lueedde-Neurath, R. 1988. "State-intervention and Export-oriented Development in South Korea." In *Developmental States in East Asia*, edited by G. White. London: Macmillan Press.

Macedo, J. B. 1986. "Collective Pegging to a Single Currency: The West African Monetary Union." In *Economic Adjustment and Exchange Rates in Developing Countries*, edited by S. Edwards and L. Ahmad. Chicago: University of Chicago Press.

Mantel, R. and A. M. Martirena-Mantel. 1982. "Exchange Rate Policies in a Small Open Economy: The Active Crawling Peg." *Journal of International Economics* 13:301–20.

Mathieson, D. J. 1976. "Is there an Optimal Crawl?" *Journal of International Economics* 6:183–202.

McKinnon, R. I. 1982. "The Order of Economic Liberalization: Lessons from Chile and Argentina." In *Economic Policy in a World of Change*, edited by K. Brunner and A. H. Meltzer, 159–85. Carnegie-Rochester Conference Series on Public Policy 17. Amsterdam: North-Holland.

Mertoğlu, H. 1987. "Increasing Indebtedness and Decreasing Investment in See Balances Expected." *Yapı Kredi Economic Review* 1(2):43–47.

Mezzera, J. and J. de Melo. 1985. "Adjustments by Industrial Firms in Uruguay during 1974–82." In *Scrambling for Survival*, edited by V. Corbo and J. de Melo, 153–210. Washington, D.C.: World Bank.

The Middle East, January 1988.

Mitra, P. 1981. *An Analysis of Adjustment in Developing Countries*. World Bank Development Research Department Working Paper.

Nas, T. and M. Odekon, eds. 1988. *Liberalization and the Turkish Economy*. Westport, Conn.: Greenwood Press.

Nas, T., A. C. Price, and C. T. Weber. 1986. "A Policy-oriented Theory of Corruption." *The American Political Science Review* 80(1):107–19.

Ng, Yew-Kwang. 1979. *Welfare Economics*. London: Macmillan Press.

Nicholas, P. 1988. "The World Bank's Lending for Adjustment." World Bank Discussion Paper 34.

Odekon, M. 1988. "Liberalization and the Turkish Economy: A Comparative Analysis." In *Liberalization and the Turkish Economy*, edited by T. Nas and M. Odekon, 29–46. Westport, Conn.: Greenwood Press, Inc.

O'Donnell, G., P. Schmitter, and L. Whitehead, eds. 1986. *Transitions from Authoritarian Rule: Prospects for Democracy*. Baltimore, M.: Johns Hopkins University Press.

Öniş, Z. 1988. *The Role of the Financial System in the Creation and Resolution of Macroeconomic Crises in Turkey*. Istanbul: Boğaziçi University.

Öniş, Z. and J. Riedel. 1989. "The Political Economy of Macroeconomic Policies, Crises, and Long-term Growth in Turkey." Paper presented for the World Bank Conference on Macroeconomic Policies, Crisis, and Growth in the Long-run, Mexico City.

Öniş, Z. and S. Özmucur. 1988. *Supply Side Origins of Macroeconomic Crises in Turkey*. Istanbul: Boğaziçi University.

———. 1988a. "Supply Side Origins of Macroeconomic Crises in Turkey."

Paper presented at the World Bank Conference on Macroeconomic Policies, Crisis and Growth in the Long-run, Madrid.

———. 1988b. "The Role of the Financial System in the Creation and Resolution of Macroeconomic Crises in Turkey." Paper presented at the World Bank Conference on Macroeconomic Policies, Crisis and Growth in the Long-run, Madrid.

OECD. 1990. *Economic Surveys: Turkey.* Paris: OECD.

———. 1988. *Economic Surveys: Turkey.* Paris: OECD.

———. 1987. *Economic Surveys: Turkey.* Paris: OECD.

———. 1980. *Economic Surveys: Turkey.* Paris: OECD.

Oyan, O. 1988. "Fonlar, İstikrar Programı ve Özelleştirme" (Funds, Stabilization Program, and Privatization) *Mülkiyeliler Birliği Dergisi*, January 20−26.

———. 1987. "An Overall Evaluation of the Causes of Use of Special Funds in Turkey and Their Place in the Economy." *Yapı Kredi Economic Review* 1(4):83−116.

Özaki, R. 1984. "How Japanese Industrial Policy Works." In *The Industrial Policy Debate*, edited by C. Johnson. San Francisco, Calif.: ICS Press.

Özbudun, E. 1987. "Turkey." In *Competitive Elections in Developing Countries*, edited by M. Weiner and E. Özbudun, 328−65. Durham, N.C.: Duke University Press.

———. 1980. "Income Distribution as an Issue in Turkish Politics." In *The Political Economy of Income Distribution in Turkey*, edited by E. Ozbudun and A. Ulusan. New York: Holmes & Meier.

Özdemir, H. 1989. *Rejim ve Asker.* (Regime and Military). İstanbul: AFA Yayınları.

Özel, M. 1988. *Dış Ticaret Sermaye Şirketleri: Japonya, Tayvan, Guney Kore ve Türkiye* (Foreign Trade Corporations: Japan, Taiwan, South Korea, and Turkey). Istanbul: Turktrade Yayınları.

Pamuk, Ş. 1982. "İthal İkamesi, Döviz Darboğazları ve Türkiye" (Import Substitution, Foreign Exchange Bottlenecks, and Turkey). In *Krizin Gelişimi ve Türkiye'nin Alternatif Sorunu*, edited by K. Boratav, Ç. Keyder, and Ş. Pamuk, 36−68. İstanbul: Kaynak Yayınları.

Petrei, H. and J. de Melo. 1985. "Adjustments by Industrial Firms in Argentina during 1976−81." In *Scrambling for Survival*, edited by V. Corbo and J. de Melo, 25−84. Washington, D.C.: World Bank.

Quirk, P. J., B. V. Christensen, K. M. Huh, and T. Sasaki. 1987. "Floating Exchange Rates in Developing Countries: Experience with Auction and Interbank Markets." IMF Occasional Paper 53. Washington, D.C.: IMF.

Rescher, N. 1989. *RISK: A Philosophical Introduction to the Theory of Risk Evaluation and Management.* Washington, D.C.: University Press of America.

Riedel, J. 1988. "Macroeconomic Policies, Crises and Long-run Growth in Turkey: Analysis of Crises." Paper presented at the World Bank Conference on Macroeconomic Policies, Crisis, and Growth in the Long-run, Mexico City.

Rodrik, D. 1990. "Premature Liberalization, Incomplete Stabilization: The Özal Decade in Turkey." Unpublished paper.

———. 1988. "External Debt and Economic Performance in Turkey." In

Liberalization and the Turkish Economy. edited by T. Nas and M. Odekon, 161–83. Westport, Conn.: Greenwood Press.

———. 1988. "Some Policy Dilemmas in Turkish Macroeconomic Management." Paper prepared for the conference on Turkey's Economic Development in the 1980s, Harvard University, April.

———. 1988. "Turkiye'nin Ihracat Patlamasinin Ne Kadari Hyali?" (What Portion of Turkish Export Boom is Fictional?) *Toplum ve Bilim* 42.

———. 1987. "Trade and Capital-Account Liberalization in a Keynesian Economy." *Journal of International Economics* 23:113–29.

———. 1986. "Macroeconomic Policy and Debt in Turkey during the 1970s: A Tale of Two Policy Phases." harvard University, Kennedy School of Government. Mimeo.

Rogowski, R. 1989. *Commerce and Coalitions: How Trade Effects Domestic Political Alignments.* Princeton, N.J.: Princeton University Press.

Roos, L. and N. Roos. 1971. *Managers of Modernization: Organizations and Elites in Turkey (1950–1969).* Cambridge: Harvard University Press.

Rustow, D. A. 1987. *Turkey: America's Forgotten Ally.* New York: Council on Foreign Relations.

Sağlam, D. 1981. "Türkiye' de KIT Reform Çalışmalarının Değerlendirilmesi" (Evaluation of State Economic Enterprises Reform Studies in Turkey). *2. Türkiye Iktisat Kongresi Kalkınma Politikası Komisyonu Tebliğleri,* October 2–7. Izmir, Turkey.

Samuels, R. 1987. *The Business of the Japanese State: Energy Markets in Comparative and Historical Perspective.* Ithaca, N.Y.: Cornell University Press.

Sayarı, S. 1990. "Turgut Özal," In *Political Leaders of the Contemporary Middle East and North Africa,* edited by B. Reich, 395–401. Westport, Conn.: Greenwood Press.

———. 1981. "The Crisis of the Turkish Party System, 1973–1980." Paper presented at the Conference on History and Society in Turkey. Berlin.

———. 1977. "Political Patronage in Turkey." In *Patrons and Clients in Mediterranean Societies,* edited by E. Gellner and J. Waterbury, 103–13. London: Duckworth's.

Saybaşılı, K. 1976. "Türkiye'de Özel Teşebbüs ve Ekonomi Politikasi" (Private Enterprise and Economic Policy in Turkey). *METU Studies in Development* 4:83–97.

Şenses, F. 1988. "An Overview of Recent Turkish Experience with Economic Stabilization and Liberalization." In *Liberalization and the Turkish Economy,* edited by T. Nas and M. Odekon, 9–28. Westport, Conn. Greenwood Press, Inc.

———. 1983. "An Assessment of Turkey's Liberalization Attempts since 1980 against the Background of Her Stabilization Program." *METU Studies in Development* 10(3):271–322.

———. 1981. "Short-Term Stabilization Policies in a Developing Economy: The Turkish Experience in 1980 in Long-Term Perspective." *METU Studies in Development* 8(1–2).

Sönmez, M. 1982. *Türkiye Ekonomisinde Bunalim.* (Crisis in Turkish Economy) Istanbul: Belge Yayınları.

State Planning Organization (SPO). 1988. *The Fifth Five Year Development Plan: 1988 Program.* Ankara: SPO.

———. 1985. *V. Beş Yıllık Plan Destek Çalışmaları*. (Support Studies for the Fifth Five year plan). Ankara, Turkey: SPO.

Sunar, I. 1987. "Redemocratization and Organized Interests in Turkey." Unpublished mimeo.

Sunar, I. and S. Sayarı. 1986. "Democracy in Turkey: Problems and Prospects." In *Transitions from Authoritarian Rule: Prospects for Democracy*, edited by G. O'Donnell, P. Schmitter, and L. Whitehead, 165−86. Baltimore, Md.: Johns Hopkins University Press.

Supplement to Euromoney. 1986. "Turkish Banking and Finance: The Markets Mature," December.

———. "The New Challenge for Corporate Turkey," April.

Swamy, G. 1981. "International Migrant Workers' Remittances: Issues and Prospects." World Bank Staff Working Paper 481.

T. C. Başbakanlık Hazine ve Dış Ticaret Müsteşarlığı. 1986−88. *Kamu İktisadi Teşebbüsleri 1980−1986 Yıllığı* (State Economic Enterprises: 1980−1986 Year book). Ankara.

T. C. Maliye ve Gümrük Bakanlığı. 1988. *1988 Mali Yılı Bütce Gerekçesi*. (Justification for the 1988 Fiscal Year Budget). Ankara.

Thomas, V. 1988. "Issues in Adjustment Lending." World Bank PPR Working Paper WPS2.

Togan, S., H. Olgun, and H. Akder. 1988. *External Economic Relations of Turkey*. Istanbul: Turktrade Publication.

Toprak, B. 1984. "Politicization of Islam in a Secular State: The National Salvation Party in Turkey." In *From Nationalism to Revolutionary Islam*, edited by S. Arjomand, 119−33. Albany, N.Y.: SUNY Press.

Tresch, R. W. 1981. *Public Finance, A Normative Theory*. Plano, Tex.: Business Publications, Inc.

Tun, W. U. and C. Wong. 1982. "Determinants of Private Investment in Developing Countries." *Journal of Development Studies* 19:19−36.

Turan, I. 1988. "Political Parties and the Party System in Post-1983 Turkey." In *State, Democracy and the Military*, edited by M. Heper and A. Evin, 63−80.

Turkey: 1989 Almanac. Turkish Daily News, Ankara.

Turkish Industrialists' and Businessmen's Association, TÜSIAD. 1989. *1989 Yılına Girerken Türk Ekonomisi* (Turkish Economy at the Beginning of 1989). İstanbul.

TÜSİAD. 1989. *Turkish Economy '89*, İstanbul: TÜSİAD.

———. 1988. *1980 Sonrası Ekonomide Kamu-Özel Sektör Dengesi*. (Public-Private Sector Balance in Turkish Economy after 1980). Istanbul: TÜSIAD.

———. 1988. *Turkish Economy '88*. Istanbul, Turkey: TÜSİAD.

Uçtum, M. 1989. "Capital Account Liberalization and Investment." University of Laval, Quebec. Discussion Paper 8907.

Van Wijnbergen, S. 1986. "Exchange Rate Management and Stabilization in Developing Countries." *Journal of Development Economics* 23:227−47.

———. 1983. "Credit Policy, Inflation and Growth in a Financially Repressed Economy." *Journal of Development Economics* 13:45−65.

Wade, R. 1988. "State-intervention in 'Outward-looking' Development: Neoclassical Theory and Taiwanese Practice." In *Developmental States in East Asia*, edited by G. White. London: Macmillan Press.

Wade, R. and G. White. 1988. "Developmental States in East Asia: An Introduction." In *Developmental States in East Asia*, edited by G. White. London: Macmillan Press.

Walstedt, B. 1980. *State Manufacturing Enterprise in a Mixed Economy: The Turkish Case*. Baltimore, Md.: Johns Hopkins University Press.

Waterbury, J. 1990. "Export-Led Growth and the Center-Right Coalition in Turkey." Chapter 3 in this volume.

————. 1989. "Coalition Building, Export-led Growth and Public Sector in Turkey." Paper presented at the Middle East Studies Association Conference, Los Angeles.

White, G. 1988. *Developmental States in East Asia*. London: Macmillan Press.

Wickham, P. 1985. "The Choice of Exchange Rate Regime in Developing Countries: A Survey of the Literature." *IMF Staff Papers* 32:248–88.

Williamson, J., ed. 1983. *IMF Conditionality*. Cambridge: MIT Press.

Williamson, J. 1982. "A Survey of the Literature on the Optimal Peg." *Journal of Development Economics* 11:39–61.

Wogart, J. P. 1983. "Combining Price Stabilization with Trade and Financial Liberalization Policies: the Argentina Experience, 1976–81." *Journal of Interamerican Studies and World Affairs* 25:445–76.

World Bank. 1988. *Turkey: External Debt, Fiscal Policy and Sustainable Growth* 1, The Main Report, 7, Methodological and Statistical Annex. Washington, D.C.: World Bank.

————. 1988. *World Debt Tables*. Washington, D.C.: World Bank.

————. 1986. *Turkey: Adjusting Public Investment* 2, Main Report and Statistical Annex. Washington, D.C.: World Bank.

Yaser, B. 1988. *A Comparative Analysis of Selected Financial Ratios of Private Manufacturing Firms in U.S.A. and Turkey, 1983–1984*. Istanbul: Istanbul Chamber of Industry Publication.

Yoshihara, K. 1982. *Sogo Shosha: The Vanguard of the Japanese Economy*. Oxford: Oxford University Press.

Yoshino, M. and T. Lifson. 1986. *The Invisible Link: Japan's Sogo Shosha and the Organization of Trade*. Cambridge: MIT Press.

Yüksek Denetleme Kurulu. 1988. *Kamu Iktisadi Teşebbüsleri Genel Raporu, 1985 and 1986*. (Report on State Economic Enterprises) Ankara.

————. 1987. *Kamu Iktisadi Teşebbüsleri Genel Raporu, 1985 and 1986*. (Report on State Economic Enterprises) Ankara.

Zahler, R. 1983. "Recent Southern Cone Liberalization Reforms and Stabilization Policies: the Chilean Case, 1974–82." *Journal of Interamerican Studies and World Affairs* 25:509–62.

Index